NOW SOLO

now SOLO

one woman's record-breaking flight around the world

JENNIFER MURRAY

MAINSTREAM
PUBLISHING

EDINBURGH AND LONDON

Ten per cent of the author's royalties will be donated to
Operation Smile

First published in Great Britain in 2002 by
MAINSTREAM PUBLISHING COMPANY (EDINBURGH) LTD
7 Albany Street
Edinburgh EH1 3UG

ISBN 1 84018 720 4

A catalogue record for this book is available from the British Library

Typeset in Courier and Garamond
Printed and bound in Great Britain by
Cox & Wyman Ltd

Contents

To Simon

It is not the critic who counts; not the man who points out how the strong man stumbles, or where the doer of deeds could have done better. The credit belongs to the man who is actually in the arena, whose face is marred by dust and sweat and blood; who strives valiantly . . . who spends himself in a worthy cause; who at the best knows in the end the triumph of high achievement, and who at the worst, if he fails, at least fails while daring greatly, so that his place shall never be with those cold and timid souls who know neither victory nor defeat.

Theodore Roosevelt

Acknowledgements

I have so many people to thank for their wonderful help, support and encouragement, both before and during The NOW Challenge. Some have been acknowledged in this book, but there were many, many more, including: members of the Whirly Girls, the BWPA (British Women Pilots' Association), The Royal Aero Club, all those who sent us e-mails and all those who came to Brooklands to see us off and welcome us home. For me, one of the greatest rewards has been the friendship and camaraderie that we found and continue to have worldwide.

Another special thank you goes to our principal sponsors: to Richard Li and Network of the World, and Tommy Hilfiger, who made our challenge possible and to all our other sponsors and technical sponsors: Hutchison Whampoa, Garmin, MP Bolshaw, Bose, Honeywell, Jeppesen, Mainair, HeliAir, Lynx, Typhoon, H.R. Smith Group of Companies, Submersible Systems, Multifabs, Airzone, Skydrive, Simon Carves, Breitling, Executive Aviation Services and International Jet Services.

And for advice and input with my book: my husband Simon, my daughter Christy, my niece Hannah Mather and my friends Christina Wesemann and Brian Milton; and to my agent Robert Kirby and my publishers Mainstream for believing in me.

Finally, an especially big thank you to my family and friends for all their support and understanding and for coping with anxious times as we travelled around the world. And to my fellow pilots, Colin Bodill and Heinz Rust, my steadfast friends.

Introduction

For 54 years I had been a happy passenger. That changed in 1994 when my husband Simon bought a half share in a helicopter. It was an impulsive buy. I thought he was nuts, but he had worked hard, he earned the money and if that was how he wanted to spend it, it was OK by me. Then he told me, 'I haven't got time to learn how to fly, so you'd better.'

I presented myself at Sloane Helicopters, Sywell Airfield, Northampton, 100 miles north of London and the home of our new half-owned helicopter. It was a rather intimidating place: the efficient-looking young instructors were all 20 years younger than me, dressed in navy blue with helicopters emblazoned on their chests; and most of the students didn't look old enough to have a driving licence.

My prospective instructor said, 'So you want to do the wives' course do you?'

Wives' course? That sounded so sexist. I found myself saying, 'What do you mean? I want to do the real thing. I want a full pilot's licence.'

I suppose the wives' course, which would have given me just the basics of how to land a helicopter if the pilot were to have a heart attack, was exactly what I was looking for, but it sounded so patronising and sexist. So instead, off I went for my first flying lesson, off to a new and wonderful world.

Not that my life up till then hadn't been wonderful, and full of excitement – being married to an ex-French Foreign Legionnaire is never dull. I have known Simon, a distant cousin, nearly all my life. We met at London Zoo, aged ten. Shortly after leaving school he was steered into the family engineering firm, Mather and Platt in Manchester, as a special apprentice working in the iron foundry for four pounds a week – he was always broke. Simon was half in love with me and threatened to go off and join the French Foreign Legion if his feelings weren't reciprocated. I never took him seriously, but one Monday morning he failed to appear for work! I wasn't ready for his affections and had indicated that I needed space – but not that much space!

Five years later Simon returned from the Legion and we fell in love. Keen not to let him run away again, I happily accepted his proposal of marriage. As you can imagine, however, my parents weren't too thrilled, considering Simon was fresh from the war in Algeria, had no money and no normal qualifications – he didn't even have any A levels, having opted out of his final term at school in favour of a trip on a tramp steamer to South America, peeling potatoes. Three weeks before we got married he announced that he'd landed a job with Jardine Matheson, one of the oldest British trading companies in Hong Kong.

We spent the next 30 years in the Far East. Our son Justin was born in Thailand and our two daughters, Suzanna and Christy, were born in Hong Kong. When not busy with the children, I ran my own textile companies, first in Thailand, then in Hong Kong, designing, printing and wholesaling furnishing fabrics. Simon went from strength to strength and life was full, fun and busy. In between work we travelled, ran marathons and went trekking in Nepal and Bhutan. Then the children graduated from university, they were all grown up. I had a little time, we had a little money and the timing was perfect – I entered the world of helicopters.

I was hooked from the start, even though it was confusing and left me wondering whether I would ever get the hang of coordinating all the controls. However, like learning to drive a car, when you think you will never get the knack of letting the clutch in and out, the same applies to a helicopter, only you have one extra control. In your right hand you have the cyclic lever, which controls the angle of the main rotor head disc. So, the cyclic lever is your principal steering wheel, the tiniest movement rolls you left and right, or pitches you up and down. Your left hand is occupied with the collective lever, which controls the angle of attack of the actual rotor blades plus the throttle. There is a small switch on the end of the collective lever which engages the governor, when turned on it automatically controls engine power. Finally, you have the torque pedals. These alter the pitch of the tail rotor, which balances the main rotor torque, thus preventing the helicopter from spinning at slow forward speeds. Confused? And that was just the beginning! But when you lift off – or rather the instructor does, with you just touching the dual controls to get a feel for it – suddenly there you are, you're off the ground in a bubble with 270-degree vision. The freedom, the beauty of it all, is stunning.

After that first lesson I opted to learn somewhere closer to London. Lothar Wesemann (owner of the other half of G-IVIV, our beautiful new helicopter) suggested I go to Denham Airfield where 'Q' (Quentin Smith) operated. Lothar had been taught to fly by Q's father, Mike Smith, in Hong Kong.

I liked Q from the start, with his enthusiasm to share his love of flying along with a laid-back approach to life. He ran a one-man operation, with his girlfriend looking after bookings when she was not at college. He shared an office and hangar with a bunch of fixed-wing pilots. Q gave lively ground demonstrations in aerodynamics – enthusiastically pacing around, waving his arms and saying, 'The helicopter is the most perfect flying machine, the next closest is a humming bird. The helicopter can hover, turn, go backwards and forwards.' It all sounded wonderful, especially when he said, 'Helicopters *don't* just fall out of the sky; people *think* they do, but they don't. If your engine fails, you go into autorotation and you float down. We practise it all the time.' Floating sounded good to me.

Three weeks, forty-seven flying hours (ten of which were solo) and six exams later I was the proud possessor of a Private Pilot's Licence for helicopters.

The training was exhausting both mentally and physically – and felt wonderful. I loved the demands, the challenge of the skies. The adrenalin rush of the first solo flight was incredible, being out there alone and wondering whether I would ever be able to get back to earth. I got lost on my first cross-country flight, panicked and made a 'Pan' call for help. This is one call down from a 'May Day', which is normally only used in more dire situations. Q had instructed me only the day before on Pan calls and I thought it was the perfect solution. I couldn't find Denham Airfield, from which I had only just taken off. I radioed 'Pan Pan Pan' and heard the calm voice of Heathrow ATC (Air Traffic Control) asking me questions about my position and what I could see. He then calmly told me that the reason I couldn't see the airfield was because it was directly underneath me. What a nice man.

Passing all the written exams was perhaps my biggest achievement. Radio/telephony, air law, navigation, meteorology, technical and human performance – all involved numbers, figures and formulae, and I was certainly never a maths or science scholar. However, I found I actually enjoyed and understood the basics and even allowed Q to convince me that I was a natural engineer.

By 1995 we had our own R44 helicopter, G-MURY. I flew whenever I could around England and then further afield. Simon got his licence and together we saw Europe from the skies. Somewhere along the line we started saying, 'Wouldn't it be wonderful to just keep going?'

To begin with it was only a dream, then the dream began to firm up. A fellow helicopter pilot and friend, Michael Kadoorie, gave me Dick Smith's book, *Solo Around the World,* and that became my bible. I learnt how Dick had set off in 1982, in his Bell 206, hoping to be the first person to fly a helicopter around the world, but Ross Perot Junior beat him to it. He heard about Dick's intended flight and decided to go for an American 'first'. Dick, however, went solo, he showed the world that helicopters could 'go it alone'. He had no support aircraft, while Ross Perot Junior had a co-pilot, Jay Coburn, and a twin-engine Hercules with a bevy of technicians and, I believe, a spare engine. In 1994 Ron Bower flew solo around the world in a Bell 206B and the same year Dick Smith piloted his Sikorsky 576 accompanied by his wife Pip who took photographs. Ron went again in 1996 with John Williams, setting a world speed record in their Bell 430. The world had been circumnavigated five times – all done by men, in larger jet turbine helicopters with autopilot. G-MURY has a piston engine and no autopilot. Could it be done?

What a challenge: to be the first, a major first. I didn't think there were any 'firsts' left and I certainly never thought that I would have any involvement in one.

First of all we thought we would go in two helicopters, a pilot and co-pilot in each: Simon in one, myself in another. (We didn't want to leave our children parentless.) Q was to be the third and Lothar was keen to make us four. Then, when we came to see the amount of preparation time it would take, as well as execution time, Simon realised that he wouldn't be able to free himself up for long enough. Also, 'Someone has to work to pay for this little jolly,' he said with a grin. Lothar also pleaded work. 'Why don't you and Q go for it?' Simon said.

I went to see Frank Robinson in California, the manufacturer of the helicopter. I couldn't wait to see his excitement at the prospect of his helicopter going around the world, and I was mad keen for his approval and support. I got none. I felt crushed, Frank thought I was mad. He said, 'If you had more experience, if Q were a little older and you had done more preparatory trips you would have my full support and backing.' He gave me a one in five chance of making it and said we wouldn't get as far as Pakistan. Later I was to have the great pleasure of sending him a postcard from Pakistan.

Before that first trip I had 600 hours' experience. Q was 32 years old;

he had thousands of hours' experience. We had also done plenty of preparatory trips. I had done a lot of flying around Europe and Q had flown to and from Moscow for the World Helicopter Championships (where he'd won the solo freestyle event). Q and I had also done a two-week trip up the Norwegian coast to the most northerly point in Europe, North Cape – 300 miles inside the Arctic Circle – then turned south down through Finland and over to St Petersburg before returning to England. We had also been tested in an emergency. Two hundred miles inside the Arctic Circle on that Norwegian jaunt, and half an hour south of the small town of Tromso, we had been forced to make an emergency landing as the fan shaft had fractured.

While in California visiting Frank Robinson in 1997, I took the opportunity to visit the big Helicopter Expo at Anaheim to meet fellow 'Whirly Girls' (members of the worldwide association of female helicopter pilots) and talk to avionics and survival equipment manufacturers, in the hope of getting some technical sponsorship. I also met the world speed record holder Ron Bower, a six-foot-something Texan, who was standing on a podium in his flight suit, signing autographs with his eight-seater, twin-engine, state-of-the-art helicopter behind him. Rather nervously I waited in the autograph line, introduced myself, and asked for any advice he could give me. There was a long pause, a very long pause, while he rocked back on his heels with his hands clasped behind his back. He finally said, 'Young lady, you won't be setting any female records as your co-pilot is a man.' It seemed to be all about records. 'Well,' I said bravely, 'I was more interested in the challenge and adventure than setting records.' It's strange, though, because once you've achieved your goal you *do* want the record. You certainly don't want someone else to get it.

I spent six months organising that first round-the-world trip, trying to convince everyone I was serious – not least Q, who never believed I'd pull it off. And I nearly didn't. BP, one of the major sponsors, nearly backed out on me a month before take-off. Someone in the company had found an article in an aviation magazine quoting Frank Robinson saying that he was not happy with the venture. 'What are we doing sponsoring this helicopter when the manufacturer doesn't even approve?' asked BP. The following days were a nightmare, but I talked to Frank Robinson and Frank talked to Ralph Alexander (my big supporter at BP) who finally persuaded his fellow directors to go with me.

How I ever thought I could put it all together in six months I don't know – where fools rush in . . . that was me. Sponsors, auxiliary fuel tanks, CAA (Civial Aviation Authority) certifications, clearances, fuel, routes, raising money for Save the Children etc., but Q and I finally made it to the start line, and we made it around the world and into the *Guinness Book of Records* – the first and fastest woman to circumnavigate the globe in a helicopter. We also got the FAI (Federation Aviation International) record for 'Fastest piston engine helicopter around the world' for our trip: 10 May–8 August 1997. But no FAI female record. Ron Bower had been right, and I began to think seriously about going again, not just for the record, but also for me – to prove to myself that I could do it.

In '97 I had Q with me, a vastly more experienced pilot than I and in whom I'd always had sublime faith that he would be able to get me out of any predicament – and there had been many. I was the one who got the recognition, being the official captain and a woman, but I didn't feel that I could fully justify that acclaim having had Q beside me. Amelia Earhart received huge attention for being the first woman to fly across the Atlantic, but on that first crossing she was a passenger, she didn't even touch the controls. As the world knows, however, Amelia more than justified that acclaim. A couple of years later she captained her own aircraft across the Atlantic and made many more long distance, pioneering flights before disappearing so tragically off Howland Island in the Pacific on the final leg of her world record attempt to circumnavigate the globe. I needed to prove I could do it alone, not for anybody else, but for myself.

The first step towards realising my own solo dream came when I bumped into Colin Bodill at the Woodford Air Show for record breakers. I had first met Colin in 1998 at the Royal Aero Club. He was there receiving an award for his record-breaking flight to Australia in a flexiwing microlight and I for being the first woman to circumnavigate the globe by helicopter. On that first occasion there was little time to talk with Colin but we were destined to meet again later that year at Woodford. At that time Colin was preparing for his solo flight around the world and asked me if I had anything else planned. 'Why don't you come with me?' he said.

I thought it was a great idea but going with a microlight? My helicopter was much faster than his little flexiwing microlight. 'But I'm way faster than you,' I said. 'Do you want to bet?' came the laughing reply. We shook hands and took some photos, just in case we actually should end up going together.

I liked and trusted Colin from the word go – and still do. An 'honest Jo', straight as a die, he was of stocky build with longish fair hair and a lovely dry sense of humour. And, as I was to find out, he was also very determined and incredibly brave. A week later I phoned him and said let's talk some more. That was in July 1998. Eighteen months of intensive planning followed. Eighteen months of hope and despair.

I budgeted for £800,000 to cover four aircraft. This would include the cost of hiring a fixed-wing plane for technicians and equipment, avionics for a camera helicopter, a refit for G-MURY and Colin's microlight. We needed sponsors, but to get sponsors we needed to have guaranteed publicity in place. Sponsors are looking for PR as companies have to justify such expenditure to their shareholders. We had to be able to present a professional package to any would-be TV/Documentary/Internet company and then to other potential sponsors.

I also wanted a charity to benefit from our venture and Colin and I chose Operation Smile. This is a small charity whose headquarters are in Norfolk, Virginia. They send missions to 18 countries each year to correct cleft palates and other facial deformities suffered by children and young adults – all free of charge. I had seen Operation Smile in action in Kenya where I had run a marathon to raise money and awareness on their behalf. I had been hugely impressed with their work and was not surprised to hear that they had won the Conrad Hilton Award for the best-run charity in North America. One of the reasons we chose Operation Smile was that we knew any money we raised would get directly to those in need. Dr Bill Magee and his wife, Kathy – the founding directors of Operation Smile – were delighted about our proposal, but from a logisitcal point of view this meant that there were brochures and fund-raising plans to organise.

The route had to be checked meticulously: distances, fuel availability and clearances were of utmost importance. We had to decide where, in the London area, should be our starting point.

We first thought that the grounds of the Royal Maritime College and Observatory at Greenwich would be perfect – it was zero meridian. The director of the Observatory, Kristen Lippincott, liked the idea, so Colin and I visited the site and paced out a landing strip for the microlight. But then the College director decided that we didn't have a strong enough connection to the sea and refused permission. We tried to argue that helicopters play a large role in air/sea rescue, but to no avail. We then thought of Brooklands and the curator, Julian Temple, was delighted. Brooklands was the birthplace of British aviation. In 1908, A.V. Roe made the first-ever flight in a British-built aeroplane from there and since then Brooklands has been the take-off point of many pioneer aviators. It was ideal. Colin and I visited Brooklands with our excitement building, imagining the great 'Take-off' day.

Fuel had to be sorted, the helicopters run on Avgas 100LL – similar to the fuel that cars run on – one grade higher than 4Star. Jet fuel is more readily available than Avgas so we knew that we would have to arrange for fuel to be shipped in to various places around the world (like Russia), or carried on board our support plane, if we got one.

The calculation of distances over water was also critical. The maximum range for both the helicopters and the microlight was approximately 830 statute miles. The crossing of the Pacific would have to be from Eastern Russia, across the Bering Strait to Alaska; and the Atlantic crossing would have to be from northern Canada to Iceland.

Many of our clearances could be organised by Dave Gannon and Mike Gray at Overflight on the Isle of Man who had done a great job for Q and me on our '97 trip. However, I knew that east of Thailand it would be up to me, namely clearances for Vietnam, China, Hong Kong, Taiwan, Japan and Russia. All British Embassies en route would have to be notified and many of the clearances would have to go through diplomatic channels.

The actual plotting of the route could be done on our computers using Jeppesen's excellent Flite Star programme – an essential for anyone planning any kind of trip. With the Flite Star programme you can put in routes and get airport information, programme times, fuel consumption and fuel availability (though the latter should always be checked). For a world record we would have to cover at least 23,502.80 statute miles (20,437.22 nautical miles, 36,787.559 kilometres).

We needed charts giving topographical detail and charts plotting airways – all the countries heading east (as we would be doing) between Europe and Alaska would require us to fly airways just like any commercial airliner, although not at their altitudes. Chart plotting was fun, your imagination runs free – mine more than Colin's. He was looking for direct routes all the time, while I was happy to make minor detours for ultimate scenery.

Technical sponsors were also needed. G-MURY was equipped with everything required for long-distance travel from my '97 trip. The most important item required was an auxiliary fuel tank which held a further 60 US gallons (240 litres) of fuel. I needed another one for G-JEFA, the brand-new R44 that was delivered in January 2000, which I was going to use as the camera helicopter. At least this time I knew who to go to as finding the auxiliary tank from our previous trip had been a nightmare. Premiere Fuels, the only British company I could find who had the capability and the CAA certification, was running at full production making fuel tanks for 60 per cent of the world's racing cars and had said they could not help. I found a company in the USA who could make one, but it meant that G-MURY had to be American-owned and registered. I was going to sell it to a friend for a dollar (with a signed proviso that I could buy it back for the same amount!) Then Premiere said they could do it after all, but the CAA said it would have to be tested and that the tank would have to be able to withstand a 40-foot drop. I argued that the tank would be the only thing to survive such an impact and to carry out the test would require making a second tank – I could afford neither the time nor the money. The CAA were finally persuaded to forgo the test but insisted on frequent inspections. I ended up with a state-of-the-art, double-skinned, foam-filled tank with two electrically operated pumps. That was '97, this time I knew the route to go.

Besides the fuel tank I needed GPSs (Global Positioning Systems), radios, fuel low meters and survival equipment consisting of life rafts, survival suits, life jackets, EPIRBs (Emergency Radio Beacons) and three-minute air supply units (small canisters of air that we would strap onto our flight suits for water crossings – a life-saver if you are trapped inside a fast-sinking helicopter).

The support plane needed to run on jet fuel, be cheap, economical to run, have a good payload and have a minimum airspeed as close to ours as possible. Islanders and Cessna Caravans fell into that category so Colin and I started to search for either of those. There was just so much to organise.

I was pretty much on my own in the planning for the first few months, although Colin and I were in constant communication by fax, e-mail and phone – oh the joy of modern communications. Colin lived in Nottingham, some 200 miles north of London, making a living as a microlight instructor with a young family to support. When not working he was helping his partner Michelle with their children, Sarah aged nine and Peter aged six. They are lovely children, but Peter suffers from brain damage and is a diabetic requiring round-the-clock care. Colin had promised Michelle that he wouldn't go on another venture unless he could raise enough money for a down payment on a larger house. On his last trip to Australia, much to Michelle's dismay, he ended up selling his car to meet the costs. I had also assured Simon that, if I took on another challenge, it wouldn't cost him a penny, that I would have it all covered by sponsors. In '97 he ended up being the principal cash sponsor but I hoped it would be easier the second time round. I felt confident that, with Colin and I both having a track record, sponsorship wouldn't be too much of a problem . . . I was horribly mistaken.

Getting round safely the first time was not a bad advert for the helicopter. I had high hopes that Frank Robinson would support me on the second round-the-world flight, this time solo. I wrote to him, telling him of my plans and how I thought I had met all his previous requirements. I was now much more experienced and had done a major preparatory trip. I got a four-line letter back: 'Jennifer, you are absolutely mad, or else you take a sadistic pleasure in putting me through three months of not knowing whether you are going to make it or not. Anyway, good luck' – not exactly the response I was hoping for!

In January 1999, Simon's godson, Jamie McCallum, came on board to help me with fund-raising. He had recently formed his own sports marketing consultancy firm after four years with Damon Hill and two years with IMG. Jamie designed a very sexy brochure and we sent out hundreds of them, but we got virtually nothing back.

Our first priority was to find a TV/Documentary/Internet company who would be interested in getting involved, as that would cover both PR and sponsorship. Jamie suggested we get in touch with Quokka Sports, an Internet company making extreme sports websites. It was a young and vibrant set-up with headquarters in San Francisco. We had many meetings with them and at one point it looked as though they might come on board. We even got to the stage of working out details such as the cameramen who would be required. Disappointingly, though, they then got a new head of programming who was more interested in sport than extreme sport and Quokka fell by the wayside.

British Aerospace, for whom we did presentations at Farnborough and Woodford, looked good for a while, as did Iridium whom we visited in Washington DC. They were a white-hot hope, until they went bankrupt.

Whilst in Washington, Colin and I had a meeting with Russell Lee, curator of the Smithsonian Air and Space Museum in Washington. They had already expressed an interest in having my helicopter G-MURY for permanent display after my first trip. We suggested they might like to have Colin's microlight as well, if, of course, we both made it round. Russell was enthusiastic and thought it would make a very interesting display in their new museum, due to open at Dulles Airport in 2003. This was good news – potential sponsors would fully appreciate the PR value of their logo being viewed year after year by millions of visitors.

HSBC looked like a possibility at one stage. We attended several meetings and made presentations, but were then told 'Sorry, but no.' Morale was proving difficult to sustain.

On the more positive side, however, while we had been in America visiting Quokka, I had suggested that we also travel to New York to see Tommy Hilfiger who had generously sponsored me in '97. This time they were even more generous, giving us £250,000, meaning that we just needed another £550,000 to reach our target. Thank God for designer sportswear.

Then I met Michael Johnson, when he and his wife Susan came to lunch at our house in Somerset. Michael worked for Pacific Century Cyber Works (PCCW) in Hong Kong, of which Simon was a director. They were setting up a huge Internet 'content' production centre in London called NOW (Network of the World), which was a joint effort between Mark McCormack's IMG (who own TWI, Trans World International, the world's biggest distributors of sporting TV programmes) and PCCW controlled by Richard Li (son of Kah Shing Li) in Hong Kong. Michael was telling us all about this new venture, how it would be the first fully convergent TV and Internet company. They planned to launch a terrestrial TV channel – initially for the Middle and Far East, then hopefully worldwide – on which they would give their Internet website programmes time. They hoped that for every minute of TV time they would generate ten minutes of on-line website time. The website would be worldwide from the start. What interested me was that they were looking for extreme sports programmes.

'Michael, I think I am exactly what you are looking for,' I said and went on to explain what I was planning. He was excited and said, 'As luck would have it I am having dinner tonight with the head of programming for TWI, Bill Sinrich. I will pass it by him and see what he has to say.' Bill Sinrich liked the idea. The following week Michael saw Mark McCormack in Hong Kong who also liked it. Richard Li immediately agreed. Michael confirmed: 'We're on'. I immediately phoned Colin with the news – celebrations all round.

That was in June 1999, and it all seemed too good to be true. I asked Michael about acquiring other sponsors and was told, 'We have hundreds of people whose job it is to raise millions of dollars, the best thing you can do is do nothing.' Wonderful? It certainly appeared to be. I finally got a full-time secretary, the lovely Jo Jo (Joanna Peyton-Jones) who provided some much-needed help in the office. Jo Jo is a friend of my daughter Suze, and one of life's great enthusiasts.

One month, two months, three months passed; time was ticking away. We had nothing in writing from NOW and Michael never answered my phone calls. I appreciated that he was working flat out trying to get his new company launched by the end of the year. In the meantime, however, I was eating into Simon's bank account and saving the Tommy Hilfiger funding for the journey. We heard from NOW that there were delays and still more delays. I couldn't afford to do nothing but sit and wait, so we went ahead with looking for technical sponsors. There was so much that we needed: all the avionics, survival equipment, charts and a fuel sponsor. We couldn't wait for those hundreds of people to raise millions of pounds. We had felt so confident that NOW would come up with the sponsors, but now panic started to set in as it began to look as though things weren't running as smoothly as we had thought.

Jamie took on a partner, James Barker, and Jamie's friend, Nick Harris, who ran his own small PR company, took on our account together with Jason Brake who worked for him. Jo Jo's friend, James Fletcher, pitched in with invaluable computer and technical support. The pace was fraught and we just prayed every day that NOW would come through. We were haemorrhaging cash and I was desperately trying to keep calm.

The fuel situation was critical. If NOW didn't come through we desperately needed a fuel sponsor. I contacted Tommy Thompson, a good friend of Simon's who lives in Texas and is, or was, in oil. On the fuel front he couldn't help, but when I mentioned my concerns about Russian clearances he said that I must meet Maestro Mstislav Rostropovitch, the world's greatest living cellist and one of the greatest conductors on earth. The Maestro was passionate about a charity called Medicalogic, of which he is chairman. Medicalogic organise and raise funds to vaccinate Russian children against childhood diseases – polio, measles etc. – vaccinations that we take for granted in the West. Tommy thought we might be able to do something together for our respective charities. Operation Smile, the charity that Colin and I were supporting, is very active in Russia and has operated on over 1,500 children there and would be operating on a further 350 in Tomsk later in the year. That all sounded good on the charity front, therefore, but didn't help the fuel situation.

Another problem area was the route, which had to be changed so many times. Originally we had planned to go east, straight through Russia from St Petersburg to Provideniya, across the Bering Strait, then loop down through North America, into Central and South America, going about 300 miles up the Amazon before turning north and enjoying a slow passage through the Caribbean. I had hoped to get a large fuel sponsor on board who would treat the whole route through Russia as a major challenge and PR event, but this didn't happen and the quote I got from the Russians for fuel was US$250,000. A route change was called for.

To qualify for a world record you have to do the mileage, but you also have to cross 'x' number of meridians within the Tropics of Cancer and Capricorn. This latter criteria was introduced by the FAI (Federation Aviation International) after Mike Smith (Q's father) and Steve Goode's record attempt in 1997. Mike and Steve were attempting a speed record in Steve's Hughes 500. They were hoping to beat Ron Bower and John Williams' record of the previous year. What Mike and Steve did was fly around the North Pole (a very, very brave venture), which dealt with all the meridians, and then they flew up and down in the States until they had achieved the mileage. The FAI said it wasn't in the spirit of the game and argued that they were short of the pole by several hundred yards. The judgement was very tough, their instruments weren't reading accurately due to magnetic interference and they were unable to prove that they had made it. They planned to make another attempt but Steve tragically died the following year whilst flying his Hughes 500 with a friend in Germany.

Having decided on a new route we had to get clearances, and at this stage we didn't know for sure how many aircraft were going and who would be on board. This also caused a problem with the umpteen visas that were required. Jo Jo was working hard on these with visa agents, Visa Express, while Dave Gannnon was working flat out on clearances as far as Thailand. I was getting on with the rest of the clearances and coordinating the whole show. Jim Cunliffe at Mainair, the manufacturers of Colin's Blade 912S flexiwing microlight, generously came through with full sponsorship of the aircraft. Colin would be installing all the avionics.

All this planning was going on but we still had no confirmation of sponsorship from NOW. Then, just seven weeks before our intended departure, disaster struck – heart-stopping news. This is my diary entry from that terrible day:

> To think that Michael Johnson gave us a verbal contract last September and then I have a phone conversation with Rob Banagan from NOW – eight months later. I asked him why the continued delay over approval of the budget and he said – 'Well, your dates don't fit with ours and we're not sure that we are prepared to finance it.' Went cold all over, just felt numb. [I was in France, all on my own, Simon was in Hong Kong.] Glorious day outside, all our plans in tatters, feel like giving up, no more strength. After all the sweat and effort and MJ having told us not to look for any more sponsors, and then this, it's sickening. Got to get a grip of myself. Took the dogs for a walk – think, plan, this is why other people haven't done it before etc. – be positive.

I put all the facts in an urgent fax to Simon. I spoke to him on the phone and told him that we could delay our departure by three weeks in the hope of being more compatible with the delayed launch of the NOW website, now scheduled for the last week of June, but that was the very latest we could go. It left us with little margin for the Greenland crossing, but if NOW backed out we'd be going nowhere.

Simon was seeing Richard Li the next day and would talk to him. I couldn't sleep that night so I watched a harrowing movie in French, cried and phoned Simon again at 2 a.m. my time. At 8 a.m. he phoned, he was 'yet again my hero', all was sorted and Richard Li had said 'consider it done, I will phone Michael Johnson right away.' Sure enough, suddenly, thankfully, it was all action in the NOW camp.

Then I got a call from Tommy Thompson, 'Can you come to lunch next week in Paris with Slava Rostropovitch and myself?' I agreed, although it felt a little extravagant going all the way to Paris for a lunch. (Tommy, I later found out, came all the way from Texas, a 24-hour turnaround, just for the lunch.)

I was thrilled at the prospect of meeting the Maestro in person and I was not disappointed, what a gentleman. He had a lovely twinkle in his eye as he said, 'but Jeffokha, I am already a little in love with you and now I am going to worry about you for three months!' He also said, 'Jeffokha [his Russian interpretation of Jennifer], I think you should come to Moscow to meet the people who have made your journey possible.' So off I went and I asked Q to come too, as Colin was up to his ears doing all the electrics on his microlight.

We never underestimated the importance of our Russian clearances or the work involved. There is so much you must put in place, so many people you must talk to, a route to be agreed upon and a final application to be made through both the civil aviation and diplomatic channels. We had done it all before, but that time it was only for one aircraft. Moscow was a priority.

Slava was a star – he opened every door. We met Gennady Velikovsky, Head of Air Traffic Control for all of Russia, a man who had only been a voice to me for many years, and through whom I had got our '97 clearances. We also met his boss (I had previously assumed Velikovsky was the top man), Andrei Andreev. They couldn't do enough for us, all because of Slava. Slava has near God-like status in Russia, and here he was giving me the time of day; me whom he'd only met once before in a restaurant in Paris.

Meanwhile NOW continued in high gear – at last. We would be called 'The NOW Challenge' and yes, they did want the Cessna Caravan as a support plane, and yes, they did want a camera helicopter. The excitement was building, 'D-Day' was fast approaching – and we had the money!

The engineers at HeliAir were servicing my helicopter, G-MURY. They had to reinstall my auxiliary fuel tank, fuel flow meter, new Bose headsets, new Sky Force GPS and a Garmin GNS430, but they went into overdrive in order to fit out the new camera helicopter G-JEFA for which all the same avionics had to be installed, plus a radar altimeter and a turn and bank indicator. (G-MURY only has a seven-hole instrument panel, G-JEFA has a nine-hole with room for the extra avionics.)

Our technical sponsors (who had all come on board during the agonising wait for NOW) – Steve Gubbins at Garmin, Dick Merriott at Bose, John Prior at Bendix King (Honeywell), Alan Lathan at Jeppesen's and Andrew Dawson at H.R. Smith – all came up trumps with yet more sponsorship on their products.

Then NOW said they absolutely had to have satellite communication tracker systems in my helicopter and Colin's microlight so that people could follow our every move on the website. This required a major modification certificate from the CAA – a process that normally takes around six months. The CAA were also extremely helpful, pushing it through in a matter of days. But it landed Colin, beavering away in his garage in Nottingham, with a mammoth increase in electrical installation on his microlight, and, of course, increased the workload for the engineers working on G-MURY.

Jo Jo was rushing around in ever-tighter circles; together we were fielding the increasing barrage of phone calls, faxes and e-mails and she now had to get visas for five more people: the cameramen and pilots of the support aircraft. The take-off from Brooklands required yet more of her time in organising tents, catering, press conference facilities etc. James Fletcher was talking with our technical sponsors and getting supplementary charts for the other aircraft from Jeppesen's, and Jamie McCallum and James Barker had the task of sorting out our contract with NOW and making sure all our sponsors were happy. I agreed to everything that NOW requested as I was so desperate to ensure their sponsorship and to avoid further delays. I even signed away all editorial rights and royalties on video footage.

Colin and I went for a meeting with Rob Banagan at NOW, who asked whether we had any special criteria for cameramen. 'Yes, they need to be lightweight and have the spirit of adventure, prepared to rough it and be team players.' Rob thought we should have fresh cameramen every couple of weeks, or at least every month. He thought they would get burnt out if they had to stay the course. I argued for keeping the same team all the way for continuity and added that I thought any cameraman would be reluctant to be taken off such an amazing challenge. Colin was less certain, saying that cameramen probably weren't as crazy as us. He was right! God,

I wished that I'd listened to Rob's advice but at the time I didn't appreciate just how exhausting their workload would be.

Al Edgington (director, cameraman), Pat Davey (cameraman, technician) and Dave Ullman (technician) joined the team (although Dave would be 'on and off'). They all seemed very pleasant and enthusiastic. Al, aged 28, failed dismally on the lightweight proviso as he was 6 ft 2 in. and weighed in at 15 stone. Easygoing Al looked apologetically down at himself and said 'Will I do?' His credentials were good; he had been on many overseas assignments in tough places and, it turned out, was at prep school with my son Justin. Pat, gum-chewing Pat, whose conversation was constantly punctuated with 'cool', met the weight spec and seemed well-suited to the task. Dave, also slight of build, was friendly with everyone.

There was no time to get to know each other before the expedition, to see whether we worked well as a team. I accepted them, weight, chewing gum, cool and all.

The camera helicopter was to be flown by Q, who was now looking the part, sporting wavy blond locks down to his shoulders, a ginger moustache and goatee beard, which he was constantly stroking. Q is a superb pilot, intelligent, entertaining and full of charm. His flip side is that he's lazy, has chronic time-keeping and is prone to erratic bursts of energy that surface at inopportune times. All in all, he's good news in small doses. He had caused me a fair amount of stress on our first flight around the world and many people advised me against having him along on the second trip. Colin and my family were among those with reservations, saying that there were thousands of ace pilots who would give anything to go on a trip like this. I argued that we had already worked together as a team, I liked him, I thought I could count on his loyalty and support – and I guess there was an element of better the devil you know. There were lots of reasons for choosing Q. The helicopters were serviced and maintained by his family company and, besides, he was virtually 'family'. His sister Sasha is married to my sister's son John, I had introduced them and Sasha was about to have a baby. I reckoned that he would be a great support, that the rest of the team wouldn't tolerate prima donna behaviour and lateness. I was wrong, however, and my mistake was to make for difficult times ahead.

The Cessna Caravan was a single-engine turbo prop aeroplane piloted by Heinz Rust, 62 years old, and co-pilot James Davey who was in his early thirties. The cameramen, Al Edgington and Pat Davey, would alternate between the two aircraft. I have known Heinz and his wife Barbara for many, many years, they are good friends from Hong Kong. Heinz is very experienced: a good fixed-wing pilot and more recently a helicopter pilot.

He's flown the world and sailed the seven seas and looks a bit like a pirate. In fact he's Swiss, a successful architect, very methodical and imbued with plenty of the spirit of adventure. On this adventure, Heinz and Colin turned out to be the best teammates you could possibly ask for. Without them I wouldn't have made it.

James Davey, a nice, dark-haired, good-looking young man came with the Cessna Caravan, G-EELS, which was owned by Peter Wood. We had finally found G-EELS at Gloucester Airport where it was available for hire. Peter Wood runs a small business out of Gloucester Airport ferrying glass eels around Europe. Happily for us, the timing of our challenge was 'off season' for glass eels, so James and G-EELS were available. Peter was anxious to keep James happy and asked if James's girlfriend, Pascal Lejeune, might join us in Vancouver and travel in the Cessna as far as Boston. I told him that, much as I would like to be accommodating, the Cessna was for NOW's use and I was anxious to keep the numbers to a ninimum. But, if there was space available, we might perhaps be able to take her along for a couple of hops.

Eighteen months of planning were behind us. We had our sponsors, we were The Now Challenge and Colin and I were as ready as we could hope to be – ready to fly solo around the world. And the world was going to be able to share our great adventure over the Internet. But we were short on time. With every delay the pressure would increase. It was already the monsoon season in India and Burma. It would be the typhoon season by the time we got to Hong Kong and Japan and we could anticipate hurricanes in America. Already we were asking the question, could we make Greenland before the end of the short Arctic summer?

We had our aircraft, we had our team of pilots and cameramen – we were a team of seven (eight when Dave Ullman was with us). There were great times ahead, but from the start I should have established my authority and laid down some rules: who should do what; who was answerable to who. I failed to do so. Wrongly, I had believed that everyone was imbued with my own spirit of adventure and I never appreciated how much greater the stress levels and workload would be with a team of seven versus the two we had been in '97. The long hours, the risks, the bureaucracy, the danger, the tiredness and being confined to each other's company for so many days – all would take their toll.

ONE

Brooklands to Cyprus

31 May – 7 June

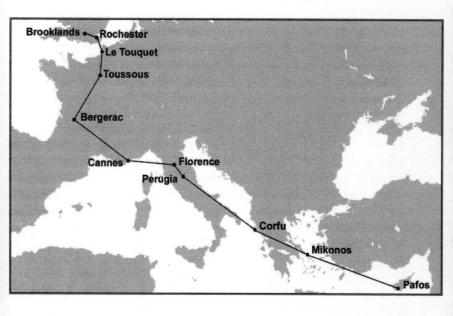

DAY 1

I woke at 5 a.m. Gone were the fears and doubts of the night before when I had lain in bed trying to sleep and the full force, the enormity of what I was about to attempt had hit me. I was about to embark on a journey that no woman had ever done before – to fly solo around the world in a helicopter. What was I doing? What had I taken on? How dared I think that I, a woman fast approaching her 60th birthday, could take on such a challenge? It would be a daunting enough prospect for anyone in the prime of life, for a young person with lightning-quick reactions and razor-sharp mind. Would my reactions be fast enough in an emergency? Or would I freeze? This time I would have no reassuring co-pilot, no companion, this time it would all be up to me. Solo – solo.

I had lain there, a bag of nerves, filled with doubts, and finally drifted into a fitful sleep. When the church clock in the square chimed 5 a.m., I looked over at Simon, still sound asleep beside me, the dear familiar face, and around our bedroom; everything in the thin morning light looked so reassuringly normal. Only the small bag of luggage and one state-of-the-art Tommy Hilfiger flight suit hung over the back of my chair proclaimed the day.

I took a quick peek out the window to see the sun rising in a clear sky. My normal confidence and optimism had returned, the forecast was good, the gods were with us and I felt surprisingly calm.

Shawn Flaherty, Simon's office driver, drove us out to Denham to collect the helicopters for the short 15-minute flight to Brooklands. The engineers were still fussing around my helicopter G-MURY, my home for the next three months, doing final last-minute checks. We had arrived with masses of time, but time has a nasty habit of slipping away. Colin was already at Brooklands and had been on the phone pressing me to hurry up as some of the press were already there and he could not move his microlight G-NOWW onto the forecourt until I landed, as I would blow him away. Next, James Fletcher phoned, urging me to hurry. I in turn was putting pressure on the engineers. John Michalakis, the chief engineer, announced that they had yet to fuel up. I checked the tanks and reckoned I might have just enough to get to Le Touquet, certainly enough to get to Brooklands. There would be plenty of time to worry about fuel later. The important thing was to get on down to Brooklands.

My luggage was already on its way with my daughters Suze and Christy and Christy's husband, Nick. The bag would be stored in the Cessna 'baggage plane'. With me in G-MURY I had one small case of charts, a video camera, two 'stills' cameras (one for colour slides and one for prints), EPIRB (my emergency radar beacon) and a life jacket.

External checks done, I climbed on board. I was about to fly solo around the world and yet it seemed like any other day. Denham looked so reassuringly normal. The hangar doors were wide open with helicopters in various stages of undress, engineers starting their day. On the grass around me there was a scattering of helicopters and Simon was walking towards his R22 helicopter.

I went through the internal checks: start-up, warm up, final checks, I was ready to go.

'Golf Mike Uniform Romeo Yankee requesting flight information for departure to Brooklands, one on board, Captain Murray, not returning today.'

Back came Nick Rudge's voice from the Tower. 'Runway 24 in use, QNH 1011, report ready to depart.' It was the familiar routine, all done so many times before. I was cleared for departure and once clear of the circuit asked, 'Request change to London Heathrow, 119.9'.

'Frequency change approved. Good luck Jennifer, see you in August.'

And so it began with the short flight to Brooklands Airfield, talking to Heathrow ATC, following the low-level route to Ascot and onwards to Brooklands, feeling a mixture of exhilaration and fear but trying to concentrate on the job in hand. Colin was waiting anxiously. We had to go through press photos and interviews and there was little time to talk with so many family and friends. Peter Wood was there with an anxious expression on his face, clutching a small 'in tray' in which sat the final lease contract for G-EELS, the Cessna. This had to be read through, but I think I would have signed anything that day. Spirits were high, the band was playing and the sun was shining on the happy crowd of friends, family, well-wishers and press, as the team prepared to depart. My daughter Christy, who, along with Simon and Suze, was coming to Le Touquet to see us off, gave me 'Bear' (her much loved and elderly bean-bag bear), saying, 'Mum, I want you to have Bear, you must have some company.'

Heinz, James, Al, Pat, and finally Q had all arrived and were surrounded by their families and friends. My mother was there, looking so proud and anxious, with my brothers, cousins, uncles, aunts and many, many friends – once again I was submitting them to anxious months ahead. We shared brave smiles and hugs, the doubts of the night before fleetingly returned and were quickly suppressed. After the happy and tearful farewells. It was time to go. 'See you in August!' we said.

I had one more quick check around the helicopter – fuel caps secure, all flaps closed – before I climbed on board. Life jacket, safety belt, check to make sure that no stray person was lurking near the tail rotor before starting the engine. Concentrate. It was difficult to concentrate, everything had been so emotional and still was. Everyone was there, 20 yards away behind the barrier rope, the marquee behind them, champagne glasses in hand. The skies were blue with small puffy clouds and the music was now drowned out by the roar of the engines. My confidence returned; I was in command. Me, it was all up to me.

Colin lifted off, closely followed by myself and then Q in G-JEFA, the camera helicopter. We did one circuit with a low fly-past down the runway then, gaining height and with a final glance and wave to all those dear faces, we turned south-east to pick up the helicopter route for the Thames.

Colin, with an escort of three microlights and several helicopters (including

Simon), was routing direct to Le Touquet, as the CAA do not allow microlights in the London Control area or, indeed, to fly over any built-up area.

Flying the helicopter route was all so familiar, but it was time to concentrate. We were flying in formation. Where did the camera crew want me? I positioned myself slightly in front, at the same time checking out the new instruments with which I was not too familiar, as the final installations and servicing on my helicopter were only completed at take-off.

I had a brand new, state-of-the-art GNS 430 sponsored by Garmin – a combined GPS and radio in which you can install two frequencies. By pressing a button you can switch from one to the other. I also had my regular Bendix King radio, also with the two frequencies. At the base of my instrument panel new switches had been installed, 'on, off' switches that allowed me to listen to both or only one radio, and another intercom switch so I could talk on either one or the other. It was not really complicated, but quite easy to have the wrong combination going. The big advantage in having the two radios was that we could listen and talk to each other on one radio, the unofficial chat channel 123.45 (used by all aircraft), and still listen out and talk with ATC on the other.

As we passed over Chelsea Bridge, the Houses of Parliament, Big Ben, Tower Bridge, the Tower of London, Greenwich and the infamous Dome I felt so proud to be English and I hoped England would be proud of me. I called Q on 123.45 – no reply. I realised the switch that I should have had on was off. I quickly switched and my peace was shattered by Q on the radio screaming at me that I'd strayed off the heli route, I was over the houses. We were not getting off to a good start and then, of course, I didn't have enough fuel to get to Le Touquet and we had to make our first unscheduled fuel stop at Rochester. I realised that I had been trying to focus on too many things at the same time and hadn't concentrated enough on the basics.

Many months later I was to see and hear Q's response to this on camera, on the Discovery Channel TV documentary produced by NOW. 'Jennifer, it seems, thinks that her press is more important than her fuel. Personally I think my fuel is more important than my press. Well, we will no doubt see about that somewhere mid-Channel!' Where was the loyalty and support I had counted on?

After passing over the white cliffs of Dover I took one last look back over my shoulder at England, my home – please God that I would return safely. I quickly brushed away a few self-doubts and thought of all the other English adventurers over the centuries who had set forth: first the sea-farers and then more recently the aviators who, no doubt, had also taken a last look back with the full realisation that they were leaving behind all that was most dear to them. They too would then have turned resolutely ahead.

I was the last but one to arrive in Le Touquet. Suze and Nick's mother, Carla Powell, arrived in another R44 ten minutes after us. After I landed Colin kindly said, 'It was quite unnecessary of Q to scream at you like that for all to hear. The last thing you need on a day of such high emotion, and besides, what's the big deal?'

Saying farewell to the girls at Le Touquet was dreadful. I have never been a good goodbyer, and, well, there was no getting away from the fact we were heading off on a high-risk venture. I had chosen to undertake this adventure and I was putting them through quite an ordeal for the second time.

Why was I doing it? I have been asked a thousand times 'why?' Why does anyone go off and do anything of risk by choice? Because we love the challenge, the thrill, the adrenalin high; to push yourself to the limits and then some, to do something that has never been done before. Adventurers journey forth, they go for many different reasons, but the spirit of adventure is the same for one and all. As the saying goes, those that have the spirit will never ask the question, while those that ask the question will never understand the answer. And, of course, you step out of your normal, everyday world – it's real-life movie time. For years I'd been a good housewife and mother, and loved it. I wouldn't have had it otherwise and would never knowingly have done anything involving risks of this sort when the children were young. I lived my life for my family. I still do, but there's time for me now too. The children are grown up, it's 'selfish' time again but, unlike those wonderful, penniless, carefree days between school and marriage, there is a little more money around – and time. Time to pamper yourself a little. Some people visit the beauty parlour for a few nips and tucks. As for me? I had the good luck to discover flying, and I felt wonderful.

I parted from Suze and Christy with hugs and tears and then watched them become small dots, as we headed south to Toussus on the outskirts of Paris. Simon would be accompanying us for the next two days, as far as Regagnac, our house in the south-west of France. Colin, however, had to go into the small airfield of Saint Donnolly, some 20 kilometres to the north-west of Toussus. He had said to me at Le Touquet that he didn't think Toussus would accept microlights. I hadn't appreciated that microlights were so restricted in Europe.

We had friends waiting for us at Toussus. Claude and Chantal Bouilly, good French friends who lived nearby at Vaucresson, had been at the airport for over an hour, as we were late. By the time we arrived they were sitting on the airport terrace with the airport manager, happily finishing a bottle of cold, dry white wine in the late afternoon sunshine.

We had a quick change and shower at the nearby large, clean, efficient Novotel Hotel and then went to the Belle Epoque restaurant, just a few kilometres away in the centre of the old village of Chateufort. It was a haven of peace and quiet after the hurly burly of the day. Madame told us that the terrace was still '*hiver*' – the chairs tipped against the tables. But she agreed that the evening was warm and 'but of course we could have a *coupe de champagne dehors*', with a look that said it all about the mad English.

What a day it had been. It was a joy to sit on the terrace, with the place to ourselves, looking out over a small wooded valley. When I say 'we', the group was not complete for that first glass of champagne, there was just Simon, Heinz, Barbara (Heinz's wife who was accompanying us in the Cessna as far as our next stop), Claude, Chantal and myself. Next to arrive were Mike Miles and Ian McCallum, both very good friends of ours and on Simon's board. (Simon had strategically organised his board meeting for the following morning in Paris.) Then the lovely Slava arrived. He came by car, an hour's drive from Paris, to wish me well. He couldn't even stay for dinner as he had a long-standing dinner engagement that night, but he insisted on coming for a drink. He said to me, 'Jeffokha, I have something for you, I want to give it to you in a quiet place.' We went indoors. 'Jeffokha,' he said, 'two days ago I was in Israel, I went to the tomb of Jesus and I got this for you.' He had been holding one hand against his chest, which he now opened to give me a small icon of Jesus, and made the sign of the cross. We both had tears in our eyes. As he was leaving he told me to contact him if there was anything he could do to help. We were later to need that help desperately, and he didn't let us down.

Pat and Al our cameramen had had to cry off, they had work to do. They had to cut and edit all the day's footage and send it back to NOW for the web site. Their main work began when ours ended and they often worked until two or three in the morning. James Davey opted to stay with them, so our original numbers were somewhat depleted. Colin and Q, who had gone to pick him up at Saint Donnolly, arrived as we sat down to dinner.

Low cloud, mist and rain greeted us the next morning. Q and Colin managed to lift off early for Saint Donnolly. Q was going to drop him off then come back and collect Pat. Unfortunately, the cloud base lowered and the airfield declared it was IFR (Instrument Flight Rules) only. Q by now was circling just to the south and being refused permission to land. I was two-way on the radio with him. We decided it made more sense for him to continue south with Colin rather than circle around for hours, burning fuel with no certainty of a landing. We were beginning to appreciate the logistical problems involved in ensuring that four aircraft departed and arrived at the same locations each day.

There was no point in the Cessna hanging around either. They were IFR rated, they had the instruments and they had autopilot. I was VFR (Visual Flight Rules), without the luxury of autopilot to see me safely through cloud. The rules for VFR flight are that you have to stay visual with the ground at all times. To be able to fly straight and level in a helicopter in cloud with no autopilot is difficult and dangerous. Helicopters, unlike fixed- wing planes and microlights, do not fly naturally straight and level and if you do find yourself in cloud and get disorientated, which is easy to do, you have a real problem. You must believe your instruments. 'Believe your instruments, believe your instruments, always believe your instruments' is drummed into helicopter pilots during training. I imagine that disorientation is what happened to John F. Kennedy Junior. He was inexperienced, he flew with no horizon, he got disorientated and lost it.

If you have ever fringed on disorientation in a small aircraft you will know what I am talking about. It is very, very frightening, I've been there and I know. You find yourself in cloud, it's a white-out, but it's moving, light and dark flickering, it's all around your plexi-glass bubble. You focus on your instruments, the artificial horizon, the VSI (vertical speed indicator), the altimeter and the ASI (air speed indicator). It can only be a matter of time before disorientation. Suddenly, all your senses tell you that you are screaming off to the left or right or up or down, but when you look at your instruments they tell you otherwise. You feel they must be wrong and think to yourself, 'Christ, now my instruments have packed up,' because all your senses tell you the opposite of what the instruments say. That is when you must repeat and repeat 'believe them, believe them' and with a bit of luck you'll hang in there. You don't have to be in cloud, haze can cause the same effect. Thankfully, after the first experience of disorientation, you know what to expect and are far less likely to panic, but it is still a difficult sensation to overcome.

I remember my first experience clearly. I was flying from my parents' house in Cheshire to our house in Somerset and was on my own with only some 70 hours of flying experience. I was at 1,500 feet in haze and the foothills of the Welsh mountains were ahead. I decided to climb above the dusty, polluted inversion layer (a layer of cold air trapped between two warm layers). Looking directly upwards I could see blue sky; 'it can't be more than a few hundred feet,' I thought. I climbed and climbed: 2,000, 3,000, 4,000, 5,000 feet. I finally came through on top at 7,500 feet. I had seldom been so high and never on my own. It was very beautiful and very, very lonely, and suddenly all I wanted was to be back within smelling distance of the grass. Looking directly down I could just see the ground – I was legal – but to get there I needed to look straight ahead.

I tried to remember all that I had been taught: 'no jerky movements, do everything slowly and remember the instruments don't lie.' And so I started my very slow descent, or what I intended to be a slow descent. I thought 300 feet per minute would be good, and thought I was only doing that. Then I looked at my VSI and it was saying 1,000 feet per minute. I just didn't believe it, but then heard a voice in my head saying 'believe it, believe it' and I slowly, slowly raised the nose and slowed my speed. Twenty of the longest minutes later I got to smell the grass. It was only minor disorientation but a salutary lesson.

The Cessna left. I sat twiddling my thumbs, remembering my conversations with Colin all those months ago. 'But I'm faster than you,' I'd said. It looked as though I might still be on the apron when Simon arrived to collect his R22 after a full morning of meetings. I hoped that we would make Regagnac before nightfall. Serge and Veronique Pardoux, our neighbours, were preparing a feast in our honour. Finally, around noon the fog began to lift, pilots emerged, we had VFR conditions and I was on my way.

I arrived at Belves Airfield in the Dordogne, a couple of kilometres from Regagnac, two minutes after Colin and, to my surprise, eight minutes before Q – it turned out that he had stopped at a Chateau hotel and enjoyed a lunch of smoked salmon and foie gras in the garden. Colin, with a 22-knot head wind and ground speed of 38 knots, had been in the air for hours.

The chairman of the Belves Aero Club was happy to hangar Colin's microlight. We pushed it into the hangar and Colin joined Q in G-JEFA for the two-minute hop over the trees to our house, but G-MURY, my helicopter, wouldn't start, not a murmur. It was dead as a dodo – the first of my mechanical problems.

A scenario of 'too many cooks' then developed. Q and Colin could not agree. Colin had 30 years' experience of building, stripping and rebuilding microlights, while Q had a working knowledge of helicopters, but neither were certified engineers. Finally it was agreed that the problem lay in a sticky starter motor, which was cured by lying under the helicopter and giving the starter motor a couple of bangs with a heavy spanner. It worked, but what if it conked out permanently in some less-friendly spot? OK, the starter motor doesn't affect you in flight, it means that you won't actually get into the air, but Colin also spotted that a nut had been forced on crooked, stripping the fine thread on the solenoid. The mechanic who did it must have known. Was he hugely pushed for time? Was he over-tired? Too much pressure? The last few days at Denham had been manic – what else had been done too hastily? My normally sublime confidence in my machine was shaken. I argued that my fears were groundless, that the engineers at Heli Air at Denham were first class, that John Michalakis was the best and had already seen me once around the world, but

G-MURY wasn't getting any younger at four and a half years old with 1,200 hours on the datcon (the instrument that shows how many hours the helicopter has flown). Once things start going wrong . . . I had to snap myself out of these negative thoughts.

When we arrived at Regagnac all the Cessna crew were relaxing by the pool. Everything was so normal and familiar at our holiday home, far from the madding crowd, deep in the forest of La Besede. We had bought the ruined village 22 years earlier from Serge and Veronique Pardoux, and we had been rebuilding and renovating ever since. It consisted of 14 very small dwellings that had been abandoned at the end of the First World War, during which all the men of the village had been killed. One of our neighbours told us that one day all the women and children just packed up their belongings and left. Simon had wanted to renovate the entire village, but we ended up with two principal houses, an annexe and a cottage for the *guardienne*. Our two lovely dogs (in quarantine between Hong Kong and England) were there and then Simon arrived.

That night we had a feast to end all feasts. Veronique's superb food was accompanied by local French wines as we sat at the long table under the catalpa tree on the chateau terrace. The night was warm under a star-filled sky and Veronique, a cook *par excellence*, had surpassed herself with ten courses of the Dordogne's gastronomic best: Terrine de Foie Gras, Asperges, Sendre, Maigret de Canard, Girolles et Cepes, ending with a crescendo of flaming Omlette Norvegienne! It was a banquet to remember in the lean times to come.

The next day Colin made his first emergency landing.

NOW in London were upset that none of the landings had been filmed and took it out on James Fletcher, all of which we learnt later when James had to make an emergency dash to Florence.

We were all meant to fly to Cannes and stay overnight there before going on to Florence, where the Contessa Maria Fede Caproni (of the Caproni Aviation Museum) had organised our stopover in Italy, including permission to fly around the Leaning Tower of Pisa. Instead, everyone except Colin was in favour of staying an extra night at Regagnac and flying direct to Florence and just refuelling in Cannes. It was a good idea as it gave us all a chance to relax, but Colin said he would rather push on and break the journey with an overnight at Fayence, a 'microlight friendly' airfield to the north of Cannes.

Colin, totally focused on the challenge, with his sights firmly set on the long way round to London, rather sensibly said he would like to take advantage of clear skies. 'It's over five hundred miles to Florence and it's going to take me a good six hours just to get to Fayence with this head wind.' Colin, I was to find, never saw the silver lining – perhaps that's how he managed to stay alive. However, I was quickly to find out that 'fear' as most people know it is an alien concept to Colin.

Two hours after his departure for Fayence my phone rang. It was Colin on his mobile. 'I'm on the ground at a small airfield called Saint Afrique – hello, hello? It's Colin, can you hear me?' I told him I could, but the line wasn't great and what was the problem?

'Yeah, I have a bit of a problem, it's my exhaust, I had to make an emergency landing!'

All this was announced in such a quiet, slightly frustrated matter-of-fact fashion you'd think he'd just missed the bus. It took me a moment or two to register. My voice went up a couple of octaves.

'You what? An emergency landing?' Al, who had been filming rural France, whipped round. He had his first drama.

'The exhaust pipe blew. There was a big bang, I was at 7,000 feet. I cut the engine, couldn't have pieces flying through the prop. I spotted this little airfield and luckily was able to coast in here.'

'Christ, Colin, are you OK? Can you fix it? We had better come down there.'

'No, no, I'm fine. It's not as bad as I thought. A couple of the spring clips need replacing, I shall try and fix it, but there's no one here. There's a large hangar, I don't really like to go inside without permission. Perhaps I can nick some wire off a fence and do a temporary job.'

I was not reassured and must have sounded like a fussy mother hen. Colin asked me to phone the manufacturer, Jim Cunliffe at Mainair in England, having tried himself to get through to Jim without success. I said I would have a go and then I would call him back.

I couldn't get hold of Jim, and then I couldn't get Colin. In desperation I phoned Michelle, Colin's partner. I didn't want to alarm her, so I told her that Colin needed some spares and that I couldn't get through to Jim – had she got Brains' (Paul Hopewell, commonly known by all as Brains due to his terrifying intelligence) phone number? Brains finally located Jim (it turned out that Mainair was changing factories at that precise moment and were 'off air' for two hours), then Jim had no idea what spares Colin might need besides the clips: 'Was the exhaust pipe damaged?' Jim was very reassuring, he knew Colin better than any of us and said, 'It will take more than a couple of clips to stop Colin, I have every faith in him as an engineer, he could strip and rebuild his machine with his eyes closed'. Three hours later we got a call from Fayence, 180 miles south of Saint Afrique. He had indeed done running 'fence' repairs and couldn't think what all the fuss was about.

Mobile phones worked well in Fayence and Colin kept us abreast of events. He decided not to bother with a hotel and said he would sleep rough on the floor of the hangar beside G-NOWW. The next phone call was from a little café. 'I'm having a pizza and a beer with this bloke, he's ever so friendly, I think he has invited me to go and stay at his place, can't understand a word he says.' (Colin knows not one word of French.) Next he was in the Frenchman's car. 'This is crazy, I don't know where we are heading, we've been going for hours up some mountain road, we're miles from the airfield and this guy is as drunk as a lord, he keeps bumping into the barrier, it's madness.' Actually, he sounded as though he was rather enjoying himself, but then he spent a very uncomfortable night in a sort of storeroom getting little sleep as the dog of the house took up a position outside his door at 1 a.m. and barked till dawn. Daylight revealed an immensely battered car bearing the scars of many a drunken journey home.

The rest of us had a lovely evening and the following morning went our separate ways, Barbara accompanied Simon northwards back to England in his little R22, while we headed south-east. This was my final farewell to family and home. 'See you in Hong Kong,' I said, trying to hold back the tears. Simon was very cheerful, which helped.

Cannes, Florence, Corfu and on to Mikonos. We rendezvoused with Colin at Pisa. He had had a good flight, following the coast and enjoying a fleeting 'overview' glimpse of the Grand Prix at Monaco, while we, the two helicopters, took a direct over-water route from Nice as we were running late.

We passed over the Leaning Tower, the river Arno, the terracotta tiled roofs bathed in golden late afternoon light and flew on to Avia Mondi, a small grass strip high in the hills above Florence where we were given an enthusiastic welcome by the lovely Contessa Maria Fede, a regiment of Italian Generals, our own Jamie McCallum and Sheelagh Bailey from the British Women Pilots Association who had arranged everything with the Contessa. There were interviews, photos and then an al fresco dinner at a small restaurant in Bivigliano, perched high on the sienna-coloured hills, amid cedar and olive trees.

Tired and happy, it was a perfect evening marred only by one small incident. I asked Al if he would take a photo of us all with my camera but he refused, saying he was too tired. Al had been a passenger in the Cessna that day and had made a two-and-a-half-hour direct flight. Perhaps he was having a bad day but he had me worried. His manner was offensive – this wasn't just tiredness. We were only four days into our trip, with another eighty to go, and something was eating at Al.

James Fletcher had agreed to fly out from London bringing the precious spring clips for Colin. He arrived at the Giotto Park Hotel where we were staying in the small hours of the morning and told Colin and I that he had taken a lot of flack from NOW for our lack of coordination and feedback while we were at Regagnac.

James said, 'They're looking for trouble, really looking for trouble that lot.'

'In what way? Why are they looking for trouble?' Colin asked.

'Oh, I had Lawrence Duffy [Al and Pat's boss at NOW] on the phone jumping up and down because I hadn't told them that you weren't flying to Cannes that day. As it happens I didn't know myself, but I didn't want to make out that I didn't know. And then they were really pissed off that you weren't filmed landing the night before – Bergerac, wasn't it?'

Colin said that only the Cessna had landed at Bergerac, but their cameramen knew we were all going to Belves.

'Well,' James said, 'never mind where you guys landed, the point is you landed separately and you weren't filmed and I seem to be the fall guy.'

Colin cut in saying, 'Yes, but what is odd is that I filmed these guys coming in, as I got there first, and I was filming myself with my front-mounted camera as I landed, so we were all on film and I handed over the film to Al.'

'Well, somehow they didn't get it and they seem to hold me accountable,' said James and went on, 'We appear to have a "them and us" situation developing. I said to Lawrence, "Look, you've got two guys out there on your payroll with all the kit in the world and if they weren't able to tell you that they weren't flying to Cannes that day, then I'm sorry but it's not fair to ring me up and give me a hard time, that's why you've got two guys in the field." But as Jamie rightly says, "they are our principal sponsors and we have all got to try and pull together and keep them happy."'

I agreed and said that Colin and I were in part to blame as we hadn't done our 'bat' phones. NOW had given us an automatic answering machine number in their office that we were meant to be phoning every morning and evening, giving a short update on events and onward plans. I remembered the small incident with Al the night before. The warning signs were all there. I should have cleared the air, established some rules and leadership and defined who was accountable for what. I can argue that NOW only came fully on board in the last few weeks and all was manic in those last hectic days before departure. I had not fully appreciated the workload of a team of seven, together with the added stress and demands of flying solo. If I'd known then just how bad things were going to get . . .

Italy was behind us: the coastal towns, all whitewash and terracottas; the harbours with their ancient forts; and the beaches, colourful with Sunday afternoon Italians and tourists; the white chalk cliffs and the breathtaking turquoise Aegean Sea. We left the coast 30 miles south of Brindizi and the water crossing to Corfu was like glass. Then, mountains to the north of Kerkira appeared out of the haze.

Colin took a straight-line route from Corfu, while the helicopters enjoyed a meandering course, island hopping. Colin was once more well ahead of us at Mikonos. The Cessna had landed hours earlier. So none of us were on hand when Colin landed, the wind gusting up to 30 knots. When you have 120 square feet of sail that can be a big problem. It's reasonably OK when you are moving, but once you come to a halt you need several people to hold down the wings, otherwise you are in danger of being blown over. Colin had a battle on his hands. He was trying to summon help from a group of men from Olympic Airways who were idly passing the time of day, sitting in the shade of their hangar doorway. They thought Colin was being friendly and just waved back until they finally cottoned on to the problem and ambled over.

The wind and associated turbulence close to land made life interesting for the helicopters too, and made photography almost impossible for me. The first blast of turbulence had me moving fast out to sea. When the air is calm, you can take the left hand off the collective lever, but the right hand has to stay on the cyclic lever at all times, keeping the craft straight and level. Taking photos with the left hand becomes tricky. However, I was getting quite good at one-handed skills like changing films, opening chocolate bars and bottles of water – except in turbulence. It was frustrating. Everywhere I looked was picture postcard perfect: all those whitewashed houses with their blue doors and window frames, the parched earth colours, white-sand beaches and emerald seas – we meandered and bounced slowly towards Mikonos.

I had not known that the island of Mikonos was famous for its wind, there were windmills scattered everywhere. Whilst the camera crew and I were bumpily admiring the islands, Colin had dismantled G-NOWW, and having found no hangar space, was not in the best of tempers.

'Why did you choose Mikonos of all places?' He was full of doom and gloom. 'We could be here for days, the locals say that once this wind picks up it usually lasts for at least ten days.' And then he said 'Why was no one here to help me? Where's Heinz?' Heinz, it turned out, had come out to the airfield several times on a hired motorbike to help Colin and on the last trip he had skidded on some oil on a corner, fallen off, and was nursing a badly grazed arm, and bruised pride, but thankfully nothing more.

Boys – and there I was trying to cope with six of them; six, all very different in character. Colin, rock solid as always. Heinz, an adventurer and a meticulous planner, very organised and dependable, good company and tolerant, except when it came to sloppy and slow check-outs at hotels where we soon found we could depend on him to bark orders and get action. Later in the trip, Heinz's tolerance was to be tested to breaking point, by our own people. Al – big Al appeared easygoing. He had a great sense of humour, loved his work and the desolate places, but he was never a kindred spirit. And Pat – I never really knew Pat, he was good at his job, the typical modern reporter at large, standing in front of the camera, 'This is Pat Doyle reporting to you live from . . .' He made cocky, quick movements and had staccato speech, but his eyes were cold. Or have I forgotten the warmth that might have been there in those early days? James Davey was the quietest of the pack but ready to follow. Al, Pat and James were all good people, but put the seven of us together, then start adding tiredness, stress and long hours, take away respect and I had a problem. Only one week into the trip and it seemed that we were already developing, as James Fletcher had said, a 'them and us' set up. Colin, Heinz and myself versus Al, Pat and James, with Q, the mercurial, clever, lazy, charming, arrogant 'go-between'.

Workloads varied. Al and Pat had a busy time of it once we landed, cutting and editing and then sending NOW the footage. The one who flew with Q in the helicopter had a longer and more tiring day, while the days in the Cessna were relaxed by comparison. Al and Pat had to have hotel rooms facing the right direction for their numerous satellite dishes and their rooms were always awash with equipment. Q and James Davey had the most relaxed time on the ground, James especially. Heinz did most of the airport work for the Cessna: filing flight plans and paying all the airport charges, ground handling and parking fees and, in some places, he sorted out the navigation and Met reports. He was also employed (unpaid) as the accountant and much more. I had asked him, before departure, whether he would mind keeping tabs on expenditures, little appreciating how much work it would involve, and he was meticulous. He brought along his little Sony computer plus a small printer and kept immaculate accounts, filing all receipts and sending weekly statements to NOW. He handled all the bills. As the Cessna crew always checked out of the hotels last it meant the rest of us could just say, 'Mr Rust will pay.' He would also print us out each a copy of the airways routes and reporting points for the next day.

Colin had the longest flying days. G-NOWW had an airspeed of 60 knots. The helicopters averaged 90 knots and the Cessna 180 knots. But Colin didn't have much to organise outside the airfield. My days were long and I had never appreciated how much more ongoing work four aircraft and seven people would entail. There was so much organisation to be done: e-mails, faxes to be sent, clearances, confirmations on fuel, updating the home team who were in turn doing a whole mass of organising on our behalf. We were still waiting for many clearances to come through, Russian and Chinese clearances were a particular concern, and there was constant worry as to whether they would come through on time. There were always key people en route to be contacted. The overall organisation was my problem. I was the one with the contacts, I was the one who knew the people we needed to pull the strings – much needed for places like Russia, China, Burma and Japan. We were also attempting to raise money for Operation Smile, there were press interviews and press conferences to go through and I was also trying to keep an audio journal.

The time spent at airports between Europe and North America was excessive, anything from one to three hours on both take off and landing. De-rigging and rigging Colin's microlight took time, as did refuelling, filing flight plans, getting Met forecasts, paying landing fees, navigation fees, ground handling charges – and invariably all were in different buildings.

Clearances for Iran had still not materialised. I decided we would have to route via Bahrain and Dubai from Kuwait to Karachi, which had always been the safer option as mechanical problems could be more easily handled. I had been keen to visit pastures new, having been through Bahrain and Dubai before, and I had heard that the Iranians were very friendly. However, the Bahrain route would also save a day – a major plus – so I e-mailed Dave Gannon at Overflight for the route change.

The winds grew stronger. Colin and I arrived at the airfield at 7 a.m., too late as the wind had already gathered strength, and then Colin gave me the 'I told you so's.

'I just knew it, I just knew we should have come out earlier, I just knew it. When I looked out of my bedroom window at 5 a.m. there was no wind in the grass, but at 6 a.m. it was already bad and I just knew we were too late.' A lost day.

There were mutterings of 'There's no way Colin is going to make it', and 'What is the cut-off point? This is all a big mistake – the microlight will jeopardise the project.'

'We're in this together. We, Colin and I, are the project' I replied. 'I'm not going on without him. If we can't make the northern crossings this year then we'll just have to wait till next year!' Brave words, and not what any sponsor wanted to hear, but at that time I never doubted that we would both make it.

The next day we decided to go for a dawn departure when the winds would be at their lightest. Colin, Q (who hadn't been to bed) and I were at the airfield an hour before sunrise. There was no sign of the film crew who had said they would be there to record the threatened hairy take-off, and a helping hand would not have gone amiss. Assembling Colin's microlight is no easy task. Basically, if he cannot get hangar space he has to take the wing off, and to do that the fuel tanks have to be taken out, the wing laid flat on the ground with the fuel tanks weighting it down so that it doesn't blow away. If the fuel tanks are already full, as they were that day, reassembling requires a lot of brute strength, something I don't have much of, but at least on this occasion we had Q to help us.

Q and I held a wing tip each. The winds were strengthening with every passing minute, and Colin was doing nothing to ease my worries: 'I hope the wing doesn't break.' Q's response had been: 'Well, you won't know until you try!' We then ran along the runway as fast and as long as we could, clutching the wing tips, then stood and watched the critical moment as Colin took to the sky. Despite Colin's dire warnings 'that the wing could break in two, that never before had a microlight taken off as heavily laden in such a strong wind,' and several graphic descriptions of wings breaking catastrophically, he made it aloft. These men weren't world champions for nothing and that left me asking myself a few questions.

Once airborne from Mikonos, Colin had an uneventful flight, as did we all, with 21 knots of tail wind and a safe landing in Cyprus, where we faced the possibility of another day's delay. I wanted a fully functioning starter motor before leaving Europe so Simon Gale, the Heli Air engineer, had arrived with a new starter motor for G-MURY and we had decided to have the 50-hour services on both helicopters done. This worked out well, as the 100-hour service would now be done in Hong Kong, where my son Justin was living, rather than Calcutta as originally planned. Justin conveniently worked for Cathay Pacific at the new international airport, Chep Lap Kok. Happily Simon was able to change the starter motor and complete the services on the afternoon of our arrival so no delay was incurred.

The flight to Cyprus had been the longest water crossing to date – 439 miles. Four and a half hours over water for the helicopters, six and a half for Colin and a comfortable two hours and ten minutes for the Cessna. Water crossings so far had been the English Channel, the Mediterranean from Nice to Pisa and the Aegean Sea from Brindizi to Corfu, plus some Greek island hopping. We had already passed over a lot of water but there was a great deal more to come. We would be crossing over 7,500 miles of water before finally arriving in Scotland. Our flight to Jordan the next day would take us over another long water stretch.

I was never very happy over water. The time between those last secure moments of leaving terra firma and the relief of eventually seeing that distant smudge on the horizon was always filled with a quiet anxiety. My ear was always attuned to the engine, acutely aware of any change or suspected change in engine noise, and with good reason. Engine failure in a single-engine helicopter over water is bad news – helicopters sink like a stone.

We had all done the 'Dunker Course' at the Royal Air and Sea Base at Yeovilton before departure. You get in a capsule, strapped in full harness, and are then dropped 20 feet into water. The capsule rapidly sinks and turns upside down as it does so. Blackness floods in and you are blind, panicked and already screaming for air. There are four people scrambling to get out with water flooding in, the helicopter falling and falling, deeper and deeper. Arms and legs and feet flail in the dark and everyone is trying to get to the door – and that's only training. The real thing? The very thought of it made me sweat. Everyone was agreed that, without that training, one's chances of ever making it out of a sunken helicopter were near zero.

I believe the military never fly solo and their helicopters are large enough to have a built-in life raft for a seat cushion, which is attached to their flight suits. They also have ejector-type window panels and most have pop-up floats on the skids of their helicopters. Our R44 helicopters had none of these; we had neither the space nor the weight for such luxuries. So, when my right magneto blew up on me at 9,000 feet over water and one hour from the nearest land it was like being hit in the stomach with a sledgehammer.

TWO

Cyprus to Calcutta

8 - 17 June

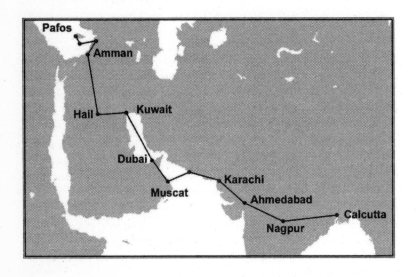

DAY 9

Cyprus, our last European stop. The day started badly. Clearance to overfly Israel had been denied, so instead of a 322-mile leg from Pafos to Amman in Jordan, we were looking at 485 miles, having to make a dog-leg to the north to overfly Syria and Lebanon.

Colin had gone to the airfield on his own as I had to make phone calls. He spent hours up in the Tower getting everything sorted and filing everyone's flight plans, and was fed up and frantic by the time we arrived. He had planned a 6 a.m. take-off and he finally departed at 10 a.m. followed by the helicopters at 10.30 a.m. and the Cessna shortly after that.

The weather was fine but hazy and within minutes we were out over the water on an initial heading of 110 degrees before turning on a more northerly heading. There was no horizon. For a time I could see the mountains of Cyprus, which gave me something solid to focus on – over water in haze if you lose your horizon you have to rely heavily on instruments and it demands continuous concentration. We climbed slowly (being very heavy with fuel) through the dust-laden air to 9,000 feet, the height of the inversion layer where the skies were clear. At that height and heavy with fuel, the helicopter does not perform at its best. The air is thin and you tend to get a lot of vibration and blade slap, the latter leads you to think of nasty things like 'blade stall', which is exactly what it sounds like – a catastrophic situation.

So there I was at 9,000 feet, a height I never normally fly at, when BANG! There was a noise like a pistol shot, like a car backfiring in my headphones – quite literally heart-stopping. I tried to kid myself that it had just been some sort of radio interference. I adjusted my 'noise reduction' Bose headphones, I checked my Ts and Ps (temperature and pressure instruments), RPM, manifold pressure (power), exhaust gas temperature – and then the low RPM horn sounded (engine revs per minute) and the red warning light was glowing. The continuous shrill sound of the low RPM warning, signalling 'stall', is very frightening, and when it refuses to stop it is nerve-shattering.

I lowered the collective lever a fraction, reducing the blade pitch and at the same time rolled on the throttle. Everything returned to normal, everything except my heart which had gone into overdrive. Had the aircraft yawed to the left? I didn't think so. I didn't want to believe it as that would mean loss of engine power. I wanted so desperately to believe it was just radio interference, but logic told me the RPM had nothing to do with radio static. I had company close by, but I was alone, very much alone, and I needed no reminding that it was all up to me.

My life raft was positioned behind my head. I reached back and pulled it over onto the seat beside me with the handle beside the collective lever. Mentally I did a quick run through emergency procedures for ditching at sea: check wind direction, send a May Day call, check speed, check rotor RPM, tighten safety belt, undo both door latches, flare at 40 feet, level off, collective up – and get the hell out. My locator beacon was in one of the leg pockets of my flight suit and my precious Spare Air (three minutes of bottled air) was zipped into the front of my suit for quick access.

How could I have thought I had the expertise and courage to fly solo around the world? I didn't have what it takes, I just wasn't up to it – I was really, really scared. We still had another two hours before we would see land. It seemed like ten, time dragged, my confidence in myself and in G-MURY was in tatters, and then, with the Syrian coast in sight, it happened again, another terrifying explosion in my ears. This was definitely no radio interference, but I had no idea what the cause could be. 'Please God just let me get over land' was all I asked. The next 30 minutes were the worst in my life, knowing something was wrong and waiting for something ghastly to happen. I was in the grip of cold, sweaty fear.

I made it to land and relaxed a fraction. But something was badly amiss. My helicopter was five years old and had had some hard flying. I wished, not for the first time, that I was flying the brand new G-JEFA, the camera helicopter that Q was piloting. I had opted for G-MURY as I was hoping to have both of my world records in the same aircraft.

Should I press on for Jordan or should I stop in the Syrian sands? I decided to press on and stay high; the ground was flat with endless autorotation landing spots. I was completely shattered. It was the most exhausting flight I had ever made; not the longest, but the most demanding and the most unnerving. After the sea crossing, we hit severe turbulence, then a sandstorm, then yet another explosion and finally I had to contend with the shimmering desert heat. I was bordering on disorientation with the mirages, the burning, relentless sun and fatigue. I don't really know how I made it to Jordan's International Marka Airport in Amman, but I did and the relief of crossing the threshold of Runway 24, of taxiing to the apron, finally shutting down and being safely back on the ground was overwhelming.

The two helicopters arrived at the same time as Colin, landing in formation, albeit somewhat ragged, much to the happiness of a small gathering of journalists waiting on the hot and dusty apron in front of aircraft hangars dwarfed by an immense Jordanian royal crown. Colin, although slower, had taken a more southerly route through Lebanon over the mountains – where Lebanon ATC insisted on a minimum flight level of 11,000 feet (too high for the helicopters) to clear the highest snow-capped peaks. The Cessna had passed Colin over the mountains at 14,000 feet, and to a man they were in awe. Heinz said to me later, 'There sat Colin, open to the elements in that fragile little toy of an aircraft, so frail, so vulnerable, high, high in the heavens, high above the snow clad peaks, chuntering along and giving us a brave wave!' Colin's comment had been, 'I was that cold, but I was above the turbulence.'

I had been so tired on landing that I hadn't even checked out my aircraft. It wasn't until the following morning when doing the checks that I found out what was wrong. I had lost my right magneto. I was going nowhere and Colin had already left. I tried to get him on my radio, no luck. Colin was on his own, heading into the 'Empty Quarter', hundreds of square miles of desolate sand with midday temperatures in the high 40s and, knowing Colin, he had probably taken little water. Brian Milton (who flew round the world with Keith Reynolds in a microlight in 1998 – the first and only team ever to do so) had been critical of our taking this route, the route through the Empty Quarter. Brian had also been critical of our breezy landing on Mikonos. 'Mikonos is famous for its winds,' he'd e-mailed us, asking, 'Why the hell are you there?'

I should have asked the Tower to relay a message to Colin but was just too preoccupied with my own problems. How long would it be before I could get an engineer out to Jordan? Robinson helicopters don't have a worldwide infrastructure, engineers are few and far between and parts have to come from the factory in Los Angeles. Also, being a UK registered helicopter, we could only have CAA certified engineers tinkering with the helicopters. A mechanical problem like this could mean a long delay.

To compound all these problems, it was Friday – a day of rest in Jordan. Everyone was on holiday. The airfield was deserted and the hangar doors were closed. A couple of members of the press were there and a certain Sami Zogby. Sami, a microlight enthusiast, had been following our progress on the NOW website and had come to the airport to meet Colin. Sami had a friend who was an engineer, who was in bed. He was finally roused and proved to be not only an engineer but a certified Civil Aviation engineer for piston engine helicopters and – a further miracle – deep in the supplies shed he found a replacement magneto (the magnetos are not made by Robinson). Sami, the engineer and Q worked all day to make the repairs. This was a day when I had only good thoughts about Q.

I went back to the hotel. It gave me a chance to check on our Indian clearances and to see how Justin was getting on with the Chinese Civil Aviation Authorities. After Hanoi we hoped to overfly China to Hong Kong, rather than make the long sea crossing from Danang, and then I needed to talk to Dave Gannon at Overflight about Burma and Thailand. I didn't get much done, however, as I fell sound asleep and only woke when Q phoned at 3 p.m. saying 'I can be ready to leave in an hour!' I was half-asleep and still feeling shattered from the traumatic flying of the previous day. I opted for another night in Jordan – not even promises of wonderful desert sunsets and the warning of another day lost could sway me. The onward flight to Saudi Arabia would take four hours and, as it turned out, Q was over optimistic, it was another three hours before G-MURY was ready.

Colin arrived safely in Hail, having tried for hours to raise us on the radio. Then he waited at the airfield for an hour and a half for Simon Walters from the British Embassy in Ruhad, the British Embassy had been on our case for months and Simon flew in especially to ensure our safe passage. Colin was not very happy and said to me the next day, 'What if I had had a problem? What if I had gone down in the Empty Quarter?' He had taken his EPIRB, but only one bottle of water. Later, however, we were to be glad that he had been alone that day rather than two days later, my birthday and a day I will never forget – ever.

We made it through to Hail the following day. But, within minutes of take off, I noticed that my cylinder head temperatures were into the red, and that the clutch light was coming on for long periods. Although the cylinder head temperatures were high, the exhaust gas temperatures were normal – was it just the dial misreading? I couldn't just assume that was the case. If it was an accurate reading and the cylinder heads were seriously overheated my engine would seize. Very, very slowly I climbed to 8,000 feet where the air temperature was a pleasant 26 degrees centigrade. By running on reduced power I was just able to keep the dial out of the red. In normal circumstances the clutch light will come on briefly from time to time when the actuator is adjusting the drive belts (the drive belts turn the drive shaft that turns the rotor blades). But if the light stays on for more than about eight seconds you must pull the clutch circuit breaker and land as soon as possible. The chances are you have a malfunctioning actuator which continues to loosen the belts until the drive shaft can no longer turn the rotor blades. It could of course just be a faulty instrument light, but there is no way of knowing. I was counting clutch seconds. The clutch finally settled down but the cylinder head temperatures remained high all the way to Hail and I had to stay high and worried, instead of being able to relax and have fun like the camera crew who were skimming the sand dunes.

We had no sandstorms, the skies were clear and we had a steady 20 knots of tail wind pushing us along. Even with my mechanical worries and having to fly high it was a good day and it was reassuring to see endless perfect landing spots. The sand reached forever and ever, changing and shifting in the Empty Quarter – the very name itself has a fierce magic about it. Finally the volcanic Jabbal mountain range came into view, in all its awesome beauty rising to 10,000 feet before plunging once more to the 5,000-foot high desert plateau and the town of Hail.

We were given a very warm welcome by Abdul Kareem Al Shammary, representative of the Governor of Hail, and a team of dignitaries: white-robed gentlemen with hawk-like features, uniformly wearing the red and white checked, cloth headdress. Colin was also there with Simon Walters.

In Hail we met with nothing but kindness, generosity, friendliness and great attempts at efficiency. And, as in '97 when Q and I had gone through Saudi Arabia via Jiddah and Riyadh, I met with no prejudice as a woman. We were escorted into a vast, carpeted VIP lounge with gilt chairs lining all four walls that were covered with pictures of Sheiks and Government officials. There we were presented with tiny cups of bitter and surprisingly refreshing tea, poured with great ceremony and accuracy from a teapot held several feet above one's small cup.

Later, we were escorted into town in a convoy of air-conditioned Mercedes-Benz cars, along wide, palm tree and bougainvillaea-lined avenues and into a fairly hotchpotch town of 1950s-looking whitish buildings where a lot of construction was taking place. A new, half-built hotel was proudly pointed out to us. We ended up at the 'old hotel' which was perfect. I'm glad we were there before the new one was finished as I stayed in it the following year and it lacked all the charm of the old one. Our hotel was small and scruffy but clean. We had rooms with school beds opening onto a central tiled hallway and shared two enormous bathrooms consisting of a basic shower in one corner, a loo and hand basin in the other, with acres of tiled floor in between.

That evening Abdul Kareem Al Shammary and friends took us out to dinner where we sat on the floor in a traditional-style, high-ceilinged, white-washed building and ate huge platters of lamb and rice, raisins and dates, chicken and camel with our fingers. It was delicious.

At the airfield, while refuelling from barrels with the camera crew filming, I had discussed my cylinder head problem with Heinz and Colin. They were both of the opinion the dial was misreading, that possibly a wire had been disturbed. Later I spoke to Q and made the mistake of saying 'Heinz thinks . . .' Q, with great sarcasm and many gestures retorted, 'Oh well, if *Heinz* thinks so, then I'm sure Heinz must be right, oh yes, I think Heinz is the person you should be listening to.' Then, pacing up and down and waving his arms he went on to say, 'It's all much more complicated than that. I am the one who fitted the magneto, and you don't know the half of what I had to do . . .' I interrupted saying, 'Q, what do you mean by "I"? Where was the civil engineer? What was he doing?'

'Well, they don't know everything, they're such wankers.'

I tried to calm him down and said, 'Look, Q, I really appreciate all the work you put in yesterday but this is my helicopter, I'm the one flying it. It's my life at stake, I need to know, and I'm not happy. I just don't need the trauma of a malfunctioning helicopter, I want it in perfect running order and it's not. We're flying over a lot of hostile terrain in remote areas. I want one of your engineers to come and get G-MURY sorted out.'

Q made me feel I was making a big fuss over nothing and that it wasn't necessary for an engineer to come out. But I insisted and it was finally agreed that an engineer would come out and meet us in Dubai. It turned out that my fears were justified and I was very thankful that I had dug in my heels.

DAY 12 – 11 JUNE

My 60th birthday – old age pensioner and all. It was certainly an original way for a 60 year old to celebrate her birthday, high over the deserts of Saudi Arabia. It turned out to be a day of high drama.

The wind was from the north and the air was full of dust and sand as Colin took off, lifting fast and quickly disappearing from sight, swallowed in the swirling dust; visibility was down to 300 metres.

We gave him an hour's start and then we were on our way. Once more heavy with fuel, we climbed slowly through the sand-laden air, flying all the time on instruments. We could see nothing: the limitless desert and blue skies of the day before were gone. We were enveloped in a strange, disorientating world; a world filled with ever-moving mirages, twists of light and formless shapes. We climbed and climbed. The sands of the desert below quickly became indistinguishable from the sand in the air. When looking directly heavenward, the blue sky through the haze seemed so deceptively close but was thousands of feet up. It took us nearly 45 minutes to reach the top of the inversion layer at 8,500 feet – a lonely world.

My clutch was once more playing up and the cylinder head temperatures were also once more on the edge of the red. I was fully occupied, constantly checking instruments, staying orientated and contending with blade slap and lumpy air – there is nearly always lumpy air at the top of the inversion layer, but at times like that you wonder, 'Is it turbulence or is it the helicopter?' My confidence in G-MURY was at a low ebb and I was nervous. I wasn't enjoying my birthday at all.

We were by now all two-way on the radio: Colin, myself, the camera helicopter and the Cessna. Colin was 70 miles ahead of me, enjoying the 28 knots of tail wind and in stable air at 13,000 feet. He was happy although the climb had been 'horrendous' – life for Colin was either good or horrendous. The Cessna was some 30 miles behind. All seemed to be OK. Then Colin came on the radio, 'My exhaust pipe has blown, not sure I can hold it!' He sounded seriously alarmed, which in itself was worrying. Colin is never alarmed, always the quiet, understated, matter-of-fact voice. Q quickly asked him for his coordinates. We got his position and we all altered course to be near at hand, though God knows what we could do other than give the reassurance that we were close by.

'I'm going to try and get a strap around the exhaust – got to stop it going into the prop,' he said, and we could all imagine, all too vividly, the desperate struggle.

Several minutes passed. 'It's not the clips, there's a sodding great hole in the exhaust – burnt my hand,' he said.

Heinz in the Cessna radioed that King Kallid Military Airfield was 40 miles right abeam of Colin's present position. My own problems forgotten, I weakly encouraged him to 'hang in there'. I asked for another position fix – silence. 'Colin, are you there?' and again 'Colin, are you there?' Still silence. I imagined the worst, we all did: the exhaust had separated, it had gone into the prop, the prop had shattered sending a thousand pieces into the wing, shredding the wing. With no wing he would hurtle to his death on the desert sands 13,000 feet below.

This couldn't be happening, it couldn't have happened. I could still picture his smiling face when, just a few hours earlier, he had given me one of those Yasser Arafat tablecloths for my birthday. He just couldn't be lying crumpled somewhere on the desert floor. How would I tell Michelle?

It was the worst of times. For 20 minutes we flew in silence except for intermittently asking, 'Colin, do you read? Colin, are you there?', always followed by silence. This could not be real, and yet all I could see in my mind's eye was wreckage in the swirling sands thousands of feet below. Then – unbelievably – Colin came on the air. 'Hello, hello, anybody there?'

The relief was overwhelming – thank God. Oh thank God.

Over the static-filled radio (Colin's radio always seemed to have static), he told us what had happened. Whilst twisting and stretching out behind himself to try and get a strap around the exhaust, he had inadvertently pulled the intercom cable out of its socket in his headphones. He had been so occupied – literally fighting for his life – that it was some while before he realised that things had gone silent. Then he thought his radio was on the blink until he finally discovered the disconnected cable.

Colin managed to get the strap around the exhaust, but was holding onto it for the next two and a half hours, all the way to Kuwait, having decided to 'go for it' rather than divert to King Kallid. He was far from out of the woods. Negotiating a one-handed (the other was holding the strap) descent through 11,000 feet of unstable, sand-laden air lay ahead of him. Anxiety, though lessened, was still palpable. Would the exhaust hold out? Would he be able to hold on?

The Cessna was ahead and reported that visibility was down to 500 metres and that there was a fair amount of turbulence at the lower levels. A 'fair amount' of turbulence for the Cessna meant that it would be near catastrophic for Colin.

'Blimey' was Colin's only comment.

Worrying over Colin helped to alleviate my own fears a little, or rather take my mind off my own forthcoming descent. I wasn't at all confident about going back down through all that sand and turbulence. I had my Beatles CD playing and I remember thinking that 'Yellow Submarine' was somewhat inappropriate for the desert, but wonderfully cheerful.

I had my GPS, I knew where the airfield was. Colin started his descent – a blind, straight-in, one-handed descent. I knew he would have preferred a spiral descent at 2,000 feet per minute, 'much the best in turbulence'. I remember him telling me this when he described his descent into Kerkira Airport in Crete when he flew to Australia (setting a world speed record for an open cockpit aircraft). It had been March '98 and he had hit appalling weather. At 14,000 feet, he had been above the clouds, above the storm that was raging below. He had to get down to the airport and had opted for the spiralling, 2,000 feet per minute descent. He entered the cloud and immediately the airframe was coated in heavy frost, super cooled by temperatures of minus ten degrees centigrade. He had been deadly afraid that the weight would prove too great, but he spiralled down successfully, finally bottoming out 500 feet above a storm-swept sea. At Kerkira, where all traffic was grounded, they had been amazed to see one small microlight come hurtling diagonally across the runway and taxiing straight into a mercifully open hangar.

I was a good 30 miles behind Colin, intending to start my own descent 10 miles out. Long minutes passed, and then Heinz reported that Colin was safely on the ground. My own descent proved manageable; I was getting better on my instruments, and I landed safely. But these demanding days were proving exhausting: constantly monitoring instruments, mechanical problems, coping with near-zero visibility. I spent most of the time feeling scared – how long could I go on? The men, other than Heinz, were years younger than me and vastly more experienced. I tried to conquer my fears by focusing on the fact that we had all made it back to the ground where we were delighted to see an all-in-one-piece Colin.

My birthday had a happy ending after all and Heinz generously treated the whole team to a birthday dinner. With fruit juice (Kuwait is dry), we toasted my 60 years and Colin's merciful return to earth. We had been going for 12 days and had another 74 to go (or so we thought). We were 2 days behind schedule.

There was a déjà vu feeling about the next morning. I had the same old problem – on doing my checks I found I had a dead magneto. Once again I hadn't checked on landing and once again Colin had left. If I had been more alert we could have diverted John Michalakis (our engineer) to fly direct to Kuwait rather than Dubai and Colin perhaps wouldn't have strayed into Iranian airspace.

The first we knew about Colin and Iran was an agitated phone call from Dave Gannon at Overflight in England. He had been contacted by the Iranian authorities who told him that Colin had penetrated Iranian airspace. We had no word from Colin, we had no idea where he was or what he was doing and he was overdue in Dubai. Had the Iranians forced him to land in Iran? Dave Gannon didn't know.

John Michalakis had no visa for Kuwait and it took half a day and hundreds of faxes and phone calls to get the visa at such short notice. He finally arrived late that afternoon and worked through the night, installing the new magneto that he had brought with him. He said the replacement that Q had helped to install in Amman had two points too close together; the timing was wrong, which would account for the high cylinder head temperatures, as the points were black from overheating.

Late that same afternoon there was still no word from Colin and we were all beginning to imagine him incarcerated in an Iranian jail. At 6 p.m. my mobile phone rang – it was Colin. 'Where are you?' I asked. Colin, sounding rather surprised, said, 'Well, in Dubai of course, but what happened to you?' I ignored his question and said, 'Thank goodness, we thought you might be in Iran. Do you realise that you penetrated Iranian airspace?'

He was even more surprised and then full of righteous indignation when I told him that Iran was on the warpath. 'I went into Iranian airspace? I never did! I stayed right on Bravo 416, which is the airways route. I talked to Kuwait and I was talking to Tehran all the time,' he said. It all seemed very strange. He then went on to say that there had been an American aircraft carrier on manoeuvres in the area and that they had monitored him all the time to make sure that none of the jets came near him. It turned out that he *had* been on the wrong airway, however, and the authorities were anxious that the rest of us flew on the correct airway closer to the Bahrain side, well clear of war games. It was odd, though, that the Kuwaitis had cleared his flight plan on the other route and that Tehran had accepted him. Colin had been totally unaware of all the excitement he was causing. His next sortie into hostile air space was to be far, far more dramatic and was to make world headlines.

John Michalakis had had no sleep for 48 hours. He worked through the night and was hoping to catch the 2 a.m. flight to London. He made a final check of the aircraft and found the carburettor heater wasn't working. 'Why didn't you tell me the carb heat wasn't working?' he asked Q. Q replied that he hadn't known, neither had I, there had been no need for carb heat in the high and dry desert temperatures. 'Well, you will have to get it wired in Dubai. We'll get it fixed properly in Hong Kong,' John said. And so a whole new chapter of worry was to open for me – another malfunctioning part.

I woke the next morning to the now all too familiar sight of swirling dust and sand. At the airport we negotiated, for the last time, the long and tedious process of getting 'air side' (through customs and immigration). The camera crew headed off to the General Aviation sector and I made my way to the Kuwaiti Airlines hangar where John had been working. Little G-MURY sat there waiting, dwarfed by a Kuwait Airlines 747. Mechanics were arriving for work and even they were sand-coloured in their khaki overalls. There was sand everywhere and I saw another day of tough, demanding, no-fun flying ahead. I felt drained.

Looking back on that morning I realise what a low ebb I had reached, worn out from the days of desert flying and mechanical problems. I had lost faith in myself and my machine. Since leaving Cyprus I had been plagued with either mechanical problems or appalling visibility, or both. The conditions meant that I had been flying on instruments virtually all the time. This demanded continuous concentration as I tried not to get disorientated, constantly monitored the helicopter and, if I wasn't checking my artificial horizon, I was checking the Ts and Ps (temperature and pressure instruments). Also, to add to my woes, it was hot, hot, hot, like a hot hairdryer blowing sand. I was on my own in every sense: alone in my helicopter and the only woman amongst six men. My confidence was so low that I even felt nervous just talking to Air Traffic Control for clearance to start up and taxi.

My cylinder head temperatures were now normal but the clutch was still playing up as we once more climbed slowly up through the murk on Bravo 491 towards the Arabian Gulf and Dubai. Twenty minutes after take off we were over the sea, in haze, but the sand-laden air was improving and the Cessna, half an hour ahead of us, reported that weather conditions were better ahead. We decided to descend and fly low-level. For once, flying over water seemed positively friendly: warm waters with lots of shipping and a fair smattering of oil wells, their jets of flame looking eerie and wonderful, looming out of the haze. I had thought we were too far north for sharks until we spotted the most enormous basking hammerhead shark that wasn't the least bit frightened of the helicopters. Pat got some great video footage.

Confidence in myself began to return along with optimism. I was constantly accused of being the world's greatest optimist. When it came to pessimism, on the other hand, Colin took top honours. For Colin there was a downside to everything – the glass was always half empty.

There was one happy event while we were in Kuwait. Q's sister Sasha gave birth to a baby boy, making Q an uncle and giving my mother her first great-grandson. They called him Loris Alexander Quentin Pattinson. 'Loris' had been my grandfather's name.

Kuwait, Dubai, Oman and Karachi – Colin was ahead of me at every stop. I had suggested that he didn't hang around in Dubai waiting for us. I thought it would be sensible for him to make tracks to Karachi and perhaps break the journey, spending the night in Gwadar on the Baluchistan coast. It seemed like a good idea at the time, it's a long flight from Dubai to Karachi – 736 miles. Gwadar is just over halfway – 434 miles. So, that morning, as we were taking off from Kuwait, Colin set off for Pakistan, intending to stop in Gwadar.

In Dubai that night I was rather surprised to get a phone call from Michelle in England passing on a message from Colin. He had tried both my mobile and Q's to no avail. He finally got through to Michelle. Colin was *not* happy. Gwadar was not a port of entry and there was a major sandstorm covering the entire area. 'I could be stuck here for weeks,' he had said to Michelle and the town itself was apparently utterly godforsaken. Colin had to go miles outside the town to phone us, to the only phone with access to the outside world, where he had to join a long queue of patient Pakistanis. There was apparently nothing in Gwadar, no hotel, no water, no fuel, nothing, and the forecast was for the sandstorm to continue its unabated fury all through the following day. The tale of woe continued. He had been made to wait in the airport for three hours with the police telling him he shouldn't be there, that he couldn't be there. Finally they let him go, under escort. 'Colin says will you please check if he's still there when you reach Gwadar – don't leave him there,' Michelle said.

My own arrival in Karachi was fraught. We ran into darkness thanks to dallying over-long in Duty Free in Dubai buying new cameras and then lingering on the Baluchistan coast. The camera crew (it was Al's turn with Q) and I routed first via Muscat in Oman to refuel, as the margins for going direct were on the tight side and there was no Avgas in Pakistan before Karachi. The Cessna went direct. Shortly after take-off, Heinz called on the radio saying, 'Do you realise that you are going to be three hours into darkness by the time you reach Karachi?' We did some quick calculations and he wasn't far out – why hadn't we registered the fact? We reckoned we might just be able to make it as night descended if we could do a fast turn around in Muscat and picked up good tail winds across the Persian Gulf.

We radioed ahead to Muscat to try and speed things up. It certainly helped, but the refuellers insisted on being paid in US dollars – 950 new US dollars. We only had old. I told them that they would have to accept the old ones, as that was all I had. 'How do we know these are not fake bills? We have now to check your bills, we have too many fake.' And off they went, back to the terminal building and got a little machine that checked for counterfeit bills. Meanwhile, we sat in the shade of the helicopters dripping with sweat. It was 46 degrees centigrade on the apron and humid and seldom have I been so hot. By the end of that day Al's black t-shirt had a new pattern, a million streaks of dried white salt.

The dollar machine was useless, the notes wouldn't go through and then they said one of them was fake. Q started hopping around and waving his arms, 'I'll start up my helicopter, that should speed things up, why don't you too?' The only problem was that the fuel truck was parked right alongside my helicopter. After a long delay they finally let us go, saying they would have to trust us.

Then, as I was starting up, my mobile phone rang. It was Michelle telling me that Colin had landed in Karachi. 'The little shit!' was Q's comment. 'Do you think we should route direct and miss out the Baluchistan coast?' Q asked, adding that we were probably going to be a good two hours into darkness at our present rate.

'I really, really want to go via the Baluchistan coast – it's one of the most dramatic coastlines in the world and with a bit of luck the tail winds will strengthen – and Al will get fabulous footage,' I argued.

There were lots of good reasons: the coast was the official airways route that we were meant to be following; it meant that we would only be over water for 243 miles versus 578 on the direct route; and it was only 75 miles further. I optimistically suggested that perhaps it would only make a difference of about half an hour – and anyhow we had night ratings for the UK and I remembered Colin telling me that when he flew to Australia in his microlight he had flown the last hour of his flight into Karachi in pitch darkness with no lights of any sort, and the authorities hadn't batted an eyelid.

We set off with an encouraging 28-knot tail wind on a heading of 060 following air route Romeo 462 to Jiwani, just across the border from Iran, 243 miles away across the Gulf of Oman. The seas were calm and the tail winds stayed with us.

Colin's horrendous sandstorms had passed through and we could see the Baluchistan coast, a moonscape with its limestone cliffs rising sheer from the white sand beaches. The limestone is eroded and worn into anguished formations, great cathedral-like pinnacles of rock stretching inland as far as the eye can see, and not a blade of grass. Barren and beautiful, it is one of the great natural wonders of the world, even worth spending a night in Gwadar to see. Gwadar is 30 miles to the east of Jiwani.

We routed east, following mile upon mile of awe-inspiring savage scenery. Then I hit some of the worst turbulence I had ever encountered, and it was totally unexpected.

We had been flying a little way inland parallel to the coast. I decided to get a few more photos of the cliffs along the shoreline where there had been a fair amount of turbulence but nothing spectacular. I was flying a couple of hundred feet over the water with the cliffs towering above me and then, going around a headland, it hit me. Wham! I was slammed down towards the sea – a sickening drop. I thought I was going to go straight into the water. I desperately pulled full power. I was a toy, tossed every which way – wham – wham – wham – with terrifying violence, then hurled aloft only to be slammed down again. It couldn't have lasted more than a minute, but it was terrifying and seemed to go on forever. Really shaken, I managed to climb clear and continue on my course, staying well clear of headlands and sheer cliffs.

Night was falling fast as we approached Karachi. We were going to be at least half an hour after sunset and Karachi ATC was telling us to fly IFR, that we must make an IFR approach on the ILS (instrument landing system), all rather complicated if you are not into ILS approaches, which I most certainly am not. Suddenly a night landing didn't seem such a good idea at all.

If Air Traffic Control had agreed to us coming in nice and calmly, low-level visual flight rules, and if there had been no cloud, it would have been more or less a piece of cake. Instead we were being told to maintain 5,000 feet, and the previously cloudless sky was fast becoming a near solid cover below us. Then they asked if we were both instrument rated! I thanked God for Q's ability to never give a direct answer to a direct question, which normally drives me nuts but on this occasion stood us in good stead. 'We will be flying IFR,' he said.

I was nervous of the cloud below us. Time passed and night descended. 'Never mind this IFR, this is dangerous, there's no other traffic around, I'm getting down through the next gap in the clouds,' I said to Q. He radioed ATC: ' G-JEFA formation request permission to descend to 1,000 feet due to weather.'

'G-JEFA formation you may descend to 1,000 feet – QFE 1018 [airfield milibar pressure reading].'

A gap in the clouds appeared with twinkling lights below and then the reassuring lights of Runway 25, four miles ahead. We landed with hot and humid winds gusting up to 40 knots, and finally reached our hotel at 10.15 p.m. Everyone, including Dave Ullmann, was there. Dave it seemed had rejoined us for a few days, en route to film and climb mountains in Uzbekistan. He provided a much-appreciated helping hand for Al and Pat.

It was so good to see Colin again and listen to an account of his escapades over a late dinner that I was too tired to eat. He had made good time from Dubai to Gwadar with a 25-knot tail wind, giving him a ground speed of 85 knots. Everything had looked good until he neared the Baluchistan coast.

'It was horrendous, sand everywhere and the wind – I couldn't see my hand in front of my face, but that Sky Force GPS is unbelievable, it's so accurate. I zoomed it right in and made a spiralling descent over the runway. I was flying blind [Colin has no turn and bank indicator or artificial horizon] then, unbelievable, at about ten feet above the ground I saw the white line down the centre of the runway – it was half hidden in shifting, swirling sand. Those guys at the airfield, they just couldn't understand how I had landed without being vectored in.' He told us how he had been held at the airport for hours and the performance it had been to make a phone call. 'Who looked after you?' I asked.

'Well, a bloke who appeared to work at the airport, his name was Azam something or other, quite a nice bloke, he was trying to be helpful. I needed more fuel so he took me to this place where this bloke had some fuel, it was all in plastic Domestos and Coke bottles, all smuggled in from Iran. Then he found me this room, there weren't any hotels. There was no electricity and the place was crawling with ants. There was no water and nothing to eat and I had been wearing the same clothes for two days. I thought I better shake out my mattress, but I found these three horrendous great spiders on the bottom of the mattress with their big nests.' It all sounded so dreadful, you had to laugh – our 'Doctor Doom'. 'What did you do?' Heinz asked.

'Well, I just left them there. I thought maybe it was better not to disturb them, maybe they were eating the ants.'

Breakfast the next morning was at the civilised hour of 8.30 a.m. We had been informed the night before that Ahmedabad International Airport was under repair, only open from 8 to 9 a.m. and again from 5 to 6 p.m. This meant that we had to go for an afternoon flight with the threat of the usual thermal activity and monsoon storms. The weather forecasts for India were not encouraging. Colin said, 'Did you see the weather on the television? India is covered in zigzags, there are storms everywhere and I don't know whether I will even be able to take-off, and have you seen the wind?'

The wind was even stronger by 3.15 p.m. when Colin finally took to the air. We left the hotel at 10.30 a.m., hoping for a noon departure. Our ground handlers, Shaheen Services, were very charming and very disorganised, which was a taste of things to come. We were beginning to think we would miss our slot in Ahmedabad, another day and we would miss our 48-hour leeway clearance time for India. (Pilots have been known to have to wait as long as two weeks for clearance renewal to enter India.)

The delay gave Colin far too much time to worry about his take-off. 'Under normal circumstances I wouldn't even think about taking-off in this wind even without the weight of fuel I am carrying. This wind is even worse than Mikonos. This wind could break the wing or turn me upside down,' he said.

'Well, you made it last time – c'mon, let's give it a try,' Q said, giving Colin an encouraging push. His take-off was tough. Azam Khan of Shaheen Services commandeered two airport staff to hold onto the tips of Colin's wing, to stop him being blown over while he taxied for take off. Pat was running along behind, filming the whole scene, and when Azam Khan registered the fact that a photographer was running down the main runway of Quaid-E-Azam International Airport, he too gave chase, waving his hands and shouting 'Stop. Stop! It is not allowed. It is forbidden, you must come back!'

I was crying I was laughing so much, then my heart leapt into my mouth as Colin roared down Runway 27. He looked so small and I knew only too well the struggle he was going through as he lifted off, wobbling all over the place, up, down, left and right. It wasn't smooth, but with a strong head wind he lifted quickly, fast becoming a small speck and finally disappearing up into the cloud at 3,000 feet. He told me later the turbulence, especially in the cloud, had been horrendous. The helicopters and Cessna had to wait a further 40 minutes, roasting on the taxiway, for a procession of aircraft to take off and land, before we finally got on our way to Ahmedabad. It was three and a half hours and 368 miles away to the south-east. We were just hours within the 48-hour time limit on our clearances for India.

We were able to avoid all the storm cells and had a good flight. Even Colin had little to complain of after take-off. We flew over the notorious desert of the Raan of Kachchh where in '97 Q and I had had a dramatic time with a sandstorm building underneath us. We had climbed to a staggering 13,500 feet as the monster pushed us ever upwards until it topped out at 13,000 feet.

This time, to my amazement, the Raan of Kachchh was covered in water, about two feet of very salty water. As we flew further south the water got shallower and shallower until there was only salt as far as the eye could see. It looked like snow.

A great deal of patience is needed in India, the delays were endless. The hours spent in Ahmedabad and Nagpur airports were even longer than Karachi. Our ground handlers demanded US$1,500 per airfield for their services and were worse than useless. In Ahmedabad, we had a certain Mr Ejaz, nauseatingly obsequious, who began every sentence with, 'You must be appreciating'. In Nagpur, Mr Kumar pitched up just in time to collect his money, minutes before departure, having done nothing. We had spent four hot, exhausting hours the night before, when we really needed him, persuading the military that we wanted to stay overnight. They told us to continue straight on to Calcutta. 'Why are you here? Why you cannot be going to Calcutta this day? Why can you not going Delhi?' We told them we had always wanted to visit Nagpur, but that merely puzzled them. We said that it would take nine hours for the microlight to get to Calcutta and that we were all tired and half of us were sick.

Colin and Al were the worst affected, both were badly dehydrated with fever, headaches and diarrhoea. Colin drank far too little for fear of being caught short en route. I warned him endlessly of the danger of permanent liver damage, but the immediate present concerned him more. In the hot countries he would be sweating buckets before take-off as he had to wear his thick, fleece-lined flight suit, essential for his high altitude flying where it was often 30 degrees cooler than on the ground. And, invariably, we were delayed on taxiways, waiting for clearance to take-off and he would be overheated in his thick flight suit. It wasn't much better in the greenhouse conditions of a helicopter, but bladder control was not such a factor, we could land almost anywhere.

Delays, more delays and frustration. Colin especially needed to get away early to avoid the afternoon thermal build-up. Heinz, Colin and I went out to the airfield at 7.30 a.m. If Colin had been able to take off from Nagpur at 9 a.m. for Calcutta as planned, he would have made it. Instead he ended up spending the night in Rourkela, 200 miles short of Calcutta.

He and the rest of us had gone backwards and forwards from one hot and dusty terminal building to another in a bureaucratic maze, and then to the Tower where Bhaskar Aggarwal, an enormously fat gentleman with protruding eyes, insisted that we join him for a cup of tea. He sent one of his staff off to get the tea, which took hours, and when he did arrive he only brought two cups. No amount of insistence that 'two cups was just fine' would do, the man was sent off again in search of another cup; we complied because we knew we had to. Colin finally got away at 10.30 a.m. for the 600-mile flight to Calcutta. The helicopters followed an hour later.

Despite the delays in hot and dusty Ahmedabad and Nagpur, India was a joy after all the days of sand and mechanical worries, and I was one of the few who didn't get sick. I was able to fly low and enjoy the stunning scenery, and the weather was hot enough for me not to have to worry about having no carb heat. Even the clutch seemed to be behaving better. I flew low over the ever-changing plains and rivers, the picturesque towns and villages with their white-washed buildings and streets teeming with humanity, temples and mosques, farmers planting their rice and buffaloes wallowing on the muddy banks of the sluggish brown rivers.

The hours went by and then Colin came on the air, 'Jeffa, are you there?' I said I was and gave him my position. He said, 'Conditions are getting really dangerous, I can see horrendous storms ahead and the cumulus are building really fast. I can see ones reaching to 30,000 feet and still building. There's no way I can make Calcutta. I'm going to have to land.' He thought it would be less of a hassle to just land in a paddy field and ask for 'local help'. I thought that was not such a brilliant idea. Calcutta wouldn't like it and I pointed out that living conditions would probably be similar to Gwadar. That decided him, he opted for an airfield.

I met up with Colin ten miles before Rourkela Airfield, 210 miles short of Calcutta, but more or less en route. We circled the deserted airfield that lay just to the west of the heavy industrial town. We couldn't raise anyone on the radio. I half-heartedly suggested that I stay with him, but Colin said rather gallantly that there was no point in both of us suffering, 'It might make for double trouble,' he said with a laugh.

Colin had no money and little water. I said I would land and give him the few rupees I had and a bottle of water. We needed to be quick, though, as otherwise I risked being detained for hours. I taxied close behind Colin as he landed and headed towards the apron, and saw a car batting up the road to the airfield. As I landed beside Colin, I saw the car stop by the airport shed some 70 yards away. A man jumped out, and started running towards us across the apron. Rotors running, I opened the door and flung the water and rupees to Colin. 'Good luck,' I shouted, shutting the door and executing one of my faster take-offs.

Once airborne I looked back and could see the man standing in front of Colin, jumping up and down, whilst hundreds of people were appearing from all directions on foot and bicycle. I felt such a heel. I should have stayed and kept him company instead of abandoning him in such cavalier fashion. My only excuse was that I needed the full day in Calcutta for onward preparation.

Shortly after leaving Colin I joined up with Q and less than 20 minutes later had to go through one of the storm cells about which Colin had been so nervous. He was right, it was 'horrendous'. The helicopters got a good wash. An hour later we had two-way radio contact with Calcutta and were able to tell them that G-NOWW (Colin) was spending the night in Rourkela. ATC graciously thanked us for informing them.

Deutsche Bank had offices in Calcutta and did us proud. My husband Simon had been the chairman for South-east Asia for four years and Deutsche Bank had been a big help when Q and I had gone through India in '97. So, before departure, I had contacted our good friend Harkirat Singh who had been general manager in Delhi. We got the same treatment this time, and what a difference contacts make. Calcutta Airport was a dream, all quick efficiency and the Oberoi Hotel was the lap of luxury.

Colin arrived at noon the following day, in time for the press conference (which James Barker was busy organising). Colin had had quite a time of it. The individual who I had seen running across the apron was the airport manager, Mr Javad Chandra. He had rushed up to Colin saying, 'That helicopter, it landed, it landed! I have been seeing that helicopter, it is not allowed, it cannot be coming like that.' Colin interrupted him with reassurances that the helicopter had not landed, that it had only accompanied him in to make sure that he had landed safely! Mr Javad Chandra spoke minimal English, he was not convinced and ranted on, 'What are you here? You foreign, this domestic – you cannot be staying.' He had carried on for quite a while with an ever increasing, enthralled and curious audience. He wanted to know what the registration of the helicopter was. Colin played dumb. He was finally taken to a basic local hotel, where at least there were no spiders' nests under the bed.

Q and co. had a night on the town in Calcutta with attendant hangovers the next morning. Al, Dave and James made it for the press conference though. Pat, I never saw, but Q was on the move. I found him in the lobby with one of the reporters, who was looking rather bewilderedly at him as he was clowning around. On seeing me he said, 'Oh here's the famous lady, I'm just the person who carries the bags. This is the person you should really be talking to.' I was embarrassed and the reporter looked uncomfortable. I told Q he was being ridiculous and he stormed off. I didn't see him again until we all left the following morning.

THREE

Calcutta to Hong Kong

19 - 25 June

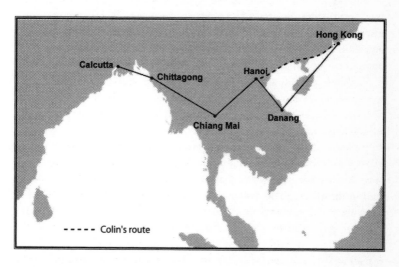

----- Colin's route

DAY 20

Tension, drama, excitement – there was to be little let up in the days ahead.

Leaving Calcutta for Chittagong in Bangladesh, we ran into a huge storm over the infamous Bay of Bengal, the breeding ground of so many cyclones. These are catastrophic storms that flatten and flood the low-lying Bangladeshi coast, wreaking utter devastation. The country was still reeling from a storm two weeks previously. Tens of thousands of people had drowned and hundreds of thousands more were homeless, human suffering on a scale that defies imagination

The Cessna had a stormscope, a small TV screen which shows you storms ahead. The screen was pulsating with activity and showing two extensive cells with large dark centres. James, reporting from the Cessna, said the storm cells were near the Bangladeshi coast, but they had no problem in circling them.

By the time we got there an hour and a half later, the cells had merged, and the entire horizon was a wall of blackness, rolling across the sea. Should we go back? Back to Calcutta with all the contingent clearance problems and more days lost? We continued: Colin at 13,000 feet, avoiding turbulence; the helicopters at 100 feet – and then the storm hit us. At 100 feet I could just see the white-capped waves, but for Colin it was obliteration. We had never experienced such rain. Colin said later, 'I just don't know how my engine kept running, how the air inlet valve got any air. I felt as though I was in solid water. It was black as black can be. I couldn't see a thing and my hands were hurting with the rain. The rain, it was that strong.'

Turbulence or no turbulence, we persuaded Colin to descend down to sea level, giving him the QNH (barometric) reading at 100 feet because it was essential that his altimeter had the correct reading. If you are making a spiralling descent at 2,000 feet per minute with zero visibility you can appreciate that it is critical to know your altitude very precisely.

Colin put the microlight into a spiral, but the turbulence, updrafts and downdrafts had him all over the place. At one moment he was descending at 2,000 feet per minute, the next he found himself being lifted by a huge updraft and screaming heavenward at 400 feet a minute. He was being thrown around like a feather in a typhoon and appeared to be getting further away from Chittagong, rather than closer. We were having a tough time too, with the blackness, turbulence and the sheer volume of water. I had water squirting into the helicopter through my air inlet, which I had to keep open to stop the inside of the helicopter steaming up, but to be totally exposed as Colin was . . . he said later it was the most terrifying moment of his life.

Colin finally bottomed-out without hitting the water and reported that he could see the waves, 'But the turbulence is horrendous and I can only see a couple of yards ahead. Are you clear yet? Can you see anything?' The answer was 'no' on both counts. Conditions were little better with us. I was even beginning to think longingly of the desert sands. Then, just as suddenly as we had hit the storm, I came out of it. I could see land. I could even see sunshine on the distant horizon.

Q volunteered to go and find Colin, give him some solid reference and guide him out. I headed as fast as I could towards that glorious, golden shore, trying not to think about rats deserting sinking ships. There was just no way I was going back there. Besides, I told myself, I'd probably be more of a hazard than a help and just prayed that Colin and Q didn't bump into one another.

As I approached the Chittagong airfield, Q reported that he and Colin were both clear of the storm. I told them to be as quick as they could as another storm was coming in fast, hurtling straight for the airfield. I landed, shut down and told the Cessna crew, who were standing on the apron, to be ready to grab the wings of Colin's microlight as soon as he touched down. The Tower gave permission for us to line up, ready, at the edge of the runway.

The storm and Colin were soon both upon us. Colin shouted, 'I've got to get under cover or I'll be blown right over, that storm will destroy me.' The ground staff, who didn't appreciate the problem, were saying there was nothing available. This was nonsense, there was a massive, empty bunker-like hangar to the north of the apron. Colin continued to shout dire warnings of approaching catastrophe. Ignoring the irate shouts of the ground staff, Heinz and I, holding a wingtip each, ran with the microlight towards the bunker. I was airborne most of the way. We just made it under cover when the storm hit with a vengeance.

The bunker turned out to be military and we were in deep trouble. Military jeeps and trucks appeared from nowhere with the Bangladeshi Air Force in a state of high excitement. They surrounded and blocked all exits, descending on us in unfriendly fashion. They said the microlight was confiscated and we were to wait there for their superior officer. The most senior officer present sternly told us 'This is not being allowed, you must be realising you have not the permission to be staying. This is military, not civilian, but no civilian can be using this place.' Then he saw my small camera and got even more agitated. I quickly put it in one of the pockets of the microlight and forgot about it – in fact the following day when I couldn't find it I thought I must have left it in a taxi. A few days later it was to prove a major embarrassment for Colin.

We were held in the bunker hangar under arrest for two hours awaiting the arrival of the officer in command. He finally arrived, looking very important, and all his men stood to attention. We were beginning to consider the joys of a Bangladeshi Military prison, and how to contact the British Embassy. The Air Vice Marshal – I imagine he was at least an Air Vice Marshal judging by the gold braid and deference of his men – repeated the fact that we shouldn't be there, that no civilian aircraft had ever, ever been inside the bunker before and that this was a gross infringement of Bangladeshi security. Then, much to our relief, he turned to his men who were still standing rigidly to attention and advised them to stand at ease. All smiles, he told us that we could leave the microlight in the hangar overnight, and 'could we please all have photograph taken in front of the microlight'.

Chittagong – noisy, colourful, full of humanity, scooters, rickshaws, trucks and cars, horns blaring, all belching filth into the already polluted air – was our home for two nights instead of the intended one, putting us two days behind schedule.

On the first morning we were all at the airport with our bags packed at 7.30 a.m., unaware of the time required to reverse the process of putting the microlight into a military hangar. By the time we had done all the paperwork and gone through the slow business of refuelling from barrels, it was midday with head winds forecast all the way to Yangon (Rangoon). It was too late to go that day.

On the second day, Colin and I opted to go to the airport at 6.30 a.m. We couldn't afford a further day's delay. 'Airport time' was averaging a good two to three hours, Colin was gloomily predicting ten hours for the 621-mile flight south to Yangon. He said he would be pushed to make it before dark.

First we had to battle our way through the throng of colourful beggars all clamouring around the airport barrier – I think they live there. They all have access to the flat roofs of the airport, where they watch the planes land, then they all hurry down to intercept the passengers as they come out. The airport staff were friendly and helpful, but it still took nearly an hour and a half to get through the bureaucracy, pay all the fees and file flight plans, by which time the camera crew had arrived. Thankfully, it was Al's day in the camera helicopter; Pat, when it came to punctuality, was nearly as bad as Q. Al, despite having a mass of technical equipment to pack up, was always punctual.

Colin was on his way at 8.30 a.m. and we followed at 9.30 a.m. We headed south along the cyclone-devastated coast, which was only a few feet above sea level and vulnerable to every storm spawned in the Bay of Bengal. It appeared to be a grey world of paddy fields; the houses that remained standing and the stripped palm trees were covered in mud. It needed little imagination to picture the poverty, hardship and misery of those still alive. We headed south towards more storms over the Arakan Yomas Mountains, which run southwards along the Burmese coast, and a temporary parting of the ways.

The day had started with clear skies and a light tail wind. Colin was clinging to the coast, the nice safe coast, well clear of the mountains. We were making good time across the mountains, but realised that with the westerly wind we would make even better time if we could route direct to Chiang Mai in northern Thailand, missing out Yangon. We could make up one of our lost days.

The Cessna was now airborne and, having a long range HF radio, Heinz was able to request Chittagong for a change of flight plan. After much chat with all the various authorities in Burma (Myanmar) and Thailand, Chittagong came back, much to our delight, and said OK.

Routing direct meant that Colin had to leave the coast and head into the Arakan Yomas Mountains. As we headed south-east across the mountains I remembered the story I had read of two Englishmen, Eric Hook and his engineer Jim Matthews, who had crashed their Gypsy Moth in these same mountains in 1930. They were attempting to beat Bert Hinkler's England to Australia record. They had set off from Lydd aerodrome on the south coast of England, only three months after Eric Hook took his first flying lesson, and were ahead of Hinkler's record when a fuel pipe burst over the Arakan Yomas Mountains. Amazingly they survived the crash and Eric Hook, although seriously injured, was able to walk, but after a few days march he grew so weak that Matthews tried to carry him. When their food ran out, Eric Hook insisted that Jim Matthews carry on alone. Ten days later Jim Matthews staggered out at the little port of Prome on the Irrawaddy. He was haggard, staggering with weakness and running a high temperature – but he was alive. The *Daily Mail* organised a search for Eric Hook. His skeleton was eventually found, identifiable only by his hair. Not a fate I fancied.

Although we had the advantage of Emergency Locator Beacons, the chances of surviving a crash in those mountains were slim, with jungle-covered peaks reaching up to 10,000 feet. Colin was uneasy about leaving the coast and reported that his horizon was a mass of storm cells, and building. The situation then deteriorated rapidly. The cells merged and built and for Colin, further west than us, it appeared to be even worse. He was in trouble again. 'This is really dangerous, it's horrendous – can't see any way out. It's building underneath me. I can't climb fast enough.'

We asked him for his coordinates (this all had a familiar ring), and kept asking for updates and making calm suggestions. 'Do a 180 – head back to the coast.' Worrying about Colin, looking for my own escape routes, awed by the sheer size of the towering cumulus building all around us and catching the occasional glimpse of craggy peaks and steaming jungle was all nerve-racking. And I now had the worry of the high humidity factor with a dysfunctional carburettor heat control. In humid conditions you can get carburettor icing with temperatures as high as 27 degrees centigrade when you are not using much power. We were at 8,000 feet and the outside air temperature (OAT) was 20 degrees centigrade. Having to dodge up and down and around the massive, building cumulus, I was constantly increasing power to climb, and then needing to reduce power to make a quick descent. With no carb heat I had to keep the power setting high. I just didn't have flexibility and manoeuvrability. My descents were shallow and fast with a juddering collective lever and a great deal of vibration.

Colin was fighting for his life for the second time in three days and I was selfishly occupied with my own problems. Yet, I remember in the middle of those great, thunderous clouds, beautiful and deadly, I kept thinking of home. It seemed to be my way of coping with the enormity of what I was handling. 'Were the family all down in Somerset?' I wondered. I could see my roses, they would be in full bloom and imagined late breakfasts; Simon, Suze, Chris and Nick there with assorted friends; Sunday papers, church bells, new mown grass, a million miles away.

Colin found a gap, a narrowing tunnel, back the way he had come, back towards the coast. 'I'm going to land at that airfield on the coast, I'll try and make a very early start tomorrow, catch you up in Chiang Mai. I'm not risking any more of this, the turbulence is still horrendous.'

I quickly checked my little red book and gave him the names and phone numbers of our contacts in Yangon, just in case he had to go that way. Ten minutes later we lost radio contact as, finally, thankfully, we were able to descend into the flat Irrawaddy plains to the east of the Arakan Yomas. Here was normality – paddy fields, small villages, white temples and buffalo – a brief respite before heading eastwards again into the mountains and the border between Burma and Thailand. Colin headed in the opposite direction towards the safety of the coast.

I was enjoying life again except, now the tension was over, I was dying for a pee. Once clear of the plains to the south east of Prome (where Jim Matthews had finally stumbled out), I followed a small river that flowed through the thatched roofed village of Bogyisakkan and into the low hills beyond until I found a flat pebble spit. I landed and shut down. There was silence. I was alone on the riverbank in the low dense underbrush. Was this the Golden Triangle? Just the possibility added an extra thrill. It was one of those special moments; life was good, even better once I had a pee. Only then did I tell Q I was on the ground. I gave him my coordinates. Five minutes later he and Pat joined me.

If it hadn't been for the worries about Colin and the ongoing nervousness of carb icing, the rest of that six-and-a-half hour journey to Chiang Mai would have been great. Mountainous jungle interlaced with fertile valleys of terraced and flat paddy fields. It was remote and wild and wonderful and I felt an extra adrenalin rush at the pure adventure of it all. Was this really me? Flying a little red helicopter over the mountains of the Golden Triangle?

At Chiang Mai it was back to the realities of airport hassle, compounded by Q being spectacularly unhelpful. Darkness came with tropical swiftness. The Cessna, which had arrived some hours previously, was parked and silent several hundred yards away across the apron from our position. The fuel truck arrived and we filled up. We trudged over to the Cessna and retrieved our luggage. No longer did we have the helping hand of the Cessna crew taking our bags to the hotels. Pat, Al and James had long ago decided they were not baggage handlers. Everybody was responsible for their own kit. A day in the Cessna was short and easy by comparison to ours, but they didn't see it that way, so no help was offered.

An hour later I got a phone call from Colin. He was in Yangon. It was 'horrendous' this and 'horrendous' that interspersed with 'blimeys' and 'crikeys'. He had made it back to the coast only to find that the airfield that he had hoped to land at was a bristling military set-up. With fresh memories of the hangar in Chittagong, he decided against another unscheduled military encounter and pressed on southwards. He reckoned he had just enough fuel to make it to Chiang Mai, if he routed south-east and avoided the high ground. But he made the error of talking to Yangon, who insisted that he came in. Thank heavens I had been able to give Colin the name and number of our contact, Ranjan, in Yangon. Colin told me that Ranjan was taking him to the Inya Lake Hotel. I warned Colin not to make any phone calls through the hotel switchboard as the charge is about US$100 per minute. I had made a couple of phone calls in Yangon in '97 and the bill had come to over US$1,200. Colin said, 'Don't worry, I know. I was here on my way to Australia and the same thing happened to me.' Colin said he was going to try for a really early start and hoped to be in Chiang Mai by 9.30 a.m.

Tired or not, I had to contact my son Justin to see if he had heard anything from Mr Zang in Guangdong Province, or any word from Beijing ATC about our China clearances. Charles Powell, my daughter Christy's father-in-law (and Margaret Thatcher's former chief of staff), had said he would have a word with Tony Galsworthy, the British Ambassador in Beijing. We had applied for permission to overfly China to Hong Kong, an altogether safer option than the long 570-mile sea crossing from southern Vietnam to Hong Kong. Justin still had no definite news but a friend of his in Cathay Pacific in Beijing said Mr Zang was on the case and that he was hopeful. It was frustrating because, if China were going to refuse us overflight permission, we should have been heading south-east from Chiang Mai rather than north-east to Hanoi.

I had the charts out all over the floor of my hotel bedroom. The southern route was green and welcoming, while the northern one, flying over Laos, was mountainous all the way to Hanoi with peaks as high as 8,000 feet and even that figure could have been inaccurate as the chart reassuringly said 'relief data incomplete'. Heinz appeared and said samlors (motorised rickshaws) were ordered, we were all going out for dinner. Bed, I longed to go to bed. But this was our one night in Thailand and I'd never been to Chiang Mai, not even during the three years Simon and I had lived in Bangkok in the '60s.

It was the monsoon season and clouds were already gathering by the time we (Colin too) lifted off the next morning heading east-north-east towards Laos and the Mekong River (we still had no word on the overland clearances). We had had the usual delays and had hung around waiting for Colin. I had tried his mobile several times with no reply, so assumed he was on his way. Finally we decided we could wait no longer, the British Ambassador in Hanoi was holding a cocktail reception at his residence in aid of Operation Smile and 'could we please try not to be late as His Excellency had a dinner appointment'.

We had already asked for clearance to start-up when we saw a small speck speeding along the runway. Colin had arrived. His first words were, 'The soldering on my exhaust pipe's gone, I'll have to fit a new one.' Luckily he had had a new one sent out to Calcutta after the Saudi saga. He quickly fitted the new exhaust, but it was by then 11.30 a.m. We had hoped to get away by 9 a.m. and the Cessna group had already arrived before we actually got away. They had an easy time of it in Chiang Mai. I had done all their paperwork for them, rushing around on the back of a scooter, filling in forms and paying out vast sums of money. Chiang Mai was the most expensive airport of our entire trip, costing US$2,400 for all the various fees, excluding fuel.

The elevation at Chiang Mai Airfield is over 1,000 feet above sea level and with the temperature at 33 degrees centigrade and the helicopters fully fuelled we had had to do a skid start, sliding along the runway until getting up enough speed to lift slowly into the thin air, not so easy on skids as opposed to wheels. The Cessna was carrying two 50-gallon drums of fuel which, together with a tail wind *should*, we reckoned, have been enough to get us to Hong Kong. There was no other Avgas available before Hong Kong.

More mountains and more storm dodging. I was up at 9,000 feet skimming the highest peaks, part hidden in cloud; the wet, black volcanic rock, stark, jagged and unforgiving, rising above the tree line of dense, steaming jungle far below. It was hostile and awe-inspiring, I felt very small, very vulnerable, and there was the continual fear of icing. I wished for the umpteenth time that the wretched carb heat was functioning. It was dangerous and in those circumstances could have been catastrophically dangerous.

Q was dancing the clouds. From time to time I got a glimpse of him, manoeuvring with ease, flaring and descending, making rapid descents through small gaps in the cloud. The best I could manage was a shallow speed descent with a great deal of vibration and kick-back in the collective lever, sort of kamikaze-bomber-cartoon-style.

I was not the only one with problems. Colin was having a repeat of being unable to outrun the storm that was fast enveloping him and coping with turbulence. He climbed to 13,000 feet attempting to find stable air, but it was a scant two degrees centigrade and he was freezing cold. He said he was looking for somewhere to land and asked us if there were any paddy fields anywhere. I told him to turn 20 degrees right which would bring him further south, closer to my track and hopefully clear of the storm which I could see some 20 miles away, very black and filling the sky on my port side. But I also told him 'negative to paddy fields'.

We battled on. Conditions, although turbulent, improved. Colin cleared the storm and with the highest mountains behind us we were able to appreciate the stunning scenery. We were seeing for real the war zones depicted in so many American movies about the Vietnam War, imagining what it must have been like to be the hunter or the hunted. Finally we saw the flat plains, the Red River and Hanoi in the distance and were clear of turbulence. Annabelle Newbigging (a friend of my daughter Suze) was there on the sweltering apron to greet us. She said she had found some fuel that she had been told was Avgas, and that it would be at the airfield at 6 a.m the following morning!

We were late for the Ambassador's reception and then the film crew said they were going direct to the hotel. I thought it a shame that neither of them were going to film the reception, where Annabelle told us that little Vietnamese children would be doing a dance that they had been practising for weeks. I suggested that at least one of them came. 'You can film it if you like,' Pat said dismissively as he turned on his heel and walked away.

The Ambassador Sir David Fall and his wife Gwendolin made us very welcome and we apologised profusely for being so late. Everyone made speeches and then the Ambassador had to leave for his dinner date halfway through the children's dance – which was utterly charming. Annabelle had done us proud and had organised freebies everywhere: transport, accommodation in the lovely old colonial Metropole hotel and a feast at the Emperor restaurant. Annabelle also secured us a lot of publicity during our time in Hanoi due to the efforts of her friend Tran Su Hoai. Briefly we enjoyed the old-world charm of the city, the night-time hustle and bustle of bicycles and street vendors. Hanoi has an enchantment, an old-world, French charm, and the people are so friendly. One night was all too short.

That night I got a call from Justin saying we had clearance to overfly China.

DAY 24 – 23 JUNE

This was the day that we planned to fly to Hong Kong. I was up at 6.15 a.m. having not slept very well as I had too many worries. China seemed to be sorted but now the biggest concern was Russia as the clearances had still not come through. James Fletcher kept making reassuring noises from London saying everything was in hand. In '97 the clearances hadn't come through until we got to Hong Kong, but that was just one helicopter. This time there were four aircraft – and one was a microlight. We had heard that microlights were unwelcome. We thought, rightly or wrongly, that Brian Milton and Keith Reynolds were to blame for that, as on their momentous flight around the world they had gone storming into Russia's Sakhalin Island from Japan without clearances and had been held for 18 days. They had done much the same with Japan where I had had a devil of a job getting clearance for Colin. It had only been thanks to the Robinson Helicopter Agent, Kenji Saito of Alpha Aviation, that we had finally succeeded in getting the clearance. Kenji had been a star, going tirelessly from one department to another. When I thanked him profusely for all his help, he laughed and said, 'Jennifer-san, I am happy to help and now I learn so much about microlight. It is very interesting, but microlight very big problem for Japan and that first microlight – big trouble, authority, they wanted to arrest him.'

So, no clearance yet for Russia, but we had Japan and Taiwan. Taiwan had been no problem at all and we also had permission to land at Chep Lap Kok, Hong Kong's new international airport. I had a fat folder full of e-mails and faxes to show for that, but Justin, David Tung and many others had been on the case and it was all sorted. The only other major clearance we still had to get, apart from Russia, was Cuba.

Everyone had been up early for the refuelling of the helicopters and the microlight. The fuel truck was there, but Annabelle's promised fuel was bright orange (normal Avgas is blue) and didn't smell like Avgas. Heinz said, however, that in 1990 he had flown into Hanoi in his Piper Saratoga and had had a fuel sample sent to Shell in Singapore who said it was OK. He assured us that what we were looking at appeared to be the same. We decided to top-up with the 'orange juice'. We had the two good 50-gallon barrels of Avgas that the Cessna had brought from Chiang Mai for the two helicopters and the microlight to share. The dilution was not great, only ten per cent would be the orange juice.

Manoeuvring the 50-gallon drums of fuel out of the Cessna and into position was tough but we had it down to a fine art by the time we got to Hanoi. James and Heinz had worked out a kind of pulley system for rolling the barrels down, using the two wooden planks (which the drums sat on when being transported in the plane) as a ramp, and the two long straps used for securing the barrels. Our hand pump wasn't working properly so we heaved one barrel on top of the other to siphon off the fuel by gravity feed; someone had to suck the fuel through the hose to get the flow going, the trick being to try and do this without getting a mouthful of fuel. We tried to get a fork-lift truck, but the airport said the charge would be US$500.

First we dealt with the microlight. We needed to get Colin on his way and it was easy enough to fill all his separate tanks which could be detached from the microlight. Colin was using all seven of his tanks for the 524 miles overland to Hong Kong, which he strapped in, on and around every available part of the framework; he was a flying fuel tank. Tanks 6 and 7 were 'bladder' tanks – transparent flexible containers that fitted under his knees. All fuelled up, Colin was on his way by 9 a.m. 'Safe flight, see you in Hong Kong!' we shouted as he taxied for take–off.

The refuelling of the helicopters took longer than expected, not helped by the airport authorities making us park the helicopters a good 200 yards from the Cessna. We had to put the wheels on the skids and push the helicopters over to the barrels, positioned in the scant shade under the wing of the Cessna. Sharing the shade was one of the double seats taken from the Cessna where those not on active fuel-pumping duty attempted to keep cool. Annabelle had arrived with lots of ice-cold cans of Coca Cola and Seven-Up.

The one-hour start that we had anticipated giving Colin turned out to be two and a half hours – and cost us our nice, safe, overland routing to Hong Kong.

We had asked for clearance to start up. The Tower said, 'Negative start up, report please to ATC.' What was going on? Hot and weary, we disembarked and headed across the baking tarmac. At that moment my mobile phone rang. 'Hello, hello, can you hear me? It's Colin!' The line was full of static interspersed with loud crashing sounds.

'Yes, yes, I can hear you, what's happened? Where are you?' I said, beckoning the others over.

'I've been forced down by fighter jets. I'm in a paddy field in China. It's really dangerous, they're dropping flares all around me. Can you hear the bangs?'

'Fighter jets? You're in a paddy field? Where are you?' The others were huddled around, all trying to hear. Al had the camera turning. Colin was shouting, trying to make himself heard above the noise of the jets and the flares they were dropping.

'I got forced off course. There was this horrendous storm. It was really dangerous, I had no choice, I'm in a military area. I think I'm in Zhanjiang province, anyway not far from the coast.' He was interrupted by an even louder bang, 'Blimey, that was close. It's unbelievable, they forced me out of the sky, these two fighter jets, they circled closer and closer and their wake turbulence was horrendous. They were going to invert me, I had to get down.

I managed to land in this paddy field.' The noises in the background continued.

'Are you hurt? What about the microlight?' I asked.

'Oh, I'm OK and the microlight's fine but I don't know how I'm going to get out of here. There are hundreds of peasants, more coming all the time. I think I'm safe enough now, I don't think the Chinese jets will harm their own people. These jets will have to go back to base soon, they'll have run out of fuel. I'm just going to stand here until someone comes,' he said. I made lots of sympathetic noises and told him we were still in Hanoi and then he said, 'Look, I better not talk any more now, must save my battery. The peasants seem friendly enough . . . But how come you are still in Hanoi? I've been trying to get you on the radio for hours.'

I told him that the refuelling had taken much longer than we had expected and that when we asked for start up we were told to report to ATC. 'I don't think there is any way they will let us take the overland route now,' I said, and added, 'Look, call again, soon as you can, let us know what is happening. Everyone's wishing you good luck!'

'OK, OK, bye now, bye,' he said and was gone. I switched off my phone, and looked at the others. 'Christ – now what?'

We all just stood there looking at each other. Was this the end of the road for Colin? Would they impound his microlight? Heinz looked grim and said, 'This will be a political issue. We must contact the British Embassy in Beijing immediately.'

I phoned Simon in Hong Kong. 'Jesus Christ! Forced down by fighter jets? He's in a fucking paddy field? Is he OK? Where are you? What the fuck . . .' I managed, between his colourful exclamations, to put him in the picture. Finally he said, 'Jeeesus, Richard's not going to like this.' Richard being Richard Li, our chief sponsor and son of K.S. Li, Number One Tai Pan of Hong Kong and very sensitive to Hong Kong–China relationships. 'I'll get on to the Embassy right away and then I better have a word with Richard – wow, he's going to love this!' he said, giving a rueful laugh. Then added, 'You're going to have the press onto this. Play it low key, say something like Colin was forced off course and the Chinese escorted him to safety.'

So the headlines the next day said just that.

The rest of us were denied overflight of China and had to go south to Danang, which added 300 miles to our route and meant another lost day. We then had the hot and weary task of hand pumping all the good fuel back out of the helicopters into the drums and putting in the orange juice. We wanted to save the good stuff for the water crossing to Hong Kong. Just before taking off for Danang I managed to get through to Colin. The line was full of static and I could only get the odd word. Something about having a gun held to his head and being interrogated, but he was OK – then the line went dead.

We flew south, down the beautiful coast of Vietnam. The engines ran well, so the orange juice seemed to be all right. Flying at 5,000 feet, I leaned the fuel off as much as I dared to a burn rate of 12.1 US gallons per hour. It was unlikely that there would be Avgas available in Danang. The Cessna was once more carrying our two 50-gallon barrels of 'Chiang Mai' Avgas. We would be setting off for Hong Kong with marginal fuel, with just half an hour in hand in 'still' air conditions. But what if we were to encounter head winds beyond the point of no return? On arrival in Danang, just to add to my already nervous state, Pat announced that he had decided to go on ahead to Hong Kong in the Cessna instead of flying with Q as cameraman in the helicopter. He said, 'I've got a gut feeling about this flight.' I was beginning to have a gut feeling about Pat!

Q and I shared out the fuel then waved goodbye to the Cessna crew as they taxied for take-off. Heinz had been anxious to be home for dinner with his wife Barbara. The others needed no encouragement – Hong Kong beckoned. Q and I took a taxi into Danang. The driver propelled us at breathtaking speed, tooting his horn through tree-lined streets filled with a million bicycles. I thought of the difference between Hanoi and Danang compared to Chittagong. All were crowded with mass humanity and noisy, but polluted Chittagong had few bicycles – everyone there had some form of motorised transport. Vietnam was still clean; the pace of life was slower (other than our taxi), and the French influence was visible in the old colonial architecture and the loaves of bread tied on the back of bicycles.

Our hotel was right on the beach. NOW always wanted us in good hotels where communication systems were good and we had no objections. I wondered where Colin was staying. I tried once more to get through to him. The phone was answered, not by Colin but by a Mandarin-speaking Chinese. My Mandarin is non-existent so I phoned my son Justin in Hong Kong who is a Mandarin speaker. Justin tried to get through but there was no reply. Things were falling apart. I got word from someone called Stephen Reid at the British Embassy in Beijing telling me that our trip was over. He said he would arrange for Colin to be deported and that Colin could forget about his aircraft. And then over dinner, just when I needed support and encouragement, Q launched a critique of all that was wrong. According to him, everything was a shambles, none of the team had any respect for me and I treated them like shit. I was tired, it had been a long day. My dinner half-eaten, I got up and left.

I went and sat on the hotel steps leading down to the beach. It was so beautiful. The warm tropical night, the cicadas, the gentle movement of palm leaves stirred by the lightest of breezes, the moon on the water – timeless, reassuring, therapeutic. I would, hopefully, be with Simon the next day. The next day – a new day – things would surely be better.

We got off to a bad start with another row. I had intended to be charming but I just can't stand people being late, and being kept waiting. I phoned Q at 5 a.m. and then again at 5.30 a.m. to make sure he was on the move. He said he would meet me in the lobby in a few minutes. I quickly put the last bits and pieces in my bag and went to the lobby to settle the bill. Then I waited and waited. Forty minutes later Q appeared, jauntily swinging his bag, hair dripping with water. 'I've been for a swim. You should have been for a swim, it was wonderful – relax, relax, it's a beautiful day,' he said with a great big smile. I had a complete sense of humour failure.

Then we got to the airport, only to find it was just opening, I had to eat humble pie and cope with the 'I told you so's! I was in no mood to be facing the longest of water crossings: 570 miles of open water across the South China Sea, potentially a six-hour journey if there was no wind. We had enough fuel for six and a half hours (with full tanks we would have had eight hours). Tail winds were forecast, but again I asked myself: what if we were to encounter head winds halfway, beyond that dreaded point of no return? 'Point of no return' has such a final, very dramatic ring to it.

We tried to find some more orange juice to top up our tanks but there was none. At least I didn't have to worry about carb icing. The temperature, even at 8 a.m., was already 30 degrees centigrade. I would not have to fly high in cool air avoiding mountains and mercifully, in Hong Kong, I would finally be able to get the carb heat fixed. I tried yet again to get Colin on his mobile – nothing. Was he going to get out? What was happening? I called Simon who said there was no news at his end but the British Embassy were on the case and were being more positive than Stephen Reid had been. No one had been able to contact Colin. I told Simon that we hoped to be in Hong Kong around 3 p.m.

Fifty miles out we had our last radio contact with Danang. We had to rely on doing relays with airliners flying at 34,000 feet, high above us, until we were able to make radio contact with Hong Kong. We were surrounded by silence and big seas, the South China Seas. Hong Kong was beyond the blue horizon. There were many miles to go – miles of open water, greater than the length and breadth of Britain, Land's End to John O'Groats – in two small single-engine helicopters. Time passed slowly.

Q and I were not in chat mode. I watched the GPS Sky Force colour moving map, the infinitely slow progress of the small dot of my helicopter moving across the vast blue expanse. I thought about our argument of the night before. Yes, I had occasionally been critical of Pat and Al, who seemed to spend most of the time filming each other or Q, but I'd also been complimentary. I thought I was sympathetic to their late working hours, but, as Colin pointed out, late working hours didn't seem to prevent them hitting the town afterwards, they always had energy for that. I certainly had plenty of arguments with Q, but that was par for the course. James? As far as I could remember we hadn't clashed. Perhaps I could have chatted to him more, but we were seldom together and in the evenings it was so obvious that they all preferred being in their 'young' group. Colin, Heinz and I got on very well – Q hadn't been referring to them. I was hurt and unhappy. Was what Q had said true? Did they have such a low opinion of me? Did they really think that I 'treated them like shit'? I resolved to have a 'get-together' in Hong Kong, but we never did.

I was also worrying about Colin – was he going to be able to extricate his microlight? What would we do if they did impound it?

We made Hong Kong with nearly two hours of spare fuel in hand, so early that no one other than airport officials and our two engineers, Simon Gale and Dan White (who had flown out from England) were there to greet us.

Hong Kong had been my home for 30 years. Justin, his wife Pinyi and their two little daughters, Nicola and Joanna (Joey), were living there and Simon was still 'half' in residence with an office and apartment there – and of course so many friends. Justin and family arrived, closely followed by Simon and Jamie McCallum.

The news on Colin was sketchy, but the British Embassy were talking about the possibility of his being able to fly out. With all the dramas over Colin, arguments with Q and just coping with each day's flying, I'd pushed the worries of our Russian clearances to the back of my mind, reassuring myself that there was really no cause for alarm – not yet. But Russia *was* a big worry. I reminded myself that in '97 we only got our clearances when we arrived in Hong Kong, and this time we had even been to Moscow and talked with the authorities. It should be straightforward, a formality. Some formality.

We spent three days in Hong Kong. I was tired, and this was compounded by all the stress and aggro. I updated Simon on Q's behavior. Simon said, 'Look, this is all meant to be fun. It's all about Q. He's really screwing you up. He's being paid to do this, he's out of line.' Then I found myself making excuses for Q.

Q disappeared on day one in Hong Kong, into the depths of Wanchai, only resurfacing on the third day to belatedly help the engineers test the helicopters. There was still no word on the Russian clearances. James Fletcher in London was, as always, reassuring. He said that the British Embassy in Moscow was on the case. Surely, surely we would hear good news any day? The Russian Civil Aviation Authorities had been so positive when Q and I had visited them in

Moscow. They had told us to submit three routes and they would approve one. We had gone to the top, we had met Andrei Andreev, Director General of Aerotrans and head of the Civil Aviation Authority. We had also met Gennady Velikovsky, head of Air Traffic Control. We had gone through the diplomatic channels via the British Foreign and Commonwealth offices in London. Alain Dacey had notified all British Embassies along our route. James Fletcher had been following up on all airfields and checking clearances. He was very confident. But there was still no word.

It was so good to be 'home', to be in our own apartment with Simon and Justin and his family and to briefly relax with them. There was, of course, all the ongoing planning: a press conference, talking with our next ports of call, Taiwan and Japan and of course Russia – it was difficult to relax even when there was the opportunity.

DAY 27 – 26 JUNE

We got word that Colin had taken off from China at 7 a.m!

We were all at the airport to welcome him. Waiting, waiting for a first sight and then seeing that tiny microlight coming in to mighty Chep Lap Kok International Airport was a great moment. Everyone clamoured around, shaking his hand, slapping him on the back, giving him hugs, barraging him with a million questions. Colin had quite a story to tell. We pushed his little machine into the shade of the big hangar and there he told us what had happened in his usual quiet, understated fashion.

'I left Hanoi and I'm flying along, I get to the border and the storm's just blowing everywhere. It was ten times worse than what I've had all the way here, the air was so unstable. I got to 15,000 feet and I thought "Right, I'll go back to Hanoi." I started to turn, looked back and no way. I had storms on three sides of me. The only clear patch was towards the coast. I was about 60 miles from there, and thought, "If I can get to the coast I can land if necessary because down below me there was nowhere to land." It was a mountainous area. The coast was the only option to save my life, because, well, you know the powers of the storm.

'When I got nearer to the coast the weather was much smoother. Then I was in a dilemma: what do I do now? Do I land and try and contact somebody and tell them what's happened? Then I didn't know what the situation was about landing in a foreign territory like China when you're not invited to land. I decided to continue along the coast to Hong Kong and try to contact somebody en route. I tried so many radio frequencies, it must have been at least an hour. I couldn't get anybody. I was just tracking along close to the coast using my GPS. I could see the sea but I couldn't quite see the coastline as there was orographic cumulus building and I was at 9,000 feet. There was a storm building in front of me, so I had to turn right 30 degrees to try and get around it, around this headland. As I turned, this fighter jet comes from nowhere with a steep bank, very slow, right in front of me, followed immediately by another one. I thought, "Oh fuck, I'm in big shit. What should I do?" I didn't know what to do. I started to climb high, trying to get around the storm and I thought, "I'll just ignore them because I can't do much about it." I climbed to 13,000 feet and they were getting closer. It got to the stage where they were that close I almost spiralled with their wake. The first jet came past, there was a hell of a lot of induced wake off the wings and it almost barrel-rolled me, then the second one came round and I got that wake as well.'

He looked at us all and smiled ruefully, saying, 'I'd had it by then so I shut the power right off and dived down. I thought the only thing I can do is to find somewhere to land. If I can get down to 20 foot they're not going to be able to move in that close to me, so I went down to the ground. I was about 20 foot above the ground, the jets were still banking tight round me but they couldn't get low enough. At this stage they started dropping anti-missile flares. I thought "Uh oh, this is getting very, very serious, I've got to land."

'I landed in what turned out to be a prawn breeding field that had been drained. So I landed, and luckily as soon as I landed hundreds of local farmers encircled the plane, so the jets had to move further away. They kept on dive bombing for about another half an hour, then they were obviously low on fuel and left.

'I sat and thought "What do I do now?" The locals were very friendly. Once the jets had disappeared they were gesturing for me to do a runner. I was tempted, but the storm was still raging and if I take off again and they catch me, then I am in trouble.

'It was so remote, it took the military 45 minutes to get there. When they did arrive all hell let loose. It was quite funny. They came running across this field, straight into deep mud and this guy in front falls flat on his face and he's all covered in mud. That slowed them right down. He was that angry, and all the farmers were laughing, and he was shaking with rage and he got his gun out and he was holding it against my forehead. Just shaking and shouting at me for what seemed like hours, but I guess it couldn't have been more than a few minutes. Then the Secret Service police arrived and he put his gun away. From then on I started building friendships.'

He had been treated well, but although everyone was friendly he was never left alone, not even to go to the loo. He was interrogated until 1 a.m. each morning, asked the same questions again and again and again. They were very anxious about whether he had taken any photos. He assured them that he had not, that he had no camera, that his camera was broken and he'd had to send it home to be repaired. He assured them all the rolls of film he had with him had been taken prior to coming to China. The second morning, an officer had come into the interrogation room swinging a small camera and had said, 'Bodill, smile, smile' and had pretended to take a photo. Colin didn't know what was going on until the officer said, 'Bodill, this is your camera!' It was of course *my* camera that I had hidden in Colin's microlight that day in the hangar in Chittagong. Colin had a lot of explaining to do.

The local hotel was taken over. Representatives of all the forces were there. It was a big event. Every time he went anywhere it was in cavalcade with motorbike outriders and sirens. He managed to persuade them to let him fly the microlight from its muddy position in the prawn field to their military airfield. When they got to the prawn field, Colin said there were literally thousands of people waiting. Word had spread about a crazy foreigner in his flying machine. They came in from miles around on foot, by bicycle and motorbike.

The authorities had drained off all his fuel, just leaving enough to get him to their airbase. Colin set off with an escort of two MIG fighter jets who circled him as he buzzed along at his max cruise speed of 60 knots. He took the opportunity to charge the battery on his cell phone. But when, after three long days, he was finally allowed to leave, Colin was told he had done more for diplomatic relations than a score of politicians! They begged him to come back (by normal commercial means) and told him that he had commanded a bigger military presence than Tony Blair. Tony Blair had only had an escort of one fighter jet.

On our last night in Hong Kong, Simon gave a drinks party at the China Club for us. So many friends came, including C.H. Tung, successor to Chris Patten, the last Governor of Hong Kong, and the Chief Secretary Anson Chan was also there.

FOUR

Hong Kong to Hokkaido

28 June – 19 July

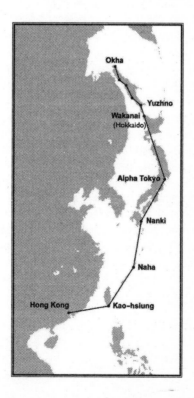

DAY 29

'It will be night long before I reach Taiwan,' Colin said.

The delay this time was G-MURY, my helicopter. The engineers couldn't get the tracking and balancing of the main rotor correct. Finally Q announced that 'it would have to do'. We taxied to the apron and slowly lifted off Runway 07, routing past the Cathay Pacific Building, and there was Justin, a small, lone figure on the roof, waving goodbye. I remembered poignantly how Justin, aged two, used to wave to the helicopters from our flat in Happy Valley, shouting, 'Hoppy, poppy, poppy, copters!' I felt such a clutch to my heart, love for Just, love for my wonderful family, and guilt that I was subjecting them to anxious times. I gave him one last wave, then headed on towards the harbour where we were meeting up with a newscopter. We passed the old airport, Kai Tak, where Q and I had landed in '97 to witness the 'Hand Over'. We had been greeted at the airport by Governor Chris Patten and his wife Lavender. They had hurried across the harbour from his last ever Legislative Council Meeting to give us a wonderful welcome, a formal one too. G-MURY enjoys the distinction of being the first and last British civilian registered helicopter to fly into Hong Kong and the first to fly out of the Special Autonomous Region (SAR) of China!

From the moment I lifted off I was appalled by the level of vibration in G-MURY. It had been fine when I had landed in Hong Kong. Why had the engineers tampered with it? And why had they had to spend over a day trying to track and balance, apparently without success? The only previous time I had experienced so much vibration was in Dubai in '97. On that occasion the bearings in the main rotor head were so worn that we had to replace the whole rotor head (the only mechanical problem of that entire trip). The Robinson helicopter factory were fantastic, getting the new parts to us with no charge and DHL set a new speed delivery record!

I radioed Q on 123.45. He had taken G-MURY for its test flight after the servicing that morning. I asked him whether he thought this could be a 'bearing problem'. 'Well, yes, I did consider it,' he said and then added, 'Yes, it *could* be possible, but I doubt it.' I wasn't reassured and I had 1,850 miles to go to Tokyo, mostly over water, before an engineer from Alpha Aviation (the Robinson helicopter agent) would be able to check it out.

It was 497 miles from Hong Kong to Kao-hsiung on the southern tip of Taiwan. Thanks to a 22-knot tail wind we arrived just before nightfall and I'm happy to say that G-MURY managed to shake and judder its way there and then onwards to all those beautiful Japanese islands: Okinawa, Naha, Nanki and finally on to Tokyo.

The Alpha Aviation team had flown down commercially from Tokyo and were there to meet us in Naha: Kenji and Shizouka Saito and their chief engineer, Ojii Sagisaka. What friends they were to prove in the difficult weeks ahead. Kenji had of course already gone to immense trouble organising Colin's clearances. Ojii made a brief inspection of my rotor head, but there was little he could do until we got to their base outside Tokyo.

G-MURY continued to have serious vibrations but remained airborne. Colin's doom-laden predictions, having watched the BBC news in Kaohsiung, of continuous storms and rain for the next three days didn't materialise. The weather held good with favourable tail winds. He completed his longest-ever non-stop flight of eleven and a half hours from Naha to Nanki – all over water. The helicopters had taken a more circuitous route, island and volcano hopping, including a rather alarming look into the very active volcano on the island of Suwanose-shima to the south of Kagoshima. It was evil-looking, with smoke billowing forth and hunks of what looked like newly-spewed black lava rocks spilling down the mountain, and the smell of sulphur, rotten eggs, was overpowering. When might the next molten lumps be hurled heavenward? I was more than happy to be once more over turquoise seas.

We finally arrived at Nanki and, amazingly, at the same time as Colin. Colin went off to see about hangar space for his machine while Q and I refuelled the helicopters. Al was once more filming Q and I tried not to feel irritated. I reminded myself that, after all, Al worked for NOW who were our principal sponsor, and the website and future documentary rights were theirs to do whatever they wanted with. Colin and I had come to the conclusion that, although we were the principal website story, Al intended to have Q playing a major role in any documentary (which indeed turned out to be the case). But it somehow just made the 'them and us' scenario worse, and it wasn't confined to Colin and I. On the apron at Kao-hsiung I'd seen James Davey make a vigorous 'V' sign to Heinz's retreating back! I asked Q what that was all about and he said, 'You really have no idea do you? You have no idea of the problems at all.' I hotly defended Heinz, a superb and highly experienced pilot. Q merely looked at me, shaking his head knowingly. Tempers were frayed and everyone was tired.

Too many negative thoughts. I tried to think nice positive thoughts, failing rather badly. I reminded myself that it had been one of the all-time great flying days, with superb weather and glorious scenery – *and* we were nearly halfway around the world.

Refuelling completed, I turned to grope around in my helicopter, sorting empty drink cartons, half-eaten sandwiches, empty film cases etc. from ongoing essentials like locater beacons. When I resurfaced, Q and Al were gone – more negative thoughts – but then Colin appeared, full of the fact that he must have achieved the longest-ever non-stop microlight flight over water – a staggering 691 miles. I'd done the same mileage, but it hadn't been non-stop, I'd made a couple of brief stops to stretch my legs (and have a pee) on the isolated white sandy beaches of coral islands. Yes, it had been a very good day.

We picked up our bags and headed off in search of transport into town. When we arrived at the hotel in Nanki we were met by a worried Shizouka (who had travelled with us in the Cessna), 'Our Civil Aviation Authorities, they are not happy. Not happy with Alpha Aviation Company. All airfields reporting helicopters not flying with microlight,' said Shizouka, looking apologetically at us all. The last thing we wanted to do was create problems for Kenji and Shizouka after all they were doing for us. One of the conditions for the microlight clearance was that we would all fly together, and the microlight would not overfly any built-up areas. The problem for helicopters was that we just didn't have the endurance to fly for eleven and a half hours at 60 knots. Also, R44's don't fly very comfortably or efficiently at that speed. We had tried to make it look as though we were all together and remained in radio contact with each other nearly all the time. But we assured Shizouka that we would all stay together for the shortish 347-mile hop to Tokyo.

I then checked my e-mail for the Russian clearances. Nothing. I phoned James in London, a complicated process as all calls had to be placed through the hotel switchboard. They phoned you back when the call came through. James was reassuring, 'Everyone is on the case.' Two days earlier I'd sent James a fax asking him to get in touch with Charles Powell. James said he hadn't called Charles, and that it wasn't necessary. He said that all was going ahead. I thought otherwise and I told him so in no uncertain terms. 'We need all the political help we can get, we're nearly in Tokyo. Charles knows everyone and his brother Jonathon is Tony Blair's right-hand man. Believe me, we need him.' I told him I would phone Charles myself – I was seriously worried now.

I put through a call to Charles. My luck was in. He travels all the time, but incredibly he was in London, and in his office. He said, 'I'll do my best, but it's Friday afternoon in Moscow, they may already have left for the weekend – too bad you didn't get me earlier . . . ' Two hours later Charles called back and said that he had managed, after several phone calls, to track down Richard Courbold of the British Embassy staff in Moscow who was at a meeting in St Petersburg. Richard said he knew nothing about our application for clearances but would look into it first thing on Monday morning! Did nobody in the Embassy know about our application? Both James and Jo Jo had reassured me in Hong Kong that 'everyone was on the case'. Russia was not looking good at all.

The next morning the helicopters and microlight took to the air together for the journey that would normally take three hours in the helicopters. Level-pegging with Colin, it would take nearer five. We would fly at 6,000 feet, above the inversion layer and clear of turbulence. We complied, which was a good thing, because abeam Hamamatsu we were joined by another helicopter. We were told it was a news helicopter but I think we were being checked out. We remained coastal. The authorities, in their desire to keep the microlight clear of downtown Yokohama, had us make a circuitous route to the north, which appeared to be in the direct flight path for Narita International Airport. It was alarming having 747s passing *underneath* us every three minutes. We had to stay high until overhead Shimotsuma (Alpha Aviation's facility), where Colin announced he was going to do one of his spiral descents. Q took up the challenge, putting his helicopter into autorotation and giving Al a great photo opportunity. I descended more sedately and joined Colin and Q overhead of Alpha Aviation with its immaculate hangars and large apron.

Heinz was on the ground with a hand-held radio, asking us to do some formation fly-pasts, and Alpha were sending up one of their helicopters with a cameraman. It was midday and very, very hot – 38 degrees centigrade at 200 feet. By the time we had played around with formation circuits for half an hour we were dripping in the enclosed hothouse conditions of the helicopters. It wasn't any better for Colin as he was wearing his fleece-lined suit.

G-EELS, the Cessna, had landed at a small grass strip a few miles away, because Shimotsuma only had helipads. Colin thought he might be able to land on the small dirt road beside the hangar. He did a low fly-past to check it out and got frantic admonishments from Shizouka. 'No, no you may not, you must go to airfield.' So off Colin went and missed out on the red-carpet arrival. I landed and the carpet was quickly unrolled, extending from the hangar to my helicopter. The hangar itself was bedecked in red and white bunting with welcome signs and flags. The mayor of Shimotsuma was there and all 30 of the young trainee pilots were lined up rigidly to attention. A lone trumpeter wavered through 'God Save the Queen'. Q and I were handed large bouquets of flowers and I could see that he was as overcome by emotion as I was. Colin arrived a few minutes later (having been flown back from the airstrip by helicopter) and was also presented with a bouquet. Then there were cold beers and light refreshments for all. Kenji and Shizouka did us proud.

We could not stay long at Shimotsuma as we were due in Tokyo at the Mitsui 'Guest House'. The Mitsui corporation were hosting a cocktail party in our honour, Simon was due there too. It was a wonderful party, with many business acquaintances and friends that Simon had got to know over the previous 30 years. We were honoured and very touched.

We had expected to spend only two nights in Tokyo before heading north to Wakanai on the island of Hokkaido, our last port of call before Russia's Sakhalin Island. It was not to be. The Russian clearances failed to materialise.

We arrived in Tokyo on 1 July. The next day Simon left early, returning to Hong Kong. That afternoon Richard Courbold phoned with the devastating news that our clearance application had been turned down. He sent us a copy of the letter.

> DIPLOMATIC NOTE NO 5312/2ED
>
> The Ministry of Foreign Affairs of the Russian Federation pays its respects to the Embassy of the United Kingdom of Great Britain and Northern Ireland in the Russian Federation. With reference to Diplomatic Note Def204/00, dated 28 June 2000, which requested diplomatic clearance of 2 helicopters and 2 aeroplanes (including one micro-light), to fly across Russian airspace from 4 to 9 July 2000, the Ministry has the honour to inform that it will not be possible to grant clearance for this flight. This is due to the complexity of the air situation over the proposed Russian leg of the route. It is also because of the impossibility to fully control the above mentioned aircraft due to the absence of suitable radar control along the declared route for aircraft of this type and also because of the absence of Russian navigators on board these aircraft.
>
> The Ministry takes this opportunity to renew its respects to the Embassy.

What could I do? I could reapply, but there was no guarantee that it would be accepted. I felt as though I had been punched in the stomach. This couldn't be happening. I was alone in my hotel room when I received the news. I sat, numbed, unable to take in the full implications, blocking my mind to the possible scenarios. The one thought that recurred over and over in my head was, 'It's my fault, it's all my fault – I put this trip together.' Later, while breaking the news to the rest of the team, I remembered Q's words about what a shambles the whole trip was, and about the lack of respect which the team had for me.

I sank into the deepest depression. I don't think I have ever been so depressed. I had told Colin and Heinz first. I could see how shattered they too were at the news, but they were supportive and Heinz immediately started an action campaign. 'We must contact everyone we can think of who might be able to help, we must draw up a plan of action.'

The days that followed were the worst and most testing time. I contacted everyone I knew who knew anyone who knew anyone: politicians, ministers, ambassadors, admirals, civil servants, businessmen – and my Maestro. I sent faxes and e-mails in the morning and then made phone calls in the afternoon when England, nine hours behind Tokyo, and Moscow, seven hours behind, arrived at their office desks. I longed for 'good news' phone calls, and dreaded a final, definitive 'no'. I contacted the British Embassy in Tokyo. I spoke with Jonathon Thompson who had helped Kenji so much in getting the microlight clearance for Japan. I spoke with the ambassador, Sir Steven Gomersall. They said they would see what they could do. We waited. What was going on? What wasn't going on?

I called Alexis Vlasov in St Petersburg. Alexis worked with Harry Fitzgibbon, an old friend, in Harry's company in St Petersburg. He had been very helpful when Q and I had visited there in the helicopter on our 'preparatory' trip in the summer of '96. Alexis was ex-KGB, but most importantly he was an old friend of Vladimir Putin's. Alexis said he would make enquiries.

Alexis got back on his mobile phone. 'It's not good,' he said. 'The Minister of Defence does not approve your trip, he is the one who is against it, he is still against it.' I asked him if he had given any reasons and Alexis said, 'I have already told you too much, I cannot say any more. It is either a "yes" or a "no".' He then said, 'Call me in my office in two hours' and the line went dead. Two hours later I called his office. Alexis wasn't there. A nice-sounding man called Valentine answered and suggested I called a bit later. Next I got Tatiana Vogdanova, pleasant but unhelpful. 'Please call again tomorrow morning, he will be here before he goes to the airport.' We could only wait.

Richard Courbold in Moscow phoned to say that he was no longer on the case, it had 'gone political' and Susan Hyland would be handling everything from now on. Was this good? Richard didn't know.

Alexis was in his office the next morning. He obviously felt he could speak a little more freely on a landline. There was no good news. 'It is still negative. Look, I will talk with people in the Ministry of Foreign Affairs, but you realise this involves many departments. The Ministry of Defence is firmly against all of this. I'll call you back later.' He called back an hour later. 'If you call the Ministry of Foreign Affairs in a couple of hours and ask to talk to Andre Voisov, he may be able to tell you some more. I am sorry I cannot give you better news.' But Andre Voisov was out and I was put on to

Marcia Salkina, a very intimidating lady who said it was not her decision.

We were all staying at the Diamond Hotel, not far from the British Embassy. The location was central but the hotel was a dreary two-star establishment. The foyer was decorated in maroon velvet and tarnished gilt, with a permanent pall of cigarette smoke. The rooms were small and poky with a view of an equally dreary-looking establishment across the road that looked like a retirement home. The sky, where we longed to be, was just a small strip high above us. Our accommodation did little to help our spirits, but by Tokyo standards it was cheap. Mercifully, I could get e-mail access in my bedroom, but for some reason my 'winfax' didn't work. I had to send hand-written faxes from the lobby.

Charles Powell contacted Sir Charles Guthrie, head of the British Ministry of Defence, and spoke to his brother Jonathon, as indeed did Charles' wife Carla. Jonathon spoke with Putin's office. I faxed Slava, dear Maestro Mstislav Rostropovitch. He phoned back the moment he got my fax. 'Oh Jeffokha, you sound so sad. Don't worry, don't worry, I have received your fax, I have contacted my friend who is the Minister of Foreign Affairs, but he is in Tajikistan, he will only just have received my fax. I will talk to him. I will call you back. Do not worry.'

I needed to contact Nikolai Selbakov who was due to bring our Avgas fuel into Russia from Alaska. Surely Nikolai, a Russian living in Anchorage, Alaska, could help? I had originally found him through the Internet in '97. After floundering in the dark, not knowing where to start the search for someone who could organise fuel for us through Russia, Nikolai had proved to be a star. He had not only organised the fuel, he had organised just about everything. He found Yuri Romanenko, our navigator, and flew to Yuzhno with Jack Lenhardt in a Volpar (a stretched version of a Beechcraft), laden to the gills with barrels of Avgas. He had also played a big hand in securing our clearances.

I told Nikolai the situation. He was concerned and puzzled as to why our clearances had not gone through – he knew the lengths we had gone to. He said he would contact Gennady Velikovsky immediately and would confirm and verify all the airfields that we intended to go to in Russia and also confirm that he would once more be looking after us.

Colin contacted his friend Michael Starkey, whose cousin, Sherrard Cowper Cole, was personal assistant to Robin Cook, the British Foreign Secretary. Robin Cook was due shortly at the G8 Summit Conference in Japan. Sherrard said he would see what he could do to help us.

NOW put out a press release and sent a large folder of press clippings to the British Embassies in Tokyo and Moscow. We had been advised that publicity might help our case. We let it be known that every day's delay meant less chance of raising money for our charity, Operation Smile. Our main fund-raising area was going to be the USA, *if* we got there. Operation Smile were active in Russia, where they had operated on more than 1,550 children over the previous few years. Surely the Russians would register this?

On 6 July, four days after receiving the Clearance Refusal, I got a fax from Susan Hyland at the Embassy. 'It looks as though there is a chance.' What a wave of relief. The fact that the Russians were prepared to talk. We dared to hope. The British Embassy in Moscow had received the following:

SUBJECT: OVERFLIGHT REQUEST

The British request for flight clearance for Russian airspace can be re-examined, with a new deadline, under the following conditions:

◆ the whole route of the flight must be thoroughly examined with the Federal Air Transport Service (Russian Civil Aviation Authority) and agreed by them;

◆ the flight through Russian airspace must begin from a Russian airport which is open to international flights;

◆ the route of the flight must be planned in such a way that there is a possibility to land and refuel in civilian airports;

◆ on board the aircraft or on one of the aircraft or helicopters must be Russian navigators.

Naturally it would take time to re-examine a request for overflight which fulfilled these conditions. In any case it would take significantly more time than that allowed by the British side in the request about 4–9 July overflight which the Minister of Foreign Affairs heard about only on 30 June.

None of this was new. The route I had submitted to the Civil Aviation Authorities after meeting with them in Moscow had met all these requirements. It was as if the authorities had never received anything. Was there no communication between departments? It seemed not.

I had originally submitted three routes. The route Gennady Velikovsky had accepted met all the requirements. We were to enter Russia at Yuzhno Airport in southern Sakhalin Island, an international civilian airport, as was Okha on the northern tip of Sakhalin Island, and Magadan across the Sea of Okhotsk on the Russian mainland. Markovo, in the middle of nowhere, halfway to Anadyr, was civilian but not international, and, finally, Anadyr was an international airfield and our port of exit before crossing the Bering Straits to Nome. All were civilian and this was the same route we had taken in '97. G-EELS had HF radio so we could remain in radio contact at all times. We could, if necessary, take on as many as three Russian navigators and I pointed out that with four aircraft, two of which were helicopters, we could launch our own search and rescue operations. I added that all of this could be verified by Nikolai Selbakov who was handling the en route logistics and bringing in the fuel to Magadan.

We sent in our second application for clearances and continued to ask everyone for help – I wasn't going to leave any stone unturned. What if the final answer was 'no'? What was the alternative? Could we bypass Russia? Costs were escalating. NOW was not happy. Lawrence Duffy, Al and Pat's boss back in London, was apologetically saying, 'We cannot fund you indefinitely, soon there will be no story. People will get bored of checking the website and finding nothing happening.' Stabbed in the back, I argued that the hype would build with every passing day, but I knew that even that would peak. Lawrence suggested that Al and Pat return to London until the clearances came through. James Davey liked the idea too.

Q, who no one had seen for some days, resurfaced. He said he was happy to stay put for the time being having found a new girlfriend. Heinz decided to go home to Hong Kong. That made sense as Hong Kong wasn't very far away. But we needed Al and Pat. Without them there would be no pictures for the website, only our bat phone messages. Thankfully they stayed and continued to feed the site with colourful scenes of fish markets and carnivals; filming street scenes and a despondent team. I bought a brightly coloured Japanese mobile phone and half a dozen scratch cards (you dial in the numbers revealed from scratching the card, which gives you 'x' numbers of minutes – you don't pay for calls dialled in).

Shizouka suggested we ask the Japanese Prime Minister for help. 'He is not popular here in Japan, but popular in Russia. Maybe the Japanese people like him more if he help you,' she said. I phoned another friend, Leo Daly in Washington DC, and left a message, a cry for help, on his answering machine. Leo knows *everyone*, he had introduced me to President Clinton when I visited Washington in '98. He called me back within hours. 'Jeffa darling, I got your message, what can I do to help?' I explained our situation. I told him that there was the hideous possibility that the final answer just might be 'no' and the only solution we could think of was to land and refuel on a container ship or aircraft carrier. Were there, by any chance, any US Fleet manoeuvres going on in the area? Some lovely aircraft carrier that could help? 'Leave it with me, leave it with me. Let's see what we can do, an aircraft carrier? A little bit of a long shot,' he said with a laugh, then added, 'I've just spent the last three days on one of the tall ships in New York

Harbour, our big Centenary Celebration. I'm in the car on my way to the airport and will be travelling back to Washington with Secretary of Defence William Cohen in his private plane which an astronaut John Glenn will be piloting, I'll get on the case first thing tomorrow. Must help our citizens in distress.' (I was born in Providence, Rhode Island, USA and still held an American passport. I'd held on to it in case any of my children needed a Green Card, perhaps it was going to have other uses.)

An aircraft carrier or a container ship were the two possible alternatives. I phoned Yonehara-san at Mitsui. Surely the mighty Mitsui must have container ships going in every direction? Yonehara-san, who had entertained us so lavishly on our arrival, was very concerned to hear that we were stuck in Tokyo. He was charming and said he would see what he could do. I also sent Alexis Vlasov an article that my brother-in-law, Mark Pattinson, had faxed to me, saying, 'I wonder if this might help?' It was an article on his great, great uncle, Sir Samuel Greig, a Scottish sea-faring captain who ended up as Grand Admiral of all the Russias! Holder of Russia's five greatest orders of knighthood and Governor of Kronstadt, the great naval fortress at the entrance to St Petersburg, he had been a hero to his men and his ruler, Catherine the Great. Mark said that when his brother had visited St Petersburg 15 years previously he had been treated like a national hero.

Everyone was helping, but the days went by and there was still no word. Hopes rose and were then dashed. More e-mails, more faxes, and endless nervous hours waiting for the phone to ring. The afternoons were the worst time, the time when we might expect that important call that would seal our fate. Then the afternoon would tick by and I would start making excuses as to why we had heard nothing. Then I would phone Susan in Russia who tried to be positive. This challenge, this whole venture, had been put together by me. I could feel the unspoken criticism, or was it my own feeling of failure? It wasn't as though anyone said as much to my face. Everyone was pulling together and trying to keep up a semblance of morale. Perhaps it was just my own feelings of having failed them all, and the ever-constant, nagging thought: 'What if the final answer is no?'

I spent hours on my computer and cell phone with Colin always ready to help in any way he could. All the while Kenji and Shizouka, Oji Sagisaka, the chief engineer, Mitsuo Aoyama, Director of Flight Operations, and indeed everyone out at Alpha Aviation were supporting us and offering to help. They made no extra charge for all the extra days of parking at their facility. Their cars were always available, their office in town was ours to use any time and they told us that if we wanted to go further north to Hokkaido while waiting for the clearances, they had some apartments available. To cheer us up they even organised a superb barbecue out at Shimotsuma, attended by their staff and pilots. Everyone was fantastic.

Sir Charles Guthrie contacted his opposite number in the Ministry of Defence from where the main objection had been raised. Alexis Vlasov put in good words for us as and where he could with all his numerous connections. Charles Powell was keeping in constant touch with both the British Embassies in Tokyo and Moscow, who were in turn in daily contact with the Ministry of Foreign Affairs. Robin Cook, now at the G8 Summit Conference in Tokyo was, we were reliably informed, sending memos on our behalf and Slava assured me that his friend, the Minister of Foreign Affairs, was now back from Tajikistan and 'would sort everything out'. Surely, with so many influential people doing so much to help, somehow, someone somewhere would finally relent and give us the go ahead?

We did have a few diversions. The first was when someone, I think it was Pat, found that our Russian visas were only valid for one week. Why only one week? Jo Jo had asked for a month. Q's visa, for some inexplicable reason, was the only one valid for a month. Lengthy hours were spent in the sombre precincts of the Russian Embassy where we got off to a bad start. Al had decided that all should be on camera and, despite warnings from us that the Russians wouldn't like it, proceeded to film the proceedings. An enraged officer (who had obviously been watching on some hidden camera) charged in and grabbed Al's video camera out of his hands and ripped out the film. Al was lucky they didn't keep the camera.

Then typhoon Kirogi came sweeping into town causing widespread flooding and destruction. Q suggested that we should fly straight into the typhoon and be catapulted to the US without having to bother with Russia, whereupon Al volunteered Pat to shoot that leg, he reckoned he'd had enough excitement! G-EELS and G-NOWW had to be moved from the little grass airfield to higher ground. James Davey and Colin, with Pat to record events, spent a happy day out of town and a few, even happier minutes in the air. Shizouka phoned the next day to say the area where they had previously been parked was under seven feet of water.

Colin and I joined the early morning joggers along the shaded path that follows the vast moat surrounding the Royal Palace grounds. Heinz, the architect, took the opportunity to visit modern Tokyo. I went with him to the City Hall that looked like something out of *Star Wars* and the Fuji TV Centre with its twin towers and suspended ball. The three of us would have breakfast at a small pâtisserie shop across the road from the Diamond Hotel (whose restaurant only opened at lunchtime). The tables and chairs were doll-like in size. Heinz, who is more than six foot tall, looked all out of proportion sitting on his little chair with his knees tucked under his chin. We went shopping a couple of times and got hopelessly tangled in the subway where all the signs were in Japanese, we went through Ginza station three times. Al and Pat 'discovered' Tokyo, keeping the website followers entertained.

We all took the bullet train to Minikami for the weekend. We went high into the mountains to the north-west of Tokyo to stay in a little skiing chalet belonging to my friends, Martin and Noriko Barrow. The peace and quiet and clear mountain air did wonders for morale. Everyone relaxed, team spirit was high and thoughts were positive. I felt that Q had exaggerated the problems and that there was no need for a pep talk. We bathed in the local hot springs and climbed Mount Tanigawadaki. Everyone joined in cooking in the tiny kitchen, and we ended up with a wild game of poker using matches, bananas and plums for money; matches were worth 10 yen, bananas 100 yen and plums 1,000 yen.

We planned to stay for three or four days in Minikami, but on the Monday morning my mobile phone rang. As always my heart gave a little lurch and everyone had held their breath. It was Susan Hyland. She said, 'Things are looking better. We are expecting a phone call from the Ministry of Foreign Affairs with, I think, a positive answer within twenty-four hours!' We immediately went back to town. We had been waiting ten days with no news, and now perhaps we could at last expect something positive.

Leo Daly phoned to say that he had spoken with Vice Admiral Gregory Johnson, Senior Military Assistant of the Office of the Secretary of Defence at the Pentagon. He had also spoken with Admiral Fargo, head of the Pacific Fleet; someone would shortly be in touch with me. Nikolai Selbakov told me he had spoken with Gennady Velikovsky who confirmed that it was out of his hands, but if Nikolai put in writing that all aspects of our route through Russia complied, he would pass it on to the Russian Ministry of Foreign Affairs. Nikolai told me an Antanov 26 was on stand-by to take the fuel into Russia and that he personally would be in Magadan (our first stop on the Russian mainland after Sakhalin Island) in three days. Susan Hyland said she had never talked to so many high-powered people. 'I could write a book about it,' she said.

But still no word came. Eleven days, twelve days. Would it never end? What was their biggest objection? Was it the microlight? Had they heard about Colin being forced down by fighter jets in China? Could it have anything to do with Brian Milton entering Russia illegally in 1999 in his microlight? Did four aircraft pose a threat? Or was it simply a new government and things were different?

BBC world news had done nothing to dispel concerns in that area. The news report on our twelfth day of waiting said, 'Mr Putin's devotion to democracy is uncertain, he's pushing some legislation which will allow him to sack elective members of Russia's Upper House at will, and he has appointed seven regional governors, most of them from the KGB and Military, to run the country for him.' The reporter then went on to say: 'The KGB headquarters, the Lubyanka, has reacquired a plaque to Mr Putin's old boss, Andropov, best known for his persecution of dissidents. Mr Putin doesn't flinch from such symbols of totalitarianism. There's a new plaque to Stalin too in the Kremlin. The use of an onslaught on press freedom was heightened recently. The paramilitary has arrested the owner of Russia's most political media outlets, but Gleb Pavlovsky, seen by many as the brains behind Putin's policies, says, "It's what the people want."' Perhaps we should have been talking with Pavlovsky. I switched to Sky Sport and watched Venus Williams beating Lindsay Davenport on the Wimbledon Centre Court.

DAY 44 – 13 JULY

We arrived in Tokyo on the afternoon of 1 July; thirteen long days and nights had passed and we had still heard nothing positive. Thirteen days at the Diamond Hotel with just the one little break. We were going crazy. We should have been in San Francisco. It was difficult to concentrate on anything other than who else to contact. What other tactics could we use? What other strategies were there? I stayed by the telephone. Tokyo was very, very expensive.

We debated flying north to Hokkaido, but our Russian visas still hadn't come through, and then Shizouka told us that the JCAB (the Japanese Civil Aviation Bureau) had contacted her and told her that we were strictly forbidden to fly anywhere. They were monitoring our every move and we were going nowhere until the Russian clearances came through. 'Please, please,' she said, 'you must not go anywhere. We will all get into trouble, it will be very bad for us.'

Our Russian navigator, poor Yuri Romanenko, was still on standby. He was kicking his heels in Moscow. Like us he had been on hold for two weeks, stalling other jobs with Aeroflot, telling them that our flight was imminent. Yuri had been our navigator in '97 and we had had some good times together. He had also attended the meetings in Moscow when Q and I had visited Andre Andreev and Gennady Velikovsky with Maestro Mstislav Rostropovitch. Yuri could, however, stall no longer with Aeroflot. 'Jeffa, I have to go to Siberia, I will be away for four days. Please wait for me?' I told him that the chances were that we would still be sitting in Tokyo when he came back, but had reluctantly added that if we should get the go-ahead, we couldn't hang around – we had to get on our way. 'But I have been waiting for two weeks for you,' he said.

'I know Yuri, I know, we are all waiting. I am so sorry, there is nothing I can do, I am so sorry. You must go on your trip. We will talk, I am sure, when you come back.' I added a few more apologies, I felt so bad. I brought him more or less up-to-date on the situation at our end and asked him if he had heard anything from Gennady Velikovsky or Irina Groushina. He said he hadn't and we said our goodbyes.

Irina Groushina. Why had I not contacted her? Lovely Irina who practically ran the Moscow Aero Club single-handed, who had been such a help on our previous Russian escapades and looked after Q and myself when we visited Moscow, trying to secure these very clearances. Irina had met us at the airport, organised a hotel, escorted us everywhere and had even taken us to a magical performance of *Swan Lake* by the junior Kirov Ballet troupe.

I immediately phoned Irina. 'Why did you not telephone me sooner Jeffa? I will see immediately what I can do. Have you spoken with Mr Velikovsky? I will talk to him, I will call you back.' I had not forgotten Irina. I just felt that I had already contacted so many people in Russia and Irina had done so much for us on so many occasions that I shouldn't trouble her yet again. But now Irina was also on the case.

Shizouka suggested that we move to the Daichi Hotel at Tsukuba, because it was closer to the Alpha Aviation base at Motshuma. 'It has a swimming pool and restaurants,' she said. That was already a plus on the old Diamond. But someone had to stay to collect the Russian visas, which still had not come through. Q, of whom we had seen little, was only too happy to stay put in Tokyo. The rest of us packed our bags and thankfully left the Diamond Hotel which had been our home for so many days. We were just happy to be on the move, even if it was only by car.

I had a call from Steve Kunkle, Head of Operations for the Pacific Fleet. He told me that sadly they had no ships in the area. They had a reduced presence in the Pacific and he was very sorry that they couldn't help. He gave me his phone number and told me to call any time. It was good to know that we had the sympathy and encouragement of the US Pacific Fleet. But the waiting and uncertainty was pushing me to breaking point. How long could we hold out? And what if the answer was 'no'?

I had heard nothing from Yonihara-san at Mitsui regarding a container ship. It was highly unlikely that there was much progress there but I phoned anyway. To my surprise and delight he had made lots of enquiries. Mitsui had two or three container ships that operated out of Kushiro and they all had helipads. They flew Bell 216s off them. They also had refuelling facilities, albeit for Jet fuel, but no doubt we could organise Avgas. Yonihara-san said he had a good friend in the coastguard who was willing to help. 'But,' he said, 'this not our decision – final decision is with Government.' He was also not sure just how far out the ships operated. He was making more enquiries. But it was a small ray of hope if all else failed.

One of our team, I think it was Al, located through the web an obsolete Russian aircraft carrier in Vladivostok, which was available for hire for US$6,000 per day! Another possibility and surely NOW would love the publicity and video possibilities; we had another last resort.

We got our visas. Q collected them and joined us at the Daichi Hotel along with a girl called Natasha. They joined us for dinner. Natasha spoke not a word of English. Q told us he was learning Japanese, that it helped to pass the time!

On 17 July, as usual, we had a whole morning to fill in before Russia woke up. 'Come on, we have got to do something, I'm going crazy,' Colin said. 'Let's go to that movie complex the others went to yesterday. They've got a bowling alley there too.' We went and for three wonderful hours we almost forgot our worries watching *Mission Impossible 2* with Tom Cruise, followed by a game of bowls with Colin patiently showing me how to hurl the ball without losing my thumb in the attempt. Then we had to go back to the hotel, back to reality, and a black cloak of depression once more enveloped me. We looked in on Al, Pat and James slumped in Pat's room, listless, helpless, waiting. The look on my face told the story – no news.

I went to my room and waited till 4.30 p.m. Tokyo time. The British Embassy in Moscow had been open for an hour. I phoned Susan Hyland, she was not at her desk. 'Please phone back later,' I was told. I phoned Irina who sounded quite confident. 'I think you will hear something from the Ministry of Foreign Affairs tomorrow,' she said. But that was what we had been told the week before.

I really felt as though I was cracking up. I couldn't go on. I was so depressed. I tried to get a grip of myself. 'Go for a walk, do something. Don't just sit here feeling sorry for yourself, be positive,' I told myself. I stood and looked out of my hotel window, at the small park-like area below. A green square surrounded by a tree-shaded gravel path. I started to put on my sneakers. Someone knocked on my door. I opened it and Colin was there. Had I spoken to Susan? I was just telling him 'no' when the phone rang. It was Susan, back from her meeting. She didn't sound very cheerful, so it took me a second or two to register what she was saying.

'We have heard from the Ministry of Foreign Affairs. In three hours they will be sending through your permission. We still have to get the approval of

the Deputy Minister and there are certain conditions, but it's looking good.'
I stood there stunned, hardly daring to believe that this really was *it*. I made
'cautiously optimistic' signs to Colin who, in turn, was looking as though he
too could hardly believe there might be good news. Susan said a few more
things about faxing through the clearance and contacting the Civil Aviation
Authorities, and said she would call me as soon as they had received the fax.
I could have hugged her. I kept saying, 'Oh wow. Oh my God. Oh I can't
believe it. Oh Susan, what a star you have been . . .'

I hung up and turned to Colin and we just couldn't stop smiling. Neither
of us said anything as we stood there letting it sink in, still hardly daring to
believe. 'Come on, we must go and tell the others,' I said giving him a big
hug and hurrying down the corridor. They were just as we had left them, the
picture of despondency. But then they saw the looks on our faces.

'It's come,' I said.

Like us, they reacted slowly. We had waited too long with hope dying,
had too many disappointments and lost too many days. 'We will be getting
faxed confirmation in a couple of hours,' I said. It was so good to be able to
tell them that we would soon be on our way. It wasn't until three hours later,
when the confirmatory fax came through from the Ministry, signed by the
Deputy Minister, that we dared to really believe it. Even then none of us
gave great whoops of joy. We were emotionally drained. I got a few quiet pats
on the back and a 'Well done'.

We had pulled through. Everyone had coped in their own way. Now, after
17 of the longest days of waiting, we were once more taking to the skies.
Russia beckoned.

We had so many people to thank. Help had come from all over the world.
What had finally tipped the balance? I like to think that it was a concerted
effort and not a little patience that finally won the day.

It was all go, gone was the black depression. Heinz had luckily just come
back from his second trip to Hong Kong and Yuri Romanenko was back
from Siberia and would be arriving on Aeroflot's morning flight at Narita
International Airport.

It was pure pleasure to set my alarm clock for 4 a.m. By 6 a.m. we were
all at Shimotsuma. Everyone from Alpha Aviation was there to see us off.
Shizouka was joining us for the first leg, piloting her little fixed-wing,
single- engine Trinidad together with Mitsuo. They would accompany us as
far as Hokkaido, deeming it a good opportunity to visit their operations
there.

It was so wonderful to be on the move again and I prayed that we might
still make the northern crossing. We were five and a half weeks behind my

original timetable (having delayed our take-off by three weeks for our sponsor NOW). But on that day we were a happy team, revelling in the early start. Problems became a pleasure, setbacks were accepted – the low cloud and poor visibility – nothing could dampen our spirits. We filled in our flight plans and felt the joy of once more going through the familiar routine: getting the Met forecast, luggage stowed, charts folded, final checks, fuel full rich, a few twists of the throttle and finally the sweet sound of the engine coming to life, the rotor blades slowly starting to turn.

We routed over to the west coast, just to the north of Minikami, over the mountains where we had spent those two therapeutic days at the Barrows' ski lodge. Then we flew north following the coast to the beautiful island of Hokkaido where we saw some mega volcanoes, three of which were busy erupting. One had coated a town in dust and we learnt later that half the buildings had been evacuated. Then it was on to Wakanai, the most northerly town in Japan, 744 miles away and 16 degrees centigrade cooler than sweltering Tokyo. The air was clear and the sky so blue as I looked north, across the sea to the far horizon where Russia awaited.

The helicopters and microlight landed in formation, our timing was immaculate, and ATC were happy. Next came Shizouka and Mitsuo in the Trinidad and finally G-EELS, the Cessna having gone to Narita to collect Yuri Romanenko. It was great to see Yuri's smiling face and he was dressed more appropriately than in '97 when he had arrived in full Aeroflot uniform, gold braid and hat. This time he was wearing a sensible windcheater and grey trousers. One of the first things Yuri asked me was whether there was a survival suit for him. There was but it wasn't exactly made to measure as it was my one from '97. Yuri, in his early 50s with short grey hair, of medium height, medium build with twinkling blue eyes set in a square, good-looking face, was all set for another adventure and he brought us pounds of fresh blueberries that he had picked in Siberia. They were only a little the worst for wear after their long journey and were delicious. He also had his habitual thermos flask and the 'never-to-be-without' bottle of vodka.

Yuri does a fair amount of 'off-the-normal-beat' flights. He had been Prince Philip's navigator some years previously when he had visited Eastern Russia. Besides coping well with all the navigation and officials at airports, you could always depend on Yuri to produce goodies like hunks of dried meat, or to locate the local source of smoked salmon and caviar which we had enjoyed in '97 – even though the salmon was more dried than smoked and the caviar came in plastic bags secured with a rubber band.

We arrived in Wakanai at 2.15 p.m. and finally got to our hotel at 7.30 p.m., having spent the usual lengthy time refuelling from barrels which

Shizouka had organised for us, and then we had to push the helicopters into hangars and back out onto the apron as there were so many flights landing and taking off between 3.30 and 5 p.m. when the whole apron was required for manoeuvring traffic. The planes were full of Russians eager to go shopping in Japan. Then we went to the airport canteen and had a late lunch of noodles and ice cream while waiting for the Cessna to land – a novel experience. We were then told that the following day was a national holiday and that customs would be closed. We had to make a mad dash into town where the customs house was located, getting there just before they closed.

The Hotel Ana boasted an excellent tapinyaki restaurant where we sat around a cooking table with the chef in the middle throwing and tossing sizzling meat and vegetables on hot plates while we got thoroughly mellow on warm little tots of sake. Not even Colin's predictions of lousy weather for the morrow could dispel the happy, tired mood.

We woke to a cloudless sky, a fresh south-westerly and the cry of the seagulls as they circled the returning fishing boats. Tail winds were forecast for Yuzhno and we needed them. We were looking at marginal fuel conditions until we reached Magadan, where Nikolai Selbakov's Antanov 26 would be flying in from Anchorage, Alaska, with 15 barrels of fuel. I could have arranged to have the Antanov come to Okha, in northern Sakhalin, but it would have doubled the costs which were already prohibitive. As long as we weren't faced with head winds I thought we should be all right.

Nikolai, like everyone else, had been on stand-by during those long days of waiting in Tokyo. He had gone to Magadan where he had made arrangements and waited. He had waited for ten days, phoning and e-mailing me every day, anxious and apologetic (apologising for Russia), and enquiring as to the situation. He had spoken with Gennady Velikovsky and Yuri. He finished all his other business and then he had to get back to Alaska saying, regretfully, that he would probably have to send someone else to meet us in Magadan as he had problems with his visa.

Magadan was on the Russian mainland, 1,099 miles to the north, with no available Avgas in between, and the last 450 miles of the journey were across the Sea of Okhotsk. Every mile counted; I had inadvertently done a 'straight line' fuel calculation from our present position to Yuzhno on Sakhalin Island, instead of following flight paths, which both the Russians and the Japanese were insisting on for the mileage from Wakanai to Yuzhno. So instead of the 97 miles I had calculated, we were looking at 275 miles. We needed to cut a few corners but the last thing we wanted to do was to upset the Russian authorities and have our precious clearances revoked. We decided that our best strategy would be for the Cessna to fly the air route, while the helicopters cut corners and Colin took a direct, low-level, silent stealth-mode route.

The Cessna was carrying two barrels of Avgas. The helicopters and microlight were full to the brim. Colin had his number 6 and 7 bladder tanks tucked under his knees, and we all prayed for continued tail winds. Yuri, now the official team navigator, was flying in the Cessna and was happily unaware of our strategy, as he was fully occupied getting himself into my survival suit for the short-ish water crossing. The rest of us had decided to wait for the Arctic waters further north between northern Sakhalin Island and Magadan on the Russian mainland before donning our suits, but Yuri had no faith in single-engine aircraft. We said goodbye and a million thanks to Shizouka and Mitsuo before heading out across the Sea of Okhotsk to Russia.

FIVE

Russia

20 - 26 July

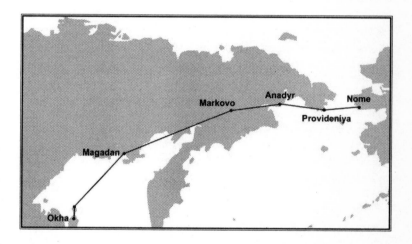

DAY 51

We all took off within minutes of each other, with Colin peeling quietly off on his northerly heading. Q and I headed north-east towards the second reporting point Argov, while Heinz, handled all the radio talk, heading south-east to the first official reporting point at Animo.

The weather was lovely and the tail winds held. Colin told us later he had seen thousands of dolphins – 'I didn't know there were so many dolphins in the entire world,' he said. We successfully cut the corners and Yuzhno let us route the last 50 miles direct, leaving out the last of the zigzags. We wondered if there was something they didn't want us to see but all we could spot was a lighthouse badly in need of a coat of paint, a rocky coastline and barren hills. Closer to Yuzhno we saw several small, depressed-looking settlements, the houses with corrugated iron roofs and the streets unpaved.

Yuzhno wanted us all at different heights, and to come in with ten minutes' separation, which required a little reorganisation and used up precious fuel. They gave us heights in metres rather than feet. It was all very confusing and rather dangerous as they kept up a non-stop dialogue in Russian with Yuri and Yuri would then give us onward information in English. Visibility deteriorated, there were cloud layers and no one could see anyone else, or the airfield. I was meant to be at 1,600 metres, Q at 1,200 and Colin at 900, all interspersed between several broken cloud layers. It was nerve-racking. Heinz had had to take cautionary action and do a 'go around' when he saw me coming in on Runway 09 just a couple of hundred yards ahead of him. But we all landed safely and were given a very warm welcome by Alexsandrovitch (Denis) Shvyrev. Q and I remembered him well from '97. He had been the cool, gum-chewing, chain-smoking dude about the airport, running errands. He was now the airport manager.

I later asked after his predecessor Nikolai Shevchenko and his wife Polina. Were they still around? Denis had said with a laugh and a shrug of his shoulders, 'Oh Nikolai Shevchenko? Not so good. So much trouble, he had to go.' I was sorry to hear that. His wife Polina had looked after us in '97 during three frustrating days when we had been delayed due to weather and I had brought her a small gift of some paints and paintbrushes. She was an amateur artist and, on hearing that I was also an artist, had taken us to her apartment. She had covered the walls with her watercolours for our benefit. They were childish and unformed, but fascinating in their Salvador Dali concepts (she had never heard of Dali).

Yuzhno Airport had had a face-lift and change was in the air. All the way through Russia we were to see changes for the better. A little money was finally getting through, unlike the last time when the endless refrain was, 'Life has changed since perestroika. There is no money, there is no hope.' I had been telling the team how depressed and poor the whole area was; how tough it would be and that we should bring masses of food with us. James Davey took me the most seriously and had brought his own small primus stove. In Tokyo we had filled an aluminium trunk full of packets of freeze-dried instant meals, cookies and candy bars, most of this got dumped in Alaska. Although conditions had improved, by Western standards they still had a long way to go. The road from the airport was full of potholes, the houses looked drab and what few shops there were had no window displays. Most business still seemed to be conducted from little kiosks on the pavements which principally sold vodka.

On reaching our hotel, Colin, Pat and Al went off in search of a beer. The beer in Russia is graded from 1–9 in potency. Colin, not knowing the grading system, went for the nicest looking bottle, and got pie-eyed on No. 9. He finally returned to the hotel with a great big silly grin on his face declaring, 'These people are really wonderful, they're wonderful people, these are my sort of people. I really, really like Russia!'

Yuzhno was the most prosperous of our stops in Russia and although the Sakhalin Sapporo hotel was drab on the outside, the inside had a sort of 1930s plush Parisienne-style opulence: there was lots of maroon velvet and chandeliers. Colin, for reasons I couldn't fathom, kept remarking on how Japanese it all was, whilst staring fixedly at a large bowl of artificial flowers. We had an excellent candle-lit dinner in a small dining room. I had the 'deer', as did most of the others, having been advised by the waiter that the rabbit was tough. The deer turned out to be a delicious filet of venison and the wine was a good table Burgundy. Things were looking up – until the next morning.

While waiting for Q I thought I would put through a call to Nikolai Selbakov in Anchorage, to confirm all the details of his fax, which Denis had handed me on arrival the day before. Nikolai said that the fuel was secure in Anadyr and that the AN-26 would leave for Magadan on Friday or Monday, depending on our schedule. Dima, his employee in Russia, would be there to look after us. I got through to Nikolai, he told me that Markovo, Anadyr and Provideniya airports would be closed at the weekend! We were due in Markovo on Saturday and Anadyr on Sunday.

'What, what do you mean?' I exclaimed, appalled at the prospect of yet more delays. 'Are they always closed at the weekend?' Nikolai said yes they were. 'But why didn't you *tell* us?' I said, looking over at the rest of the group. Heinz and Colin were looking concerned. Al and Pat looked fed up, with Pat raising his eyes to the ceiling as if implying 'Here we go, yet another cock-up.' Why hadn't Nikolai told us? His answer to that was that as we were originally meant to be in Markovo on a Tuesday, it hadn't been an issue. 'What about Chaiburkha?' I asked. Chaiburkha was the alternate to Markovo, but my memories of the place were not great. Last time we had been forced to sleep overnight in the long-disused airport terminal building with no facilities. 'Chaiburkha is also closed, the only one open on the mainland is Magadan.' Nikolai sounded very apologetic. Normally his sentences were prefaced by 'no problem, no problem', which in itself was always a bit of a worry. What were we going to do? We couldn't afford these delays. Were we going to have to route direct across Canada and miss out the USA, Mexico and Cuba? Our sponsors would be deeply unhappy and our ability to promote Operation Smile would go by the board. I reminded myself that I had to do the mileage to qualify for a world record. Every day counted.

I asked Nikolai if we could pay the airfields to stay open. 'That would be very, very expensive, Jennifer,' he said. 'It would cost a minimum of US$10,000!' He explained that you have to pay for all the airfields along the route to stay open too. 'But surely Chaiburkha is the only one we would overfly?' He agreed, but said it would still mean paying the airfield of departure and arrival to stay open for the entire time we were en route – and we were talking close on 11 hours for Colin. It looked as though we would have to spend two days kicking our heels in Magadan.

All of this agonising turned out to be academic, however, as the 'heel kicking' took place in Okha, our next port of call in northern Sakhalin Island.

When Q arrived we set off for the airfield with Denis. We had asked Denis the evening before if we could get hold of some reasonably high-octane petrol, thinking it wise to supplement our fuel if possible. He had looked a bit dubious but said he would see what he could do. He arrived with an assortment of battered five-gallon jerry cans. We stopped at an equally battered-looking fuel station and filled the cans with some suspicious-looking fuel. You can usually reckon that if there are Mercedes and Rolls Royces around, then the fuel should be OK. Yuzhno, I'm sure, had never seen either. However, filtered through a chamois leather and well diluted with our good fuel, we were certainly better off than finding ourselves with dry fuel tanks 20 miles off the coast of Magadan. The forecast was for 10- to 15-knot tail winds, but we ended up getting close on 30 knots of tail wind for most of the journey. So, even with a fair amount of deviating from the direct track, and stopping to have a picnic with some Russians on a beach, I found I still had 55 US gallons in my tanks on arrival in Okha.

I had been nervous about that journey north. I remembered all too well the last time I had flown that way and how, after the three days of delay in Yuzhno, we had finally decided to go for it. The weather had been marginal, cloud base 500 feet, but the forecast was for improvement and conditions were already good further north. In '97 we had routed north along the east coast and all would have been fine if ATC and Yuri had allowed us to remain coastal. Sakhalin Island is a narrow island just over 500 miles long and only 84 miles wide at its widest point. The south is mountainous, dominated by the Vostochno Sakhalinski Gory mountain range, which gives way to flat plains further north. We had headed happily north along the east coast, unable to see much of any land due to the low cloud. Yuri had said that we had to follow the air route, which left the coast at Poronaysk, and followed a narrow valley between the mountains, where the highest peaks reached up to 5,000 feet. Yuri had been explicit: 'If you go off course they will shoot you down.' We had been inclined to believe him. We had read the warning on our aeronautical chart, which said, 'Aircraft infringing upon Non-Free Flying Territory may be fired on without warning.' We had to leave the coast, and in the mountains we were hit by turbulence and a white-out. It was crazy. We should have been more patient and waited for better weather, but once we were on our way it was too late for such thoughts.

'This is utter madness,' Q had said, 'we're going to die!'

'Climb to 3,000 metres, heading 004,' said Yuri's disembodied voice from the Volpar, our escort plane. Yuri, an Aeroflot navigator, had no experience of low-level flying and VFR procedures, or the limitations of small piston engine helicopters. He expected us to follow the procedures for major jet airliners. We had zero visibility, our eyes were glued to the instruments as we tried not to get disorientated and fought to suppress the weird feeling of screaming off to the left or right. We had been wrapped in a cotton wool world, buffeted by turbulence and heavy with fuel, and had climbed agonisingly slowly through the white-out, praying the GPS was totally accurate. We could not have afforded to be more than a couple of hundred yards off course for fear of bumping into a mountain. We finally managed to climb to a safe altitude and half an hour later we broke into sunshine.

I had been so thankful for Q's flying skills. But that was then, this was now, I was on my own. Could I handle such a situation? I had been asking myself that question ever since I decided to go solo. I reminded myself that I had already coped with more testing situations than your average pilot ever faces: tropical storms, sand-laden air, severe turbulence and a series of mechanical problems like the failed magnetos. Still, I had not yet had the pleasure of a full-on white-out. I was going to have to wait a few days for the chance of that experience.

This time, flying to Okha, an enlightened ATC had us routing coastal, first on the east coast, then crossing over to the west side of the island to the south of the Vostochno Sakhalinski Gory mountain range. Visibility was good. The mountains were beautiful, and it was lovely to actually *see* them.

At 3,000 feet I soared over the foothills to the west coast, flying over scattered, puffy cumulus, enjoying the scenery and once again thinking how incredibly lucky and privileged I was to be doing what I was doing. I know it might not be every woman's idea of heaven, but it was mine. There I was, flying my little helicopter in Russia's Sakhalin Island, glorying in being on my own, high in the sky with 'Bear' for company, the little bean-bag bear that Christy had insisted that I take with me, way back at faraway Brooklands. Bear always looked so human sitting on the seat beside me.

I was having a good time but for Colin things were not going so well. He was having an appalling time and once again put me through some anxious moments. Unlike the east coast, where there had been no turbulence, the west coast was proving bumpy and producing lots of complaints from Colin. He was being forced higher and further out to sea in his efforts to clear the turbulence and, having thought he was going to be over land all day, he had no life jacket or life raft with him. He was, naturally, quite unhappy about that. 'I'm halfway to Vladivostok, I'm freezing cold, I'm at 12,000 feet in sleet and I'm being thrown all over the place. I've not got my life jacket or life raft. If I go down no one will ever find me.' I made sympathetic and concerned noises and asked for his coordinates but never got them, he was too busy just hanging in there. 'My wing is going to be torn off, don't think I can hold it, it's horrendous.' His radio was crackly and the last sentence, in my imagination, sounded as though he had been cut off. I had visions once again of Colin hurtling down, this time into the cold seas – a watery version of Saudi Arabia. Then, just as in Saudi Arabia, he went off the air.

Ten minutes later, much to my relief, Colin came back on the air. He sounded much calmer, just unhappy. 'It's pouring with rain, I'm soaked through and I haven't got my waterproof suit on. But the turbulence isn't quite so bad, and I'm heading back towards the coast.' I felt guilty because I was having a good time, despite unexpected pockets of turbulence, with mountains to my right, scrubland below and the sea off to my left. Then Q radioed me to say that he and Al had landed on a beach where a group of young Russians were camping and said, 'Come and join the party!' I was a little way ahead, but I doubled back and spotted G-JEFA on a narrow strip of sand at the base of the cliffs. Smoke was rising from a campfire and I landed on the beach where lunch was underway. There were four young Russian campers and two dogs. We gathered they were from a small town called Alexandria. They had a tiny tent and several fishing rods. A good fire was burning with a rather suspect-looking fish stew brewing in the coals while a blackened kettle hung suspended by a chain attached to a couple of bits of driftwood. Communication was difficult, but we managed with lots of signs and everyone talking their own language. Fresh bread and even fresher red caviar were produced and we had a feast. Al, between delicious mouthfuls, said, 'Well, who would believe this for a Friday? It beats anything, doesn't it? Eating caviar on the beach in north Sakhalin Island, how's that for laughs?'

I did cast a small thought in Colin's direction, battling the elements, and hoped he was once more over land. He missed so much up at his customary 11–13,000 feet, but he was a focused man, his sights set on far away England and achieving the near impossible.

How different that picnic was to Western picnics. I thought of all the modern conveniences we have: the picnic accessories, all the prepared this and that and the huge choice and variety, with every possible container to wrap it, pack it, keep things cold and keep things hot. Our new Russian friends were having a ball with the most basic of basics – if you can call red caviar basic. They had caught it, or rather the fish. They had five large sea trout sitting in their 'fridge', a small pool they had dug beside this icy-cold spring (a well-chosen camp site). Half an hour later, after farewells and thank-yous, we were once more on our way, Q clutching a jam jar full of red caviar that they insisted we take. He subsequently kept it too long for a 'special occasion' and it practically blew the lid off when he finally opened it in Markovo.

Meanwhile, Yuri had spent a frustrated time trying to get us on the radio. I told him that we had been forced to detour for bad weather. He didn't believe a word of it and when we landed he said, 'Jennifer, you really must make correct procedure in Russia. The authorities, they are very strict, and where did the red caviar come from?' shaking his head with a worried twinkle in his eye. We didn't conform to Aeroflot rules, but we were a long way from Moscow.

We landed at Okha within minutes of each other, Colin coming in just before us. The turbulence was horrendous for the helicopters, never mind the microlight. I don't know how Colin did it as the strong south-easterly winds were gusting up to 65 miles per hour across the flat and dusty plain. We were glad to be safely on the ground. Colin made a beeline for a nearby hangar while I quickly got out the tie downs for G-MURY's rotor blades (a fabric pocket with a long cord that you slip over the end of each blade then attach the cord end securely to the body of the helicopter) to ensure that the blades didn't get whipped up and down in strong winds, which were expected to strengthen overnight and didn't bode well for the following day.

Q was already on camera, sweeping back his hair, stroking his beard, leaning into the wind and giving a lively update on the day's exploits. Al was filming. Heinz said, 'I can't understand it, you are the story. How many adventure documentaries feature the camera crews? None. Like mountaineers risking life and limb, you sometimes cast a thought for the cameraman and how he manages to get the crazy shots, and you know he is probably in an equally precarious situation, an unsung hero, but you don't see him, he is not the story. This should be the same.'

There were, and still are, no restaurants in Okha. In '97, one of the air traffic controllers called Leila had taken pity on Q and myself and invited us to supper in her tiny apartment. She was still there and we got the opportunity to return her hospitality in the salubrious, very Russian, Business Centre, where Nikolai Selbakov had arranged for us to have our meals. Leila arrived with her friend Marcia and we all had a very merry evening, with a great deal of vodka being consumed. Everyone proposed toasts and Leila and Marcia needed no encouragement to happily stuff their pockets and capacious handbags with the contents of two large bowls of fresh fruit.

Business is obviously not brisk in Okha – we were the sole occupants during our stay.

On 22 and 23 July the wind and rain gave way to dense fog. For two days we endured dismal, dreary, damp industrial Okha, which ekes out a grim existence on the most northerly tip of Sakhalin Island, with very little to recommend it other than some delightful people. The buildings are all square apartment blocks with peeling paint and crumbling masonry. There are no restaurants in a town of over 60,000 people. But much to our surprise there was a nightclub and we all went there one evening. It could have been anywhere in the world, scruffy, flashing lights, total sound, smoke, beer and vodka. The DJ was in a mock aeroplane cockpit where Colin spent most of the night happily helping to 'mix' the music, declaring he had never ever danced in his whole life and didn't know how to. Then he had an arm-wrestling competition with the local champion and won. Heinz danced with the prettiest girl in the room and everyone had a fun evening with a great deal of vodka and subsequent hangovers the following morning. Colin found he had a very sore arm.

There had been a few changes in the last three years. Our hotel was new, a small building with seven bedrooms and a tiny lobby that was little more than a short passageway with one sofa and a reception desk. One of the bedrooms was occupied by a Finn called Andrew. He worked for a travel agency and he was the tallest, thinnest man I have ever seen, all of seven foot tall. Q and Colin had to share a room, as did Pat and Al.

On the second afternoon I went for a long walk. The rain finally cleared, the banks of fog temporarily lifted and there were even a few patches of blue sky. A fresh wind was blowing as I headed off alone towards the distant Sea of Okhotsk, past the drab tenement buildings. I was soon on a sandy track with coarse grass, scrub, and dunes on either side. I walked for three and a half hours, revelling in the solitude. We all needed space.

I wandered amongst the sand dunes, the wild lupins and vetch with the wind in my face, salt in the air and saw not a soul. I sat on a driftwood log, feeling the worn and weathered pattern of the damp wood, the sand between my toes, and watched the timeless pattern of the Sea of Okhotsk, the sea that we would soon be attempting to cross. I thought of the risks involved. Over 700 miles of freezing, empty water on the way to Magadan on Russia's mainland, out there beyond the distant horizon. This would be our first long cold-water crossing. We would be wearing our survival suits.

It was peaceful sitting there alone, and my thoughts turned to home and family and friends. I liked to imagine all the family together in Somerset. But Justin and his family were in Hong Kong – or were they already in Amsterdam? (His new posting with Cathay Pacific.) Maybe they *were* all together with the two little girls disturbing the morning peace. I thought of my mother in Cheshire, who might be painting or busy in her garden. I had checked our latitude the night before and realised that Okha was at the same latitude as Macclesfield, my mother's nearest town. It was strange as I felt so much further north, but then Sakhalin Island doesn't enjoy the benefits of the Gulf Stream as we do in Britain.

I sat there for a long time, just drifting, enjoying those distant shores until finally, with the fog once more beginning to roll in off the sea, I headed back towards town. I had seen no one, not a solitary soul since leaving the outskirts of town seven miles away. I thought it strange. You would imagine that on a weekend in high summer, the good citizens of Okha would enjoy escaping their dreary town. Then, still with miles to go to the town, I had a horrible fright. Out of the low brush to the side of the path appeared this drunken man. He came lurching towards me. I could feel the hairs on my neck literally stand on end and I went cold all over. There was no one else around. He had a bottle in his hand and was filthy. I turned around and started walking back the way I had come, further away from the town, and still he came towards me. I broke into a run and he just stumbled on. The next time I looked around he was flat on his face on the dusty road and I realised he was blind drunk and probably didn't even know I was there. Fear turned to pity as I turned around, heading once more back to town, giving him a pretty wide berth just in case.

Twice in Okha we packed our bags, paid the bill and asked the hotel to please hold the rooms for a couple of hours. We had returned both times. We visited the small Met office at the airfield and looked forlornly out the window at our aircraft being first battered by the elements, then hidden in them. On the third day I looked out of my bedroom window. The weather looked a little less foggy and the forecast for Magadan was quite good. Nikolai, now back in Anchorage, phoned us with daily updates for the region. We got to the airfield and decided to go for it. There was patchy coastal sea mist dispersing slowly.

Colin taxied over from the hangar, followed by a cloud of mosquitoes, and complaining heavily about his arm. The mosquitoes loved him and to add to his misery it looked as though he had pulled or torn a tendon in his arm. How was he going to be able to cope with turbulence, which required all his considerable strength, with a torn tendon? I told him to get his survival suit on quickly as it would be a good anti-mosquito shield for most of his body.

'It's going to be pitch dark before I get there,' he gloomily predicted, 'and we've got head winds.'

'Magadan won't be dark until 10.30 p.m. Even if it takes you ten hours to get there it will still be light,' I said as I helped him with his survival suit – not easy with a semi-dysfunctional arm. I was more concerned about the fuel situation. If we were to have head winds all the way we could be in real trouble. I then set about all my last-minute checks, trying to concentrate on the job in hand rather than be irritated by the fact that Al was once more videoing Q, this time donning his survival suit. I watched Colin take off, then put my own survival suit on and immediately had the overpowering need to go to the loo once more. I'm sure it's just the thought of knowing you can't go for hours that induces the urge. I disappeared off into the bushes at the side of the apron.

The latest forecast for Magadan was not so good: low cloud and rain. I called the tower. 'Golf Mike Uniform Romeo Yankee requesting flight information for departure to Magadan.'

'Golf Mike Uniform Romeo Yankee. Runway 16, QNH 1011, taxi to threshold 16 and report ready to depart.' Once more we were back into the familiar routine, the frustration of the past two days behind us – next stop, the Russian mainland.

I turned on a heading of 060 degrees, taking me over the town of Okha, which appeared far less drab from the air. The buildings looked more white than grey in the morning sunshine that was now burning off the early morning sea mist which still hugged the coastline. Clear of the town I turned north and followed the coast for the next 50 miles to the most northerly point on Sakhalin Island and then, turning away from land, I set course for the Island of Ione, five degrees north of the direct course for Magadan, so many miles away across the Sea of Okhotsk.

Ione, the only land between us and Magadan, is little more than a rock in the middle of the Sea of Okhotsk, but is teeming with wildlife: puffins, terns, walrus and seals. The weather deteriorated as we approached the island. We could just see the tip of the rock of Ione poking out above the cloud. The island is no more than an acre in size with sheer cliffs and rocky outcrops rising to close on a thousand feet. Every square centimetre is covered in birds. As we got closer we could see that there were small clear pockets in the mist, and we were able to drop through and get a look at our friends the walruses and seals, praying that the millions of birds would be able to take avoiding action. We did not need a bird strike out there in the middle of the Sea of Okhotsk, but if you keep your speed below 60 knots the birds can out-fly you (apparently). It was a mysterious, enchanting world that appeared through the swirling mist: the birds, the ghostly, glistening rocks and, in the tossing sea, hosts of inquisitive seals, their little faces peering up at us, dipping below the surface as we flew overhead, then popping up again immediately we passed over. One big bull walrus sat his ground on a large rock. Then it was time to go. I found another hole in the cloud and climbed once more safely back above the blanketing mists.

Colin, on his direct route, reported his position some 30 miles due east of Ione. We said we would turn back on track and intercept him, keep him company. It was good to finally spot, out there in that vastness, the little speck that was Colin, heading ever eastward. Despite all his gloomy predictions he was making good progress. The light head winds were gone and at 5,000 feet we were getting a couple of knots' tail wind. The Cessna, now an hour ahead, reported 15 knots of tail wind at 12,000 feet, with solid cloud cover below. We asked them to report cloud levels as they made their descent into Magadan.

It looked as though I was going to have to make my first prolonged solo descent through thick cloud, unless the skies cleared within the next two hours. This was the situation I had always hoped to avoid. The situation I had lain in bed imagining – a long sea crossing with thick cloud at the other end, with no alternative but to go down through it. I prayed that the cloud would not be down to the ground. Hopefully the Cessna would be within radio range to give us a report on conditions. The cloud had already pushed us up and we were now at 7,500 feet between two layers of stratus cloud, hoping the two layers wouldn't narrow further.

The previous time coming into Magadan, Q and I were also between two layers, which had closed in, and for more than an hour we had flown in cloud, with just the occasional moment between layers. Then, there had been two of us, so if one started to feel disorientated the other could take over and that time the skies had cleared 60 miles offshore, giving way to blue skies.

Now it looked a little different. I felt nervous but the world around me was so beautiful and calm, with patches of golden afternoon sunlight reflecting on the clouds below, and I was reassured by the sight of Q and Colin on my port side, several hundred yards distant. The Cessna started its descent. James finally reported that they were entering cloud at 7,000 feet and the airfield was giving a base of 750 feet. That was a lot of cloud and what would it be like in an hour's time? And what would the cloud base be over the sea?

The airfield was 20 miles inland, which was not too much of a problem for the Cessna who could make a precision ILS approach. We needed an added safety margin, we needed to descend well clear of land, over nice empty water, with no ugly surprises like a tall mast or unsuspected hill. But low cloud and sea can look awfully similar and I had an hour to think about it.

When in cloud, all movements should be very gentle. It is too easy to overcorrect. I thought the best course would be to enter cloud with a descent rate of 500 feet per minute, slowing down to 300 feet per minute at 1,000 feet. That would have me in cloud for about 12 to 15 minutes. If I still hadn't broken through, then I could creep down the next 500 and pray that I would see the sea before I got wet. Colin was relaxed. He had plenty of cloud experience, and the microlight flies naturally straight and level. We all hoped for a turbulence-free descent.

James reported that the Cessna was on final approach and that they had broken through cloud at 700 feet. 'Safe landings. See you,' he said.

We continued north over the solid cloud cover and then it was time to go down, get established on heading 030, level, nice and steady, pull full carb heat, lower the collective, slow down to 70 knots, a steady descent of 500 feet per minute – and in I went. I felt strangely calm, cocooned in a white world, eyes fixed on the instruments, the artificial horizon, the VSI, the ASI and, of course, the compass from time to time, but always I focused back on the artificial horizon.

I could have done with a turn and bank indicator like G-JEFA, it's just that little bit better than the artificial horizon, both would have been nice. I descended: 6,000, 5,000, 4,000, steady, steady. Then I started to feel the edges of disorientation. I closed my eyes momentarily, my heart accelerating. 'Stay calm, look at the instruments, look down, look at my lap, get a solid reference,' I told myself. I tried not to focus on the weird patterns of light from the all-enveloping white.

'You *can* control it,' I willed myself, still descending: 3,000, 2,000, no break in the cloud. With 1,000 coming up, I eased up the collective a fraction to slow my rate of descent (and my heart). I was now descending at 300 feet per minute – 900, 800, 700, 600, – I slowed down still further. Then, just as I was beginning to get that extra adrenalin rush, I came through the white into a grey and wet world with a choppy, foam-flecked sea, 500 feet below. I could see a patch of low mist hugging the water no more than 500 yards distant. I had been lucky. Q was also through, and minutes later Colin reported that he too was safely skimming the waves.

How different the coast looked from the last time. Gone were the blue skies and the sea that had been so calm that the mountains were perfectly reflected in the still, clear waters. Magadan is infamous for its gulags. I looked at the cold, inhospitable mountains and I thought of all the political prisoners brought there back in the '30s and '40s during Stalin's purge. More than three million 'enemies of the people' had perished there: teachers, artists, lawyers, anyone who had fallen under Stalin's suspicion was sent to Magadan. They worked the gold, silver and uranium mines in appalling conditions, with temperatures dropping as low as minus 50 degrees centigrade in the winter. No one ever escaped.

We flew low over the small port of Magadan, leaving the sea for the windswept plains, surprising two large brown bears, and in the distance I could see the Kolyma mountains to the north, rising to heights of 10,000 feet. Magadan was one small town in a vast area of steppes. The nearest town was Anadyr, one thousand miles to the east. No wonder none of Stalin's 'enemies of the people' ever escaped. There was nowhere to go.

We landed at 7 p.m. local time, and made yet another time change; now that we were so far north and heading east, we were putting our watches forward an hour virtually every day. Alaska was getting closer.

I saw our large Antonov 26 with our fuel sitting on the apron with the Cessna alongside looking very small indeed. (The Antanov has drive-on facilities for several cars.) A smaller aircraft would have done but Nikolai had said the Antonov 26 was the most economical one available, though this seemed hard to believe when it required three crew and our 15 barrels (more than we needed) took up only a fraction of the room in the hold. However, we had only had to charter the Antonov for a day and a half and it would not be travelling with us. The following morning they would take the remaining barrels back to Anadyr (it hadn't been possible to leave them there for fear of them being stolen) and then return to Anchorage. The Cessna would carry two barrels for us to our next stop, Markovo.

Colin, Q and I spent three and a half hours at the airfield; of the others, there was no sign, and Yuri had said he would try to arrange parking for the microlight. There were two enormous hangars, big enough for a couple of jumbos, only 500 yards away from where we were parked. Colin had gone off to see what the score was. He returned to say they were firmly closed and there was no one around. A young woman called Tatiana appeared from the distant terminal buildings, teetering across the vast and empty apron on the highest of wedge sandals and the shortest and tightest of miniskirts. Tatiana, who could speak a little English, told us that the duty officer in charge of the hangars was having his supper and that she was the assistant head of ground operations. She said she was meant to be on holiday for two days, but would be happy to help.

We set about the business of rolling the barrels down the ramp of the Antanov and across the apron to the helicopters. We had been made to park a good hundred yards from the Antanov for 'security' reasons. Eventually we were full of fuel again, except for Colin, who held off refuelling, hoping that the duty officer would arrive. He didn't want to find himself dismantling the microlight with full tanks, which he would have to do if the hangar remained shut. We waited interminably; no duty officer arrived. Eventually we dismantled the microlight and just as we were finishing we saw the great doors of one of the hangars slowly opening. 'I just don't believe it,' Colin said. We left the microlight dismantled.

As we were walking to the airport hotel, Yuri put in an appearance, looking harassed as usual. 'Where have you been, Yuri? We've been doing our nut. Where did you all go? We needed you to translate and to help with Colin's microlight,' I said.

Poor Yuri, whose job was really only that of navigator, looked thoroughly apologetic and concerned. He reminded me that we had all agreed it would be good to see if he could organise for us all to just refuel in Markovo the next day and then continue on to Anadyr, and that was what he had been doing. I felt a heel and apologised, I had quite forgotten that had been the plan. Yuri told us that not only had the authorities said 'no', but they had also tried to insist that we go to Chaiburkha rather than Markovo. He and Heinz had finally got ATC to agree to our going to Markovo, which Nikolai had described as 'his' airfield, claiming everything there would be 'no problem'. This was not quite the case.

We finally sat down to supper at 11 p.m., the end of a long, tiring day. My alarm had gone off at 6 that morning and we were at the Okha airfield by 8.30 a.m. There had been long delays, with Colin only getting away at noon and the helicopters at 1.30 p.m. Colin had been in the air for eight hours and the helicopters for six. I climbed wearily into my metal bed at 12.45 a.m., but was weary with a sense of achievement, not like the weariness of those endless days of waiting in Tokyo.

Flying in eastern Russia is wonderful and worth all the delays on the ground, which become entertaining with hindsight. Within minutes of being airborne you forget the ground frustrations in the exhilaration of the vastness, the emptiness, the wide open spaces. The knowledge that few westerners had ever been there or seen what we were seeing was intoxicating. To the best of my knowledge, the only other non-Russian helicopter that has ever flown in that area was Q and myself three years before. In 1982, during the days of the Cold War, Ross Perot Junior (the first person to fly around the world in a helicopter) and Dick Smith (the first man to fly solo around the world in a helicopter), had both routed direct from northern Japan to the Aleutian Islands, making a hazardous refuelling stop on a container ship. The other helicopter circumnavigations had all gone straight through Russia from Moscow to Provideniya, routing well to the north of our present position. In Sakhalin Island I had been told that I was the first female helicopter pilot they had ever seen!

I noted in my diary that, even if we had no further delays, it would be another month before we reached northern Canada to make our crossing of the North Atlantic to Greenland. The recommended window for VFR flight is from the first week of June to 24 July!

On leaving Magadan we had a slight head wind with grey skies that soon cleared. As ever, Colin took off first. The weather remained clear for the first 500 miles, then the sky got hazier and hazier and finally we smelt smoke. There was a large brush fire burning somewhere. Q and I continued at low level, but Colin, with whom we had now caught up, said visibility at 11,000 feet was deteriorating. He wanted to know what our conditions were like, especially turbulence and visibility. I told him there was little turbulence but the visability was poor. He thought he would try and descend a little to see if he fared any better.

Conditions got worse and worse, with visibility less than 100 metres. I concentrated on my GPS, getting the topographical detail, and hoping it was accurate for such a remote area. There was a green low-lying area showing on the GPS, so I headed for it, trying not to bump into mountains, trees and Q, and feeling thankful that there were no wires around. The acrid smell of burning vegetation got stronger as did the dense smoke. It became increasingly difficult to see, and we found ourselves having to head more south than east, 40 degrees off course. I tried to check on Colin, there was no reply, but I didn't feel alarmed at that time as I presumed he must have descended and was low-level behind another mountain.

Then I saw the flames. It was a huge forest fire!

Not only was visibility reduced to a few yards, but oxygen levels were seriously low. The air, even inside the cockpit, was now dangerously filled with smoke. I reached for a small towel that was sitting on the extender tank behind me and tried to hold it intermittently over my nose and mouth but had to give up as I needed both hands on the controls. The flames appeared to entirely block our path to the east and south-east. We had no choice but to head due south and pray that the flames hadn't already encircled us. I tried to contact Colin again, still no reply. I hoped he was faring better than us. We were using up precious fuel on this, one of our longest legs – we couldn't afford a big detour. Ten miles south, flying cautious and low, the smoke began to thin a little and we were able to turn 30 degrees east. Another ten minutes and we were once more on course, only ten miles south of our original direct track and with the smoke situation improving all the time. But there was no word from Colin.

The skies cleared. We climbed to 7,000 feet and managed to raise Markovo on the radio, now 90 miles distant. Still nothing from Colin. Perhaps he was low-level ahead of us? I reasoned that we must have lost a good half hour when we were forced south, and past experience suggested that Colin could be having any number of problems. He could even have had a radio failure. But it was a strange coincidence that it should happen at the moment when there were bad flying conditions. The real possibility was that he had descended, as he had said he was going to, and hadn't appreciated how high some of the mountains were, with visibility near zero. Even world champions can get it wrong. Once again I had visions of him crumpled on the ground.

The scenery, now that we could see it, was spectacular in the clear, golden afternoon light. The arid granite mountains, streaked with iron ore, were slowly flattening out onto vast and desolate plains. Under normal circumstances I would have been glorying in the great desolation, but I worried for Colin. Had he landed? He had been some way ahead of us. We heard Yuri in the tower at Markovo calling Colin. 'Golf November Oscar Whisky Whisky.' So Colin obviously wasn't ahead, he hadn't landed. Yuri then asked us if we were two-way with Colin. We climbed higher in the hope that even if he was on the ground we might hear him, or pick up the signal of his ELT (emergency location transmitter) on frequency 121.5. Still nothing. We were virtually over the airfield. It was time to land and organise a search and rescue. Heinz and James would need to get G-EELS refuelled immediately.

We landed and Heinz came over whilst I was shutting down. I told him we had been trying to raise Colin for the last hour and a half and that the last time we had spoken to him we had all been having a big problem with the smoke from the brush fires. James came over just as I was asking whether they had refuelled G-EELS, as I thought we would have to organise a search and rescue for Colin. James looked rather bewildered and said, 'But what do you mean?' Pointing up to the sky, he said: 'Look – there he is!' Sure enough, two miles out, high in the sky, was Colin.

Both radios had failed, or rather there was a fault in the wiring. 'I could hear you all the time. I thought you might even see me, you passed right underneath me 20 miles back.' Yuri had been in a frantic state. He said, 'Two more minutes and I would have had to call Moscow, I would have had to call Mr Velikovsky!'

Markovo – in the middle of nowhere, the poorest and most isolated of all our stopovers – looked rather wonderful in the evening light. The airfield's runway was in moderately good condition, but that was about the only thing that was. The apron was a grass field in front of a small wooden tower that looked as though it might collapse at any moment. It had a definite lean to it with a drooping wooden balcony on the top floor. Parked in the field were four lovely old biplanes – Antanov 2s. I thought their days of flying had finished many years previously. It wasn't until the following morning, when a small group of passengers arrived for the weekly flight to Anadyr, that I realised otherwise. The insides of the planes had wooden benches running down both sides with no safety belts and, as the passengers climbed on board, the plane was being refuelled with what smelt like neat paraffin, a good portion of which was slopping everywhere.

But Nikolai's Markovo, where he had said we would be so welcome and he knew everyone, was rather inhospitable at first. The Deputy Mayor Dimitri Rostrovitch appeared with a crumpled piece of paper with a list of questions that Anadyr had sent through. Firstly, did we have permission to land in their province? Did we have permission to film with our cameras? Why were we staying in Markovo? The list went on and on. We tried to reassure Dimitri that we had done everything correctly. We told him that we had permission from Moscow. 'You must have OK from Anadyr,' he said, 'you have stay here till all question answer.' Yuri came to the rescue and a long and heated discussion went on. Time was passing, and we were ready for something to eat and bed. We were all starving. Breakfast had been long ago: snacks of oatcakes and honey, Orio cookies and Coca Cola by the Cessna in Magadan as the hotel restaurant only opened at 9 a.m. James had managed a quick brew up of freeze-dried scrambled eggs on his little stove.

Dimitri apologised many times for Anadyr's question list, insisting that it was nothing to do with Markovo. Finally, more or less satisfied with Yuri's reassurances, he said we were free to go. Then came the discussion about transport. Dimitri was very sorry, but the jeep and the truck (our transport) needed fuel. They had none, he told us, and could they please have some of ours to get us into town? We told him we needed our fuel, but if there was any left over after refuelling the next day they were welcome to have it. We had decided, for security, and because we were tired, to refuel the next day. We thought (wrongly) that the fuel would be more secure in sealed drums. It was nine o'clock at night. Colin had been in the air for nine hours, the helicopters seven and the Cessna three. Nine o'clock at night at a latitude of 65 degrees on 25 July meant we had nearly 24 hours of daylight.

After the try-on for fuel, it appeared that the truck and the jeep did have some sort of fuel. The 'oldies', Heinz, Yuri, Colin and I, squeezed in the jeep, while the others all clambered into the open truck for the short ride into town. We bounced along the dirt road, passing a charming old wooden building with peeling white and blue paint standing all on its own. It wouldn't have looked out of place in a western movie. The driver told Yuri that it was the old

1942 airport terminal building. The airport had been moved to slightly higher ground because of flooding. Flooding? Everything looked dry and dusty, more desert than pasture. It wasn't until the following day that we appreciated the amount of water so close to hand. Markovo was on the edge of an endless expanse of lakes and meandering rivers to the east.

To add weight to the driver's argument, we passed a large and rusty tin boat lying high and dry beside the road. The driver told Yuri it had been beached there in '97. 'Normally it never rains in the summer,' he said, 'but in the summer of '97 it rained and rained and the airport and most of the town were three metres under water. Everyone had to go everywhere by boat.' I remembered that Nikolai had apologised for the dreadful conditions when we had had to stay in Chaiburkha in '97, saying that we would have gone to Markovo, but that it was under water – I had not appreciated just how under water.

The small town of Markovo consisted of a few dilapidated old apartment buildings, where paint was only a memory. Nikolai had arranged our accommodation. Our home for the night was in a crumbling two-storey schoolhouse. Everything was in need of repair. The three concrete steps leading up to the front door were cracked and missing large chunks. The weather-beaten door led into a dark concrete hallway with yet more broken concrete stairs leading up to the living quarters. At the top of the stairs we passed an open door showing a 'squat' loo, and the next door led into a large washroom with ten small washbasins, four of which had no tap, the other six had one for cold water. That was fine for us for one night in high summer, but not much fun one would imagine in the winter with temperatures plunging as low as minus 40–50 degrees centigrade.

There were several large rooms upstairs with 1950s flowered wallpaper and linoleum on the floor, all of which had seen better days. But the rooms were clean and the largest one had ten sagging iron beds. I got the matron's bedroom. The sheets and pillows were spotlessly clean and so inviting. But we were hungry. Heinz asked our new friend Deputy Mayor Dimitri, who seemed to have appointed himself tour leader, 'Where can we eat?'

'You need food?' he said. We assured him that we definitely needed food. 'We will have to go to the shop, there is no restaurant,' he said.

Why hadn't we brought some of our emergency supplies with us? We should have realised that there would be no restaurant in Markovo. We couldn't go back to the airport, the fuel was too precious and it was past ten o'clock. We set off, all of us except Al and Pat, who were wearily setting up their editing equipment and positioning satellite dishes in the middle of the room, optimistically hoping for satellites. Dimitri led us in search of the shopkeeper,

Sergei Novikov. He was rather surprised to see us, but obligingly took us to his shop. I think it was the only shop in Markovo. The choice was limited, although there was every possible brand of vodka and most of the 1–9 beers. Sergei had the Russian version of pot noodles, 'pot mashed potato'. We bought a good supply, plus Coca Cola, vodka and biscuits that turned out to be stale.

Sergei Novikov told Dimitri that he wanted to give me a present. He said that he so admired what I was doing. I remonstrated, saying that opening the shop after hours was present enough. 'You must accept,' Yuri said. 'He would like to give you a bearskin!' It was a lovely, generous gesture, but I said something about not wanting to encourage the fur trade. Dimitri looked surprised at this novel idea.

'We need food and we need skins. Winter time here is very cold and we have many, many bear.' Everyone encouraged me, and Dimitri said Sergei would be offended if I did not accept. I went up to his apartment, climbing up five floors of concrete stairs. Inside I was greeted by his smiling wife and his rather overweight son who, of all unlikely things, was playing war games on a computer. The small bearskin was lying in the middle of their tiny living room floor. Andre's wife proudly insisted I take a tour of the whole of their minute apartment. 'Da, da, da!' she said, pointing out with pride where the dog slept, where the cat slept and where the family slept, smiling and nodding as she showed me their home.

Later, Yuri told me that it was illegal to export fur out of Russia and Pat said he thought it was also illegal in America. I sacrificed my nice cotton Japanese kimono, wrapping my bearskin up inside it, and hid the bearskin at the back of one of the luggage pods under the Cessna.

We feasted on pot mash. I was so tired that I can't even remember how we boiled the water. I think Dimitri must have borrowed an electric kettle. There was no kitchen. We drank vodka and Yuri triumphantly produced a large hunk of smoked sturgeon that he had brought from Moscow, which he proceeded to carve up with a lethal-looking sheath knife. Most of us finally got to bed around midnight. We left Yuri, Q and Dimitri drinking toasts to all and everything. For them, the night was still young. There was light in the sky.

When we got to the airfield the next morning we found that one of our barrels of fuel had been opened and ten gallons were missing. Luckily we only had 215 miles to go to Anadyr where we had four more barrels waiting. More than enough to get to Nome.

Nome, Alaska; the great US of A! A shining light on the horizon. I really felt that once we reached the North American continent we were on the home stretch, and we would be free to fly everywhere. No more air routes and the added joy of being able to land at airfields, refuel in minutes and be on our way. The ratio of time in the air to time at airfields would be fabulous, and we needed no more clearances other than Cuba – if we got there. Ever since leaving Greece we had followed air routes and coped with endless bureaucracy, but soon that would all change.

We were hoping that we would be able to refuel in Anadyr and continue on to Nome. It would be another long day but we needed to make up time and none of us wanted to stay in Anadyr. We were, therefore, anxious to get away from Markovo as early as possible the next day, but there were the usual delays and Dimitri was moving at a slow and painfully hungover pace. Colin took off at 11 a.m. and the helicopters at 11.30 a.m. I looked fondly back at Markovo where, after the initial hiccup, Nikolai's friends had made us so welcome.

The sky was clear as a bell from the floor to the stratosphere, and we had 5 knots of tail wind. The flat plains, intersected by rivers and streams, meandered around and into a million lakes. There was as much water as land as far as the eye could see. I flew low-level in the hopes of seeing some wildlife. Sergei had said we should see plenty of moose, caribou and bear. The camera crew were keen to get some footage. We followed separate rivers, and then I spotted a female moose with her baby. I circled, taking a few photos. This was no easy task, especially when the best chance of getting clear pictures was through the little door flap close to my right hand, and my right hand had to hold the cyclic lever. So I either had to reach across with my left hand, or take the cyclic lever in my left hand and take the picture with my right, or just take the photo quickly through the plexiglass and risk reflections. I got reflections.

It was one of the great and glorious days. When the weather was perfect, when you laugh out loud for the sheer joy and wonder of the beauty; the vastness and the thrill of flying where few had ever flown, in a land far from anywhere. That day was a 'John Gillespie Magee day' – John Gillespie Magee, who died in the First World War in aerial combat, aged 18. As on so many occasions, I found myself reciting his immortal verse that said it all for every aviator.

> Oh I have slipped the surly bonds of earth
> And dance the clouds on laughter silvered wings.
> Upward I climb amidst the tumbling mirth,
> Of sun split clouds, doing a hundred things
>
> You've never dreamed of. Wheeled and soared and swung,
> High in the sunlit silence, hovering there
> I chase the shouting winds along,
> And hurl my eager craft through footless halls of air.

Up, up, the long, delirious, burning blue
I top the windswept heights with easy grace
Where never lark or ever eagle flew.

And whilst my silent lifting mind I trod
The high untrespassed sanctity of space
Reach out my hand, and touch the face of God.

God's great creation. That was a day I too reached out my hand, and I thought of my own father. How he would have loved to be on such a trip. My father who loved the great unknown, loved the big outdoors. He was always ready for a challenge and must be responsible for much of my love of adventure. There were so many times I felt he was with me and never more so than that day. My father, William Mather – Bill or Will to his friends – had died two years previously. I had at one time thought of calling my helicopter 'The Spirit of Will' after him. But G-MURY had always been G-MURY and I left it that way.

The plains of a thousand rivers gave way to rolling heather hills that reminded me of the Lake District in England, but there in those Russian hills there was no sign of man. We found no crofter's cottage, not even a path. The hills flattened out once more as we neared Anadyr and we could see the cold, blue waters of the Bering Sea.

Anadyr, like Magadan, Okha and Yuzhno, had also been tidied up in the past three years. Gone were the rusty piles of scrap and rubber tyres. Gone the atmosphere of tired resignation and apathy. There were new buildings, more activity, more traffic and even an air of optimism. By western standards Anadyr too has far to go. The apron is still loose gravel and many of the old buildings were still in disrepair. Only the new ones had a coat of paint. It just wasn't as depressing as before. No doubt the sunshine helped, and Yuri telling us that we were cleared for Nome.

Heinz arrived with a man driving a fork-lift truck with our barrels of fuel, hopefully our last barrels. From Alaska onwards we anticipated no further problems with Avgas fuel availability. Yuri went off with our passports and General Declaration documents, accompanied by two large, formidable women in military uniform, to file flight plans and do customs. I could see the camera crew doing an update for the website, no doubt saying, 'This is Al Edginton of the NOW Challenge speaking to you live from Anadyr!' We were working on a fast turnaround, and Colin was telling me that it was going to take him at least eight hours to reach Nome.

All formalities done, we were clear to go. The weather held good and spirits were high as we waved Colin off with the Russians standing spellbound at the sight of him and his absurdly small machine speeding down the runway, then lifting off into the east, across the Gulf of Anadyr to the Bering Sea. The Bering Strait was named after the Russian sea captain and explorer Vitus Bering who charted most of the area back in 1778. We had 500 miles to go to Nome – all over water other than one short 20-mile stretch of land when we would be crossing the Providneiya Peninsula.

Survival suits were once more on, Yuri had helped me pull the heavy rubber seal over my head and zip me in. I had to do a balancing act as I didn't want to get the loose gravel in my trainers. The survival suit has 'feet'. So having first put the quilted inner liner suit on over my normal flight suit, I then balanced on one foot, propped up by Yuri, then stood on one of my trainers and climbed into my survival suit. Finally, rubber-sealed and zipped, I had to squeeze my feet back into my trainers. Once hermetically sealed, we had all heaved our twice-the-normal-size selves into our respective aircraft, done all the checks and requested start-up for Nome. The helicopters took off an hour after Colin. Our next stop was the USA!

I felt a little sadness saying goodbye to eastern Russia. I would probably never come that way again (although that was what I had thought in '97). We had had some good times and seen sights and places that few will ever be privileged to enjoy, and the people had been wonderful, so hospitable and generous. I thought of Denis, the newly elevated airport manager in far away Yuzhno; our beach picnic friends and their red caviar; Leila in Okha; Dimitri the Deputy Mayor and Sergei and his bearskin, and there had been many others. Colin had been right when he had said after his No. 9 beer in Yuzhno, 'These are my kind of people.'

'Golf Mike Uniform Romeo Yankee and Golf Juliet Echo Foxtrot Alpha formation are ready to depart for Nome.'

Thirty miles out we spotted pack ice off to our starboard and decided to go and have a look. For nine months of the year Anadyr is frozen, but on that day in late July the temperature was a balmy ten degrees centigrade and we only saw the one mass of pack ice, about an acre in size, drifting gently south with the current. Q landed on one of the larger and what looked slightly less fragile lumps, keeping the rotors running. Pat got out and took a few cautious steps while I opted for the safer occupation of circling and taking photos. By the time we finally resumed course we were an hour and a half behind Colin. And it was another half an hour before we were two-way on the radio with him. He reported that he was 110 miles west of Provideniya, that he had a tail wind component of 25 knots at 9,000 feet and he was freezing cold. The outside air temperature was minus 3 degrees centigrade. I suggested he come down to our height where we still had a comfortable ten degrees, but he said he'd rather be cold and clear of turbulence. Once again he was making far better progress than anticipated.

Then Colin came on the air sounding alarmed. 'My exhaust gas temperatures are going through the roof. I'm losing power and I don't really know quite what to do.' The closest land was the Russian mainland some 30 miles to his north-west. I checked my topographical chart, but there was nothing there; only the mountains of Orvyn plunging down to the waters of the Gulf of Anadyr. I also noticed that the chart had a warning notice saying: '*WARNING:* Unlisted radio emissions from this area may constitute a navigation hazard or result in border overflight unless unusual precaution is exercised.' And another, more ominous one said: 'Aircraft infringing upon Non-Free Flying Territory may be fired on without warning. Consult NOTAMS and Flight Information Publications for the latest information.' I thought I wouldn't mention the notices as he had enough to worry about and there was little we could do about it anyway.

Once again we got Colin's coordinates and started heading his way. We were still an hour behind him and some 30 miles south of his track. Colin, as usual, was on track. He rightly said, 'Search and rescue stand a better chance of finding you if you are on track.'

He said he was going to try and make Provideniya, and then ten anxious minutes later he reported that the power settings appeared to have returned to normal. We all relaxed a little, which gave us time to think of the implications of a prolonged stay in Provideniya getting Colin's machine sorted out. More nights in Russia. My sadness of an hour ago at leaving Russia was quickly replaced with a burning desire to cross that International Date Line and hear the voice of Anchorage Control on the radio.

Gennady Velikovsky back in Moscow would not be happy either and, most importantly, we could be stuck there for days. I thought yet again of Greenland and wished for the millionth time I had been able to stick to our original departure date of 10 May from England. Then Colin came on the radio saying that he had given his instrument panel a thump and the exhaust gas temperature gauge had returned to normal.

Colin arrived in Nome 20 minutes before myself and the camera crew and an hour after the Cessna. We had been able to enjoy our brief moments over the dry land of Provideniya. Fog had been hugging the coast, but the fjords and mountains were clear and how beautiful that last glimpse of Russia had been. The evening light was casting a golden glow on the 3,000-foot mountains sweeping down to the water's edge. We flew north up the fjord, then turned east to overfly Provideniya's small airfield, where a friendly

ATC speaking excellent English wished us well and regretted that we were not coming in. We said goodbye to Russia.

Fifty miles out we crossed the International Date Line. 26 July lasted a long time and had us all thoroughly confused. We had taken off from Anadyr at 5.10 p.m. on the 26th, local time. The flight to Nome for the helicopters took just over five hours. We gained a whole day, so put our clocks back by 24-hours, but we were told on landing at Nome that the local time was 1.15 a.m on 26 July. Unknown to us there was a three-hour time difference between Anadyr and Nome.

We were able to see Russia's Big Diomede Island, 70 miles to the north, where Russia and the United States of America practically touch hands. Big Diomede Island is only separated by two miles of water from Little Diomede, which belongs to the United States. Gamble Island was to our south, King Island to the north, and then the long, low coastline of Alaska appeared on the distant horizon; hills rising from a sandy shore reaching away to Nome. We were two-way on the radio with Anchorage Control who welcomed us to America. I felt so good.

We flew along the Alaskan coast. A coast that witnesses some of the most savage gales and roughest seas in all the world, constantly pounded and lashed by storms. But for us that night the gods were smiling as we approached the small town of Nome, a little gold-rush town clinging on for survival on those barren shores, where the inhabitants proudly boast that the nearest tree is more than 70 miles away.

It was quarter past one in the morning, the sun had dipped below the horizon. There had been an hour of sunset merging into sunrise, the sky was streaked with red and the American flag was flying at Nome International Airport. A happy and tired band had all landed on the North American continent.

Nome to Los Angeles

26 July - 1 August

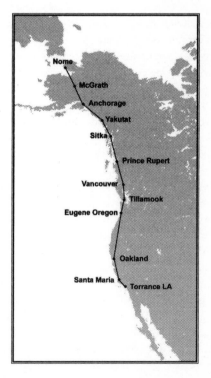

DAY 57

Nikolai was in Nome, looking a little greyer, but the same old Nikolai –
a slightly taller, slimmer version of Yuri – smiling and looking anxious as
always. We had been his main cause of anxiety for weeks. It was great to
see him in person after all the many phone calls, faxes and e-mail
correspondence of the past year, including the increasingly frantic ones
during the Tokyo wait. Nikolai had been forced to change his schedule

and all our airport arrangements and hotel bookings dozens of times.

In anticipation of a late arrival in Nome, Nikolai had bought us an immense supply of fast food: instant microwave dishes, cookies, fruit and soft drinks – pure Americana, it was wonderful.

After dinner I went straight to bed and slept like a log for the few short hours until the 8 a.m. wake-up call. We were due in Anchorage that evening. The men all headed back into town. They visited the Golden Nugget saloon, filled with memorabilia of the Gold Rush days when the population had soared to 20,000. Today it is 5,000 with a few stalwart souls still prospecting away. I don't think any of the men got much sleep that night but they managed to stumble out in time to have a quick all-American breakfast of pancakes, maple syrup, bacon and coffee at Fat Freddies before heading out to the airfield.

We flew south-east over the town, over the start-point of the famous annual Iditarod Huskie dog race where sledge teams race their huskies all the way from Anchorage and then on along the beach where small-prospectors with their sifting and draining equipment continue the endless search for gold. The weather had been marginal on take off with Colin saying 'I knew we should have got away at 7 a.m., I just knew it, I said we should have gone and there's this front coming in. I'm never going to get away – it's going to be horrendous.' However he did get away and once through the front, the weather improved dramatically. Blue skies and ten knots of tail wind ensured we had the best of flights to Anchorage with a brief stop over at McGrath airfield for fuel and a cup of coffee.

James reported from the Cessna that they were getting great views of Mount McKinley – the highest mountain in North America. Fifty miles out from Anchorage, Q told me that he and Al had landed on top of a hill to enjoy the distant view of Mount McKinley in evening light. I had been anxious to press on as two television stations were planning to film our arrival and Colin was half an hour ahead of us. We had given an ETA of 7 p.m. local time and it was already 7.15 p.m. I knew that if I said something I would get the usual sarcastic comment like, 'Oh yes, your press, we mustn't be late for your press!' I could, of course, have gone on alone but I didn't want to strain relationships even more. The friendly thing was to join them. I got their coordinates and landed near them on top of the hill. Q had shut down and the two were sitting on the ground with their backs to me. I walked towards them calling a greeting. Q half turned and gave me a brief 'Hi' before turning once more to resume his conversation with Al, who never turned around. I wandered off trying to enjoy the spectacular view. We had landed on a grassy hill, with a deep gorge plunging down one side, which looked out over forests and lakes with a river running through. In the far distance was the Mount McKinley range, all very beautiful. We finally arrived at Anchorage's Merrill Airfield at 8.20 p.m. One of the television crews had given up and gone.

Nikolai, who had flown down in the Cessna, had waited for us. He offered to take us to our hotel and I asked him to join us later for dinner with his wife Valentina and son Andre. After changing, Heinz, Yuri, Colin and I waited for the others and Nikolai and his family for 20 minutes in the lobby of our hotel. Q wandered in and looked surprised to see us all there. He said, 'Oh Nikolai phoned, he said that we were obviously all tired so they would leave us to have an early night.'

'Christ, Q,' I said, 'why couldn't you have told us? We've been waiting here for hours.' Colin muttered, 'Typical.' Heinz kept diplomatically silent, while Yuri looked puzzled.

'Well, I thought he must have told you,' said Q. 'You do things like this too, now you know what it is like.' We asked him if they would like to join us for dinner. He said they might when Al and Pat had finished editing.

We were staying in a log cabin motel, basic but nice. Doug, manning the front desk, gave us directions for Stan's Diner which was just a few minutes' walk across the shopping plaza. The four of us had excellent steaks with red wine and an entire bottle of vodka, principally consumed by Yuri. Yuri had his habitual bottle stashed in his pocket, which he fished out with a mischievous grin every time the waitress's back was turned. Yuri was going to stay with us as far as Los Angeles. Although his navigational duties were over, he had managed to persuade Aeroflot that his services were still required and that the best connection back to Moscow was from Los Angeles. We were all delighted as he had become a part of our team and he and Colin would often go off for beers together. We wandered back to the hotel in a very relaxed state of mind. Q and company never showed.

I forgot to tell Q and Pat that Nikolai would be around to take the early departure group to the airport at 7 a.m. I tried to phone them but they had all gone out. Not for the first time I wished we had an official organiser travelling with us. When there were just two of us in '97 it had been difficult enough, but with seven it got out of hand. Jamie McCallum and James Barker were always a big help when they came out for various press conferences and I was looking forward to James being with us from Vancouver to Los Angeles. But in Anchorage there was only myself. I failed to give anyone departure times, and no one had asked. I phoned Q at 6.30 a.m. and rather to my surprise he answered on the third ring – he has an amazing capacity to sleep through anything. I apologised for not telling him the night before, 'but,' I said, 'we're leaving in half an hour, at 7 a.m.'

He sleepily replied: 'Now wait a minute. Are we doing the right thing?'

'Come on Q,' I said, 'let's not waste time discussing it, Nikolai will be here at 7 a.m. and Colin really needs to get away early. We've got 650 miles to go to Wrangell.'

'But I booked a taxi for 9.30 a.m.,' he said. 'And I told you I had.'

We were getting nowhere so I compromised and said that I would go on to the airport with Colin and help him get away, and Nikolai would return for him and Pat at 8 a.m. The airport was a 20-minute drive.

The weather looked good, winds light and variable with scattered cloud at 3,000 feet. Even Colin was optimistic as he taxied for take off to Yakutat, 373 miles south down the coast, where we wanted to stop for fuel. I waved him off then headed in the direction of the airport store to buy charts. I bought four of everything available for our route through Canada and the USA and, feeling rather good, headed back to G-MURY. Nikolai was already back, but there was no sign of the camera crew.

'What happened, Nikolai? Where are they?' I asked.

'I couldn't find them. I waited in the lobby, I phoned their rooms, I don't know where they are,' he said. 'I thought maybe they had come out here, so I came back.'

I phoned the hotel and got through to Q, who had just returned to his room. He sighed and said, 'I told you I had ordered a taxi for 9.30 a.m.' I was upset that he'd mucked Nikolai up like that after all he had done for us.

'Well, I'm gone,' I said, 'I'm not hanging around any longer. I told Colin we would follow in one hour and that was 15 minutes ago. I'll see you in Wrangell.' As things turned out we didn't meet up again until Vancouver, two days later.

I apologised to Nikolai and thanked him once again for all that he had done and all the arrangements he had had to change so many times (including the very latest). I gave him a big hug, then climbed into G-MURY. The Tower gave me permission to take off from the parking lot, for that was basically what it was, rows and rows of light planes, some 800 private aircraft, in a grid pattern with taxiways for aeroplanes and cars. You had to 'hold' at intersections and check that there wasn't a car coming the other way! They know how to cater for private aviation in a country where planes are the basic mode of transport.

Freedom – I felt liberated, and I knew the treat I had in store: the majestic and awe-inspiring beauty of the glaciers, the snow-capped mountains and sea, nature in all its primeval savagery, and me, all alone to explore, to fly

ABOVE: Author and Colin.
31 May 2000 – take-off from Brooklands.

BELOW: Pat Davey, Simon Walters from the British
Embassy, Heinz, Q, the author, Colin and James Davey on
arrival in Hail, Saudi Arabia, with Abdul Kareem Al
Shammary and airport officials.

ABOVE: The Baluchistan coast, Pakistan.

BELOW: Hong Kong.

ABOVE: Suwanose-shima volcano, Japan.

BELOW: Heinz, Q, James, Al and the author with airport officials, Magadan, Siberia, Russia.

ABOVE: G-NOWW at sunset, Vancouver.

BELOW: G-NOWW over the Malaspina Glacier, Alaska.

ABOVE: En route to Galveston, Texas.

BELOW: The Twin Towers.

ABOVE: Saglek, Labrador.

BELOW: Icebergs, Greenland.

ABOVE: Ice pack, Greenland.

BELOW: Geysers, Iceland.

ABOVE: Torshavn, Faeroe Islands.

BELOW: Home again, Brooklands, 6 September 2000.

alone like a bird. I felt good. Once again I laughed out loud as I climbed steeply out on a heading of 110 degrees towards Glacier Bay. All earthbound irritations were left behind and the weather was good. I could see for ever. I put on my CD of *Great Opera Arias*.

I studied the charts. Besides checking my route, it was fun to look at all the names of the islands, the inlets, the creeks and mountains. They all told their own story, for example, which country had found them, like the Harvard and Yale Glaciers, Montagu Island, Kayak Island and Prince William Sound. Or what they were like: Ragged Mountain, Icy Bay and Seal Island; or the loved ones left behind, Esther Island and Eleanor Island – 'Eleanor', my mother's name had an extra poignancy. And I thought of my cousin Bud Ames who I would be seeing soon in Los Angeles. Bud had done a lot of flying in Alaska. He has had an impressive aviation career: at the age of 19 he was flying and maintaining flying boats in the Pacific and later became an observer and flew on one of the last Berlin Airlifts. Then, during the Korean War, he was a technical representative for Alaskan Air Command where the Air Force was flying jet fighter interceptors (F-94Bs and F-89s). He had some exciting times flying as a radar operator and it was at that time that he bought his first plane and became something of a 'bush pilot', enjoying the glory of Alaska. He had learned a lot about Arctic survival skills – skills that I hoped I wouldn't be needing.

I headed toward Harvard and Yale in College Fjord, two of 200 glaciers that flow from the mighty Fairweather/St Elias Mountain Range, one of the highest coastal mountain ranges in the world. The glaciers were sheer cliffs of ice towering hundreds of feet above the icy waters, with great wedges of blue ice calving slowly free and, with a monstrous shrug, thundering into the sea below.

I saw the Margerie Glacier flowing from its starting point atop 15,320 ft Mount Fairweather. I flew over and around the glaciers, turning and hovering around ice sculptures. I peered down crevasses of the deepest turquoise, frozen rivers of ice, forever on the move, slowly making my way down the coast towards the great Bering and Yahtse Glaciers and the largest of them all – the Malaspina – where I met up with Colin.

'Where have you been? I've been calling you for hours,' he said in a rather aggrieved tone. I apologised. I told him I had been low-level in the glaciers, while he had been skimming the mountain tops. He was also having a great day, a day clear of turbulence. 'Brilliant' replaced 'horrendous' for a few hours.

I told him that I was on my own, that the camera crew had failed to turn up. 'Typical – all these glaciers and mountains and no cameraman.' was Colin's response. I said I thought it was worth it, being such a relief to have time apart. 'They are probably saying the same thing too,' I told Colin, adding, 'It's easier for you, I'm the one they always fly with.' For Colin it *was* easier. Most of the time, since leaving England, he had been thousands of feet above the helicopters and hours in front of or behind us. And the Cessna we seldom saw, other than sitting locked up and empty on the ground or a passing glimpse and some radio talk.

I suggested that I land on the Malaspina to take some photos. The Malaspina glacier is huge and flat, a glacial delta with no great cliffs of ice dropping sheer to the sea like Harvard and Yale. I landed, not without some difficulty. From the air the glacier had looked deceptively flat. From a few feet up I could see the deep, narrow fissures and lumpy surface. I finally found a flattish, solid-looking area, landed and shut down, thinking it would be just my luck for the starter motor to play up. Then came the tricky bit, trying to walk on the slippery, uneven ice in my trainers, getting some distance away from my helicopter to take photos of Colin swooping low over G-MURY. I took some great pictures, then slithered my way back and felt so good when the engine roared once more into life. From there it was just 30 miles to Yakutat across Yakutat Bay.

I tried to call Yakutat, but got no reply. I tried again and again. It seemed strange that the airfield should be unmanned. However, it turned out that the radio was only operative when they were expecting a commercial flight. I felt a little nervous coming in to an airfield with two asphalt runways and no radio contact.

We flew over the small community port of Yakutat – a cluster of houses hugging the shore, with green fields and pine trees. It was a sharp contrast to the great glaciers on the other side of the bay. Approaching Runway 14, we looked anxiously for any opposite traffic. With the winds only light and variable, traffic could come in from anywhere. Colin managed to stop short of the bulldozers at the junction of Runway 05, which was under repair, and turned right on to the short taxiway for the apron. Ten minutes later, traffic did come in from the opposite direction, a small Cessna 204 from the south.

Yakutat airfield lies a few miles from the town, surrounded by pine trees. There is nothing much there other than the log cabin, fuel pumps and one large hangar full of light aircraft. Two men in jeans and check shirts appeared over by the fuel pumps. One was a tall, thin young man with long blonde hair down to his shoulders, the other was older and stouter with a large brown belt holding up his jeans over his beer belly.

'Good to see you folks. Ya'all can call me Dakota,' said the young one with a friendly smile. 'And this here's Tom,' he added, shaking our hands. We asked about fuel and hamburgers. 'Ya'all best be quick, kitchen closes at

2 p.m. You guys ever tasted our smoked salmon?' We smiled and said that we hadn't. 'Well, ah make ma own. Now if you folks are going to be here long enough I'll go and get ya some of ma smoked salmon, but right now yer best git in there for your burger. Tom here, he'll be around and will see to your fuel when you're done eatin'. I'll be off home for the smoked salmon.' With that he hurried off to his pick-up truck.

The kitchen was closed. 'We've come all the way from Anchorage, we've flown halfway around the world and I've been telling my friend of your wonderful hamburgers,' I pleaded (I had stopped there the last time). The cook looked sympathetic but unmoved. He had shut down his ovens and cleaned his pans. However, he did finally relent and said he could do us salmon sandwiches, which were delicious.

Everything in Yakutat revolves around salmon and trout fishing. The rivers are apparently the best. The community makes its living from fishing and tourism and anglers come from near and far to fish the waters, to which the log cabin bore evidence. Every square inch was covered in trophies and fishing memorabilia, while out the back there was an angler's dream shop selling every possible item of equipment and clothing any fisherman could ever want. The woman in the shop asked how long we were staying, and tried to persuade us that we couldn't possibly leave without a little bit of fishing. 'I can do you a half day – that'd just be the trout. The salmon you need all day.'

Regretfully we said we had to push on, that the rest of our team might take a poor view of our 'fishing break'. 'Well, it sure is a pity you folks cain't stay awhiles. Next time you be sure to stay longer.' I vowed that if there ever was another time, I would be out there on those rivers. Did I regret not staying? Yes. But all our energy was focused on achieving our goal and making that final northern crossing, so it was difficult to relax. Even when tired we were never happier than when on the move.

Tom topped up Colin's tanks and asked us if we wanted to get the weather. It was 3 p.m., we had time, and it is always a good idea, even when you are enjoying the best of weather. As the Met officer pointed out, in their part of the world the coast from Anchorage to Vancouver is renowned for some of the worst weather you are likely to encounter anywhere, and it can change very rapidly.

'Like today. You can expect a rapid deterioration in conditions further south. Low cloud and associated turbulence.'

Just after Colin took off, Dakota, in his pick-up truck, came speeding down the dirt road in a cloud of dust. He jumped out of his car and came hurrying over holding a large plastic bucket.

'Ah thought ah'd missed ya! Ah thought ah'd missed ya!' he said with a grin. And, holding out the bucket, he said, 'Here, me and ma missus put together this little tub of stuff – ah'm so glad ah didn't miss ya.'

Then, taking the lid off the bucket, he said, 'I've got some jerky. Ya'll know what jerky is?' I said yes, that I'd had some beef jerky. 'Well, this here's pork jerky, actually there's some goat in there too. It's pork and goat jerky.' The goat part, he explained, was goat's cheese. The pork had been dried in goat's cheese.

'And here's some black bear jerky.' He saw me looking a little hesitant, but assured me it was very good. 'Tastes of salmon, that's what those guys eat!' he said. 'And this here's a necklace made by my wife. My wife, she's Indian you know. Her father was the last Indian chief in the area. Took me a while to integrate but they don't call me "Yellow Hair" no longer!' he said with a laugh. And then, reaching for more goodies in the tub he said, 'Here's the smoked salmon – caught and smoked maself and, yeah, this here's reindeer sausage! It's been frozen so you'll want to do a fry up on that. And I've put in a couple of cans of Coke and a little bit of coffee and candy bars.' With a smile and a flourish he then handed me my deluxe survival pack. What a star. I thanked him profusely and asked him to say a big thank you to his wife. We shook hands and I told them we thought Yakutat was great, a special stopover. Then I climbed into the helicopter and followed Colin south.

We had decided at Yakutat to use a different chat channel from time to time instead of the normal 123.45, as we felt sure that Q must have caught us up and was operating in 'stealth mode'! We tried to get him on the radio several times, but there was no reply. We reckoned he was around somewhere, though, listening in. It was a creepy feeling. Anchorage Control frequency was on the other radio and we agreed to switch from time to time back on to 123.45 and try to raise Q.

Colin was having a ball. 'I'm flying along the beach at ten feet. This is brilliant, I've just seen three bears, and there are some more, they're just playing on the sand, and there's just miles and miles of sand.' I was also having a good time, one of our best days. I told him that I had seen whales and seals and sea lions further north.

The forecast for Wrangell had been: 'Fog banks tonight. Lowering visibility to near zero. Winds rising to moderate to strong south-east.' Back in sunny Yakutat that had been hard to believe but, sure enough, the weather slowly deteriorated and blue sky gave way to grey. And then on the radio came, 'Hello, this is Q!'

'Hi there,' I said in what I hoped was a reasonably friendly voice. 'We thought you must be somewhere around – where are you?'

'Uh, well – I'm five miles out of Sitka. We've just refuelled there.'

They would have heard me talking to Sitka on the radio. I guess they had been visual with us for some time and I imagine they must have heard us asking on numerous occasions, 'Q, are you there?' It was cat and mouse in the air! Q said that Pat would like comments for the day from each of us for the website, but no they didn't need any video, they had already taken masses when the light was good. We said our bit for the website. I asked Q about his day but got no specifics, just that they too had had an excellent day. 'See you in Wrangell,' he said.

Thirty miles south of Sitka, with Q a good twenty miles ahead of us, Colin was in trouble. We were tracking along the coast of Baranoe Island, passing Whale Bay. The cloud base was down to a hundred feet in places, the wind had picked up and the turbulence became extreme for the microlight. 'I'm going back, I'm turning around, back to Sitka – this is really dangerous.' I looked over and it was not a reassuring sight. Colin was being thrown all over the place. 'For goodness' sake – CLIMB!' I said. It looked as though he was going to plummet into the sea with every sickening drop.

'I'm trying for God's sake!' he said. 'Keep me in sight, stay close – I'm in trouble.' I got Q on the radio – just, it was very broken, we were both very low due to the cloud base – and I told him we were going back to Sitka. I think he said, 'Good decision,' confirming that it was probably even worse further south.

Colin had managed to climb a little but continued to be hurled all over the place. I radioed Sitka that we were coming back – the Tower said we were Number One, there was no other traffic. After a fraught 30 minutes we thankfully entered the shelter of Sitka Sound and touched down as night was falling on the wet and glistening runway.

Safe on the ground, we had the usual hassle of no hangar available for Colin. Everyone had gone home, so we had to dismantle the trike in the pouring rain. Then we couldn't find anywhere to stay. It was high tourist season and the town was full of fishermen, trekkers and mountaineers. We finally found rooms in a picture-perfect, minute white clapboard house with blue shutters – a B&B called The Nest. It was owned and run by a delightfully eccentric couple called Lawrenz and Ginny Ann Graham. They had come to Sitka for a vacation from New Mexico three years before and never returned. They really made us welcome. We were in a real home, my first since Hong Kong and for Colin it had been even longer (our apartment in Hong Kong only has one bedroom). He had last been in a home at our place in France.

The Nest had an L-shaped open-plan kitchen/dining room and sitting room and three bedrooms all sharing the same bathroom. Being a B&B they didn't do dinners and we were famished. Ginny Ann gave us directions to the nearest of the two big hotels, where we hoped they were still serving dinners at 10.30 p.m. We trudged over in the now drizzling rain and had delicious steak and chips. I had a glass of the house red and Colin had a beer.

Other than the testing last bit, we had had a great day. We were tired but we had to try and touch base with the others, despite having no network on our mobile phones. We went to the phone booths and found we had to buy AT&T cards at the front desk, where a large lady was screaming down the phone, 'Have you locked all the doors? Goddamit! I said have you locked all the doors?' We could hear a frightened child's voice on the other end. The large lady continued to scream. 'Where's the dog? Have you got the dog? You can't find the dog? Then find the fucking dog! He's under the bed? Where are Tess and Pete? In the bathroom?' The child was crying but, obviously her mother's child, she started cursing too! 'You can hear something outside?' The child continued to cry and curse down the phone, while the mother continued to scream at her, using the worst of language. For a good ten minutes we stood there listening to this crazy scene. Why didn't she jump in her car and go home to her terrified children? She then covered the phone with her hand and asked the other woman behind the desk if the Agriculture and Fisheries Department were on their way out there. She said yes, that they should be there soon. 'Git in the bathroom with Tess and Pete. Yeah, I said git in the bathroom and take the damn dog with you, and lock the door. Dave'll be there soon. Yeah – Dave Shannon from Ag. and Fish. Don't you unlock the door then until ya hears Dave sound the bell. Course ya'll hear the bell!'

We learnt later that a female bear with cubs was roaming the outskirts of the town. Someone had killed one of the cubs and the bear had killed a dog, badly mauled a man and had been into someone's home. No wonder the poor children were scared. The Grahams gave us a small, illustrated book entitled *The Bears and You:*

> If a bear surprises you up close . . . don't turn and run. The bear may think you're afraid and perhaps something good to eat. A bear can't see very well. He may come closer to see what you are. He may stand up on his hind feet, to get a better look at you. Yell and wave your arms. This will tell him what you are. He may talk to you in bear talk. This may sound like a dog woofing, only louder, or he may 'pop' his teeth at you. This is telling you to go away. Don't talk back. Leave slowly, always facing the bear.

We did finally get through to Q in Wrangell. He told us the Cessna was still in Anchorage as they had decided to fly direct to Vancouver, a strange decision as Pat and Al needed to be in the same place each night for editing and sending back to base. We were a well-dispersed team.

The next morning we woke to cloud and misting rain, but the wind seemed to have abated and the forecast was good further south. We rigged the microlight and Colin set off first. I was just climbing into G-MURY with sights set on Vancouver when I saw Colin coming back. 'You just wouldn't believe it, the wind was horrendous. The moment I got out of the shelter of the harbour it nearly inverted me. There's no way I can fly in that.' Suddenly, charming Sitka did not look quite so charming with the prospect of an indefinite stay.

We managed to find hangar space for the microlight, then took a taxi back to The Nest where, luckily, our rooms were still free. Ginny Ann wasn't surprised to see us. 'Ah reckoned you might be back,' she said with a laugh. 'Now you just make yourselves real comfortable. We've got lots of videos, the house is all yours, and just help yourself in the kitchen. Now you can do a fry-up with that reindeer sausage of yours!' she said with another laugh.

The town of Sitka, with a population of 8,500 souls, consists of not much more than one delightful main street, Lincoln Street, with period two-storey wooden buildings, dominated by the 'New England'-style St Michael's Cathedral complete with spire. The rest of the town was made up of neat little homes like The Nest. It took ten minutes to get anywhere, other than the airport. Colin said he wanted new spark plugs for the microlight, as his engine had been running rough. He needed the serial number of the plugs so back we went to the airport. We took a taxi and the driver, like everyone else, was friendly. 'Howdy folks, my name's Jim, now where can I take you?'

At the airport, I sat in the taxi with Jim while Colin trudged off in the once more pouring rain to get the serial number. I asked Jim about the weather. 'Does it always rain in Sitka?' I said, remembering that the weather had been equally bad in '97. He replied cheerfully: 'Well, yee-up, pretty much, but you know we had 14 real good days at the beginning of June – sun shone every day, so we ain't complainin'.' As it was by then the end of July I didn't feel too good.

'Yes, ma'am,' he said, 'but I sure hope it will be good tomorrow because ma daughter and her fee-an-cée are coming in by plane and I'd sure like it to be good on Saturday, they're getting married!' I congratulated him and he then regaled me with all the details and ended, saying with satisfaction, 'Yep, it'll be the first time in ma life that ah have ever worn a tuxedo – yes sireee!' Nodding his head, he said 'Yep, and come to think of it, the only time ah've ever worn a suit was at mah own wedding,' and gave a great roar of laughter.

Colin had no success with the spark plugs. We tried the two hardware and electrical shops but, while they had endless plugs for every type and description of snowmobile and outboard motor, they had none for the Rotax engine of a microlight. We were more successful getting analgesic for Colin's arm which was still giving him a lot of trouble, plus lightweight waterproofs, also for Colin (he'd been soaked to the skin the day before). I bought a wide-brimmed felt hunting hat in lieu of an umbrella. No one carried umbrellas in Sitka, because we were in 'huntin' country'. I also managed to find a polarising filter for my Canon camera.

In the camera shop there had been a large selection of postcards of Sitka, all taken in brilliant sunshine. I made a remark to the shop assistant about the rain, and she said. 'Yea, well, you know we cain't complain, we've had a real good summer.' I laughed and said, 'Yes, I know you had 14 wonderful days at the beginning of June!' We went back to The Nest and the luxury of relaxing in a home watching a video – *Armageddon* with Bruce Willis. The Grahams invited us to join them for dinner.

On 29 July the alarm went off at 5 a.m. and I could hear the rain still drumming on my bedroom roof. We just had to get away, these delays were mounting up. I did a quick tally of delayed days – *twenty-four*. One day in Mikonos when the winds were too strong for Colin, one day in Jordan and another in Kuwait with my magneto problems; an added day routing via Danang when Colin had been forced down by the fighter jets in China and one extra day in Hong Kong waiting for Colin and extra work on G-MURY. Then the seventeen lost days in Japan, two days in Okha for weather, but we had made up one day by not having to overnight in Anadyr. Now we were stuck in Sitka. Of course we had started the whole trip three weeks late, so were we ever going to make that final northern crossing and be able to put in the mileage necessary for a world record?

I got out of bed and drew the curtains. Colin knocked on my door. 'I think there is less wind,' he said, and added encouragingly, 'Cor, you look sound asleep! Come on, let's give it a go.' We left a note for the Grahams saying that we might well be back, could they please save our rooms until 11 a.m. and to please eat the reindeer sausage. It was still uneaten but Lawrenz had volunteered to cook it for our breakfast.

Colin was ready for take off at 7.30 a.m., his life jacket on over the top of the new waterproofs which covered his padded flight suit. He looked like a Michelin man as he climbed aboard his unprotected little trike. I stood in a puddle holding the wingtip. Start up, a brief nod and smile from Colin, already focused on the grey and wet world ahead as he taxied across the puddled apron. I hurried across to G-MURY and with relief clambered out of the wet and put on my headphones to be two-way on 123.45. I needed to know whether we were on our way before contacting Prince Rupert in Canada where we had to do customs and take on more fuel. I also had to phone the team in Vancouver giving them our ETAs.

The rain, a steady rain with no wind to move it, looked set to stay in Sitka for the rest of their summer. Cloud base was around 300 feet with occasional tendrils whispering down and across the leaden sea.

'Colin, are you there?'

'Yes,' came the brief reply – Colin is not very chatty on the radio.

'How does it look?' I asked.

'Can't see much, I'm just coming out of the harbour now, looks like nil wind, but my engine doesn't sound good. Don't be too long.'

I reminded him that I had to phone Prince Rupert and the team, then I would be on my way. I couldn't get through on my AT&T card and ended up having to go to the ATC desk for help. I finally got Prince Rupert and left a message on Q's mobile to say that we hoped to be in Vancouver, 730 miles away, by 7 p.m.

When I took off, I was an hour behind Colin. The weather was much the same – lousy. We had a long day's flying ahead of us. It was going to take Colin ten hours with nil wind conditions and head winds were forecast. If we were going to have marginal flying conditions all the way, I doubted we would make it. At least I could stay coastal if necessary, and Colin could probably fly above the weather, but it would add time and distance.

I wasn't able to get Colin on the radio for another half hour because I was having to weave my way around ghostly islands, shrouded in cloud and patches of mist. I was never more than 100 feet above the sea and constantly having to slow down and pull more carb heat. When I did get through to Colin he was unhappy and once more saying, 'Where *have* you been? I could have gone down and no one would have known. I've been trying to get you for over an hour. My engine nearly died on me twice.' Never a dull moment.

'Give me your coordinates. What height are you?' I said.

'Eleven thousand feet, I'm over the mountains. I'm trying to get back over the sea. I don't know what caused it, but I've pulled more carb heat and it seems to be running a bit better now.'

I asked him how the weather was and he told me he had solid cloud below him and could only see the tops of the mountains sticking through. 'Looks as though it's breaking up ahead, though.'

The weather gradually improved and by the time we were 30 miles north of Prince Rupert I was able to climb to 8,000 feet and managed to more or less rendezvous with Colin (I could see him up at 11,000 feet). Colin was loath to descend from his lofty height. 'There's going to be mega turbulence, I can see white horses.'

The world looked beautiful to me. The sky was cloudless as we flew high over Dundas Island with its white sandy coves and crystal clear turquoise waters. In the distance, the coastline was broken by hundreds of islands and inlets and Prince Rupert was now visible on the north shore of Digby Island.

The turbulence, for once, didn't materialise despite the strong south-westerly winds and we landed rather stylishly together. My day was made when a young Canadian Air Force pilot came up to me and said, 'I just want to congratulate you, ma'am, on that landing, that was one heck of a neat landing in that wind.' We did a reasonably quick turn-around and were on our way again within the hour, but it was already noon and we now had 10 to 12 knots of head wind. It was going to take Colin another nine hours to get to Vancouver.

I tried to get through to both Q and James Davey on their mobiles but just got an engaged signal. Then I tried James Barker but the hotel said he had checked out. I wanted to give them our revised ETA. It looked as though we weren't going to make Vancouver before 9 p.m. The only thing I could think of doing was to call the bat phone and leave a message there – it never got passed on.

From Prince Rupert southwards, Colin and I flew more or less together. I made little detours amongst the islands and narrow channels, down valleys and along rivers, flying low over endless forests and lakes. Twice I landed beside remote lakes, shut the engine down and enjoyed the solitude and the silence. I sat on a log beside the first lake, so far from anywhere, and wondered how many people had ever been that way before. An occasional Native American? A trapper? Surely no one else – and the lake was too small for a float plane to land. The surface of the lake was like a millpond; the trees, mountains and sky were perfectly reflected in the water, surrounded by spruce, black cottonwood and alder trees and wild flowers. I was a brief intruder to the home of marmot, wolf, beaver, moose and bear.

That flight from Sitka to Vancouver was the longest time either of us spent in the air in one day. Colin clocked up 13 hours and 50 minutes. I totalled 10 hours and 35 minutes. We were tired and happy as we made our final approach into Vancouver with the setting sun. It would have made great footage, but there were no cameramen. James Barker was there alone to greet us. He said the others had hung around for two hours and had left twenty minutes earlier to film a firework display. We were sad that they weren't there. I suppose we shouldn't have been surprised, but so much that I had worked and planned so hard for just wasn't working out. We were still on track, albeit somewhat late, and hopefully we would set world records and raise money and awareness for Operation Smile. But there were times that could have been fun and were not.

It was becoming increasingly apparent that the main focus of any documentary would be the pilot flying the camera helicopter. I could have saved myself the trouble of raising hundreds of thousands of pounds, and foregone having a Cessna Caravan with pilot, co-pilot and technician/cameramen and most especially the second helicopter. We could have rigged video cameras in and on Colin's microlight and my helicopter, we would have been in control of filming and, most importantly, final editing. It would have been about our challenge, and we would have been free.

Then James Barker told us that James Davey's girlfriend, Pascal Lejeune, would be staying with us all the way to Boston! Any authority I ever had appeared to be in shreds. I had considered asking James Davey to take on the job of booking hotels but was hesitant to do so as his salary was being paid by his boss Peter Wood. The problem was that we never dared book more than twenty-four hours ahead as we never knew if we were going to make the next stop on time. We had already had to pay for days that we never made.

We met up with Heinz at the Sheraton Hotel and had a great view of the fireworks from the 32nd floor. I left messages for everyone to be ready to depart at 7.30 a.m. We saw no one that night other than Heinz who had been waiting for us at the hotel.

The following morning we met up with everyone else including Pascal, a pretty and slim girl with blonde hair. I had nothing against Pascal personally but it was difficult to smile and make her welcome. I took James to one side and said, 'I can't believe that you have gone totally against what I said to Peter Wood.' I repeated what I had told Peter, that Pascal would be welcome to come for a couple of legs if there was room in the Cessna. I told him that this was never intended as a jolly for wives and girlfriends. 'You knew that and then Colin and I arrived late and tired last night to be told that Pascal would be with us to Boston.' Well, I was pretty upset.

James looked suitably chastened and apologised. He said that Pascal could be really helpful and explained that she could do the hotel bookings. There was little I could do other than say, 'Well, if NOW are prepared to take her on, and she is to be one of their staff, then I will just have to accept it, but I am really upset. You have organised everything behind my back and you haven't even asked Heinz if he is prepared to take on another passenger. You may be captain of the Cessna when flying for Glass Eels, but Heinz is the captain on this trip and what you have done is totally out of line.' He apologised again and said he would speak with Heinz.

Al told me that the fireworks had been far more interesting than our arrival and that they had waited at the airport for two hours but no one had any idea what time we were arriving and, 'Why couldn't you have taken the trouble to let us know?' Messages hadn't got through and, to be fair, waiting for two hours isn't much fun either.

Why didn't I ask for a change of cameramen and dispense with the camera helicopter? Heaven knows. Looking back, I guess it was a combination of factors. Confrontation always occurred at the end of the day when I was tired. I certainly disliked scenes and I didn't want to do anything to cause further delay. Plus, I guess I always hoped things would improve. It was my mistake. It was inevitable that we would all get on each other's nerves from time to time – that is only to be expected when you get a small group thrown together, coping with a lot of stress and tension and tiredness. But our problems were more complicated than that. Sadly, our camera team were destined to miss some major dramas because they just weren't there and tensions and tempers inevitably worsened.

We planned to stop for a drink at a small airfield called Estoria (it was so novel, after Russia, to be able to just stop briefly at an airfield). Another pilot listening to us chatting on the radio said, 'Hi guys, you ought to go into Tillamook, it's just a little bit further down the coast and has the largest wooden aircraft hangar in the world. It was built by the navy back in 1914 for a dirigible and has some interesting stuff inside.' So we landed at Tillamook, the hangar was indeed incredible and there were some great old aircraft inside. We wandered around in our separate groups and then Q and Al went and sat in G-JEFA looking bored. Al took no video footage.

In flying terms, we had an easy day of it. The weather was good, with stunning views of Mount Saint Helen and Mount Shasta and we arrived at Eugene in Oregon just before 6 p.m. Eugene is a university town and, as it was the long summer vacation, the town was dead. Everyone wanted to know why I had chosen Eugene. I had randomly put it in as it was equidistant between Vancouver and San Francisco. I had intended to check out if there was somewhere more interesting, but never did. Heinz later remarked that it was probably a good thing that Eugene was quiet. The younger members of the team had had a very late night of it in Vancouver (which might account for the slumped attitude in Tillamook) and they would no doubt be out on the town in San Francisco. I suggested that we all have dinner together, but when I got down to the lobby Heinz told me that the others had all gone on, saying they would try and find somewhere to eat down the street from the hotel. We found them in a bar playing billiards. Then Colin told Heinz and me that he had overheard Pascal saying to Q, 'Oh God, they've found us!' We decided we would go elsewhere.

I was happy at the prospect of spending the next night with my cousins Lawrie Ames, his sister Georgia Fulstone and her daughter Cynthia Muller-Racke and granddaughter Tricia, in Santa Rosa County at Cynthia's home. Everyone was invited for lunch and to stay the night, but the others, understandably, wanted to go on to San Francisco. Some had never been there and the others were keen on revisiting.

We had a great flight down. Again the weather was good and we flew over green valleys and umber-coloured hills, baking in the late July heat. Even at 5,000 feet the OAT was 30 degrees centigrade. It was such a contrast to the glaciers of a few days before. We were into the hot countries once more.

I descended into the Napa Valley to hunt for Cynthia's ranch while the others went to Napa Valley Municipal Airport. Colin paid a quick visit to Cynthia's husband-to-be, Tom Degenhardt, an orthopaedic surgeon. Colin had hoped he could do something for his arm, which was still giving him a great deal of pain. The trouble was, every time he hit turbulence he would wrench his arm and he would be back to square one. (Moral: don't go arm wrestling with Russian champions when you're flying a microlight around the world.) Tom told me later, during a quiet family dinner sitting out on the terrace overlooking the olive trees, sipping a glass of cold Napa Valley white wine, that there was little he could do for Colin. Colin had taken so many painkillers he had been unable to accurately locate the pain, and his arms are so muscle-bound it was impossible to feel. He had given him an ice pack, more painkillers and prescribed rest.

I told them of our travels and said to Georgia, with a smile, that I thought my love of flying must come from her side of the family.

Georgia and Lawrie's father, Lawrence Ames, and his brother Charles Burton Ames (my grandmother's two brothers) were both early aviators. In 1916, Uncle Burton, my cousin Bud's father, volunteered for the American Ambulance Field Service and then in 1917, when America officially declared war, he joined the US Navy as an aviator. He was commissioned as an ensign, becoming US Naval Aviator No. 193, and was later commissioned as a second lieutenant in the US Marine Corps (Aviation) – the fourteenth person to become a US Marine Corps aviator. Between 1919 and 1920 he was a captain in the New York Aerial Police Force, where he instructed in flight and ground school. He remained in the US Marine Corps Reserve until 1927 when he became a ground school instructor for the Civil Pilot Training Program at the University of California. In 1939 he was hired by Pan American Grace Airways in Lima, Peru, to establish a school for pilots and mechanics, but in 1941, just hours after the attack on Pearl Harbour, he requested active duty in the Marine Corps and was accepted as a captain. Tragically, a couple of months later, he died suddenly of a heart attack in San Francisco – just after passing his flight physical examination. Had he lived, he would have been proud of his good friend Jimmy Doolittle who was to make the first retaliation against the Japanese, just weeks after his death.

Uncle Lawrie, who died in 1981, aged 84, was a founder member of the California National Guard. He wanted to be a fighter pilot in the First World War too, but he had flat feet and was rejected. He persevered and finally did cadet training in France, flying Farman Pushers. He then went to fighter school, but the armistice was declared before he got to engage the enemy. He ended up in Santa Monica as a captain in the 369th Reserve Squadron and one of his prized possessions was a racing licence from the FAA signed by Orville Wright.

Uncle Lawrie got involved in the aircraft business with his friend Bob Gross. They heard that the Lockheed Aircraft Company was coming up for receivership and they bought it on the Los Angeles Courthouse steps. He was a director of Lockheed and Continental Airlines for many years and a test pilot for both of them. After Pearl Harbour he tested C-47s and B-17s at the Douglas Aircraft Company and served as general staff observer at Iwo Jima. He was commissioned Brigadier General and asked to form a fighter wing of the California Air National Guard. He commanded the 61st Fighter Wing, becoming Chief of Staff in 1952, and was then promoted to Major General. In civilian life he was a stockbroker and had a series of small aircraft. He was the proud owner of the first Stearman-Hammond for private use in the USA, and continued to fly until way into his seventies. Rather a tough act to follow.

Uncle Lawrie's wife, Helen, had the right spirit too. Although not a pilot, she stunned the family and the local flying club in Maui by paragliding at the ripe old age of 96!

DAY 63 – 1 AUGUST

On 1 August we were due, at 2 p.m., at the Robinson Factory at Torrance Airfield, 388 miles south of San Francisco, where we had been told there would be a lot of press waiting. It was an important PR stop on the trip and I very nearly didn't make it.

Everything started fine. The weather was good and promised to be another scorcher. I flew the short distance to Oakland Airport where I met up with Q and Al. Colin was already on his way south and the Cessna was due to follow in an hour's time. My cousin Lawrie was at the airport too. The day before at the ranch he had said that he would try to come to the airfield as he had something that he wanted to give me. It was lovely to see him again, he had been a big supporter of my flights and in '97 had organised a dinner in our honour at the Western Aerospace museum right there at Oakland's North Field. This time he gave me an original poster, yellow with age, for a world air race – dated 1915. It read, 'The Circumnavigation of the Globe, under the auspices of the Panama Pacific International Exposition, San Francisco, 1915' – just 12 years after the Wright brothers made the first-ever motorised flight and already the world was dreaming of circumnavigating the globe. While I was refuelling, Lawrie also reminded me of all the early aviators who had taken off from North Field, Oakland. These included Amelia Earhart. 'Did you know that Dad knew Amelia and her husband Putnam?' he said. I didn't, he had never mentioned it. Later he sent me this entry from Uncle Lawrie's memoirs:

> I had purchased the first Stearman-Hammond plane sold privately and the day I took delivery of it was the day Amelia Earhart was missing. Her husband, Putnam, excitedly got me on the phone and I met him at the St Francis, and we went to the Coast Guard HQ to listen for news and read the few false intercepts which were coming over. It was a sad affair and I tried to help. I persuaded the President to order the navy to put out a flat boat in search of Amelia.
>
> It became a famous and unsuccessful search and much has been written about her disappearance. I followed it all for years. She may have been picked up by a Japanese craft and eventually taken to Japan. But I know for sure that she certainly didn't fly there and land in the lagoon as some tried to claim. That is another story.
>
> We built her plane at Lockheed. I knew Amelia and liked her, but felt that, while she was a very brave girl, she was not the best pilot and should not have tried to fly around the world.
>
> Her husband George Palmer Putnam was not an attractive person, to put it mildly. He was a difficult person for Lockheed to do business with and became most unpopular.

After taking off from Oakland, everything went well for the first 60 miles. We flew north-west over the Bay Bridge, past Alcatraz and on over the Golden Gate Bridge with the early morning mist beginning to clear. Then we turned south and took a coastal route towards Los Angeles, City of Angels. Lots of memories came flooding back to me as I flew over the Presidio; I could see Nob Hill, the Mark Hopkins Hotel and could just about place California Street and Joice Street where I lived back in 1961 and '62.

It wasn't until Carmel, just south of Monterey, that my engine started missing, closely followed by my heart. Gummed up spark plug? Yet another magneto failure? I started looking for autorotation spots and checked the wind – south-west, no more than three knots. Should I play safe and just land on the first available bit of flat ground? But I argued with myself. I had flown hundreds of miles on only one magneto without it seriously affecting my flight. If it was a gummy spark plug then it might well just clear itself if I pulled more power. I decided to try that first. We had a big reception awaiting us at the Robinson Factory and if the media reception was anything like the last time it would be saturation coverage. This would have to happen when the pressure was on.

I followed Route One south with the sheer cliffs down to the Pacific Ocean on one side and the mountains rising steeply to close on 6,000 feet on the other. The only landing spots were the lay-bys along Route One, but they were close to telephone wires. I increased power, but the engine continued to run rough. Five minutes, ten minutes – no change. I had serious doubts as to whether I could manage the tight autorotation required to land in one of the lay-bys without overrunning into the sea. Could I really miss the wires or avoid hitting one of the vast juggernauts or speeding cars which were all too numerous along the route? Mentally I went through the emergency landing sequence – engine fails: immediately lower the collective lever, flatten the pitch of the blades, put the helicopter into autorotation. In a Robinson helicopter, with its lightweight blades, you have about one second to do that, otherwise you get blade stall (any wind resistance on the blades without the power of the engine to turn them will just stop the blades). With larger, heavier helicopters you have a slightly longer grace period, a yawning three seconds. Keep an eye on the rotor RPMs, flare at 40 feet above the ground to reduce all forward speed and keep those rotor RPMs high; level off, then, 10 feet from the ground, lift the collective lever. This angles the pitch of the main rotor blades and gives you, over flat ground, lots of ground inertia.

I told myself it wasn't going to happen, I was more than halfway around the world. I had had two magnetos fail on me without mishap, surely I could make it to the reassuring haven of the Robinson factory? It would look so wimpy to land with nothing more than a gummy spark plug.

I flew on south towards Hearst Castle. There was a small airfield there, perhaps I should land? I decided not, and then – yes! – the engine was definitely running smoother. I relaxed a little and when Q suggested a couple of orbits of Hearst Castle I was happy to head the few miles inland where the mountains gave way to rolling hills. We circled Hearst Castle. My engine sounded good, the castle looked great and I felt a whole lot better as we continued south with the ground becoming reassuringly flat. Then suddenly, without warning, eight miles north of Santa Maria airfield and 198 miles from Torrance, G-MURY yawed sharply to the left (indicating engine failure), the low RPM horn shrilled and the yellow warning light went on. With my heart racing I instantly lowered the collective lever and flared the helicopter – no time to ask, 'Have I still got an engine?' I looked for a suitable landing spot. I was in autorotation, descending at 1,500 feet a minute.

I slowly pulled the lever up, rolling on the throttle, hoping my engine was still there and that it had been a 'cough' rather than a cut-out. To my vast relief the engine *was* still there. But I was over-reacting, I had rolled the throttle too far, pulled the collective too high and the RPMs were going through the roof. 'Think – stay calm – function,' I told myself. I gently rolled off the throttle and let the governor take over.

With RPMs once more normal I concentrated on trying to regain some of the lost height. Height is safety. The higher you are the more time you have to organise your landing and the greater your glide-path and choice of landing places. I was flying at 4,000 feet when G-MURY yawed, and I had lost 1,000 feet. I regained about half of that, and then the whole sequence repeated itself.

Sharp left yaw, low RPM horn, yellow warning light glowing. With thumping heart, I put G-MURY into autorotation, and once again pulled the engine back in. I told Q what was happening and he urged me to regain height. The outside air temperature was 32 degrees centigrade and my hands were slippery on the controls. I didn't notice the heat but remember registering my sweaty hands. Once more I pulled the engine back in and once more I regained a little height. 'Head for Santa Maria – can you see the runway?' Q said. I could, I was fixated on that distant threshold to Runway 12, still an agonising 5 miles away. Again and again I regained a little height and again and again the engine coughed out. Every time I was getting lower. 'I've spoken to Santa Maria. I told them we have an emergency, you are clear to land,' Q said.

Four miles, three miles, two miles, one mile. I was down at 500 feet, keeping an eye on my air speed. I needed 60 knots of air speed for the kenetic energy for an effective flare and 500 feet was not a good height to be at if my engine finally stopped completely. I reached the threshold of the runway at 300 feet and quickly descended to a couple of feet above the asphalt and taxied to the apron without further mishap. I set down and with infinite relief, fully lowered the collective, rolled off the throttle, put on the frictions and slumped there.

'Christ,' I said out loud in a none-too-steady voice. I sat there shaking with wave after wave of relief flooding through me at the joy of being on the ground in one piece. I had done it. I had made it and no damage had been done. It was not exactly a *Top Gun* performance, I had not been the icy-calm hero I would have liked to have been. I know I sounded panicky – I had been – but it was comforting to know that I hadn't frozen and I had functioned. *And* I was safe on the ground.

It was very hot ground; I was getting an OAT reading of 39 degrees centigrade with the midday sun oven-like on the apron's asphalt surface there at Santa Maria Airport. I sat there, the doors now open with a wind blowing through the helicopter like a hot hairdryer, waiting for the engine to cool off sufficiently to be able to shut down.

An hour later I was once more in the air – in G-JEFA. We had spoken with Pat Cox, chief engineer at the Robinson Factory, and decided that as soon as the Cessna arrived at Torrance, Heinz would turn around and fly him to Santa Maria to sort out G-MURY. Q and Al would wait there. That way the press would never know that anything had gone wrong as the two helicopters were outwardly identical. Only the registration was different and it was unlikely that anyone would pick up on that – no one did.

Pat Cox later confirmed that it had been a magneto failure. He replaced it with a new one. He also said that, unbelievably, one of the bearings inside the magneto was missing. Robinson's purchase the magnetos direct from the factory of manufacture as a sealed component. Pat said he would be sending the magneto to the FAA for investigation. That evening, talking with Colin he mirrored my own thoughts. 'You were lucky, you know, that magneto was fitted in Kuwait. It could have gone any time. Just think of all the water we've been over, all the mountains, all the jungle and those glaciers. You were really lucky.'

We spent four nights and three days in Los Angeles while the helicopters had a thorough 100-hour service with Pat Cox and his assistants. Heinz, Colin and I stayed with good friends of mine, Jay and Susan Smith. The rest of the team stayed at the Sheraton Hotel. We only saw them twice: once when I arranged with our ever-generous sponsors, Tommy Hilfiger, for a replenishment of clothes at their elegant shop; the second time at a sad/happy farewell lunch for Yuri who had become so much a part of our team. Aeroflot needed him and there were direct flights from Los Angeles to

Moscow. For the rest of the team time apart was obviously no bad thing. It was good for everyone. The young obviously preferred their own company as had been made only too apparent with Pascal's remark in Eugene. Pascal and James had announced their engagement and I think they were celebrating the happy event.

I let Al know when Colin and I went to spend a day at the Robinson Factory (Colin to service his microlight and myself to check details with Pat and show support). I thought they might like to take some video footage. 'You can take some yourself if you like,' I was told. Martin Huberty, a very good friend of Simon's and mine and a Hollywood film director, came out with us instead and happily wielded the camera, though I believe none of his footage was used. Pat later made some very derogatory remarks about 'far too much useless footage by that friend of yours'. Martin had always been a big supporter and enthusiast and had been responsible, amongst other things, for alerting all the media in Los Angeles to our coming.

As always there was little time to relax and when there was it was difficult to do so. What with the day at the factory and onward planning and organisation – more Jeppesen Low Altitude Enroute Charts; more WACs (World Aeronautical Charts 1:100,000); more US dollars and then we found out we needed separate insurance for going to Mexico – we were busy. Jay and Susan were stars, lending us cars and rushing around doing errands on our behalf.

On our last night Susan and Jay invited the whole team to dinner at the prestigious Valley Bay Club. The team, however, not only didn't turn up, they never even let us know they weren't coming, other than Q who phoned from the Robinson factory to say he was busy and couldn't make it.

We had a high old time with Susan insisting we start off the evening with tequila slammers and dinner at the Valley Bay Club, right on the beach. We then ended up the evening on Third Street Promenade, a pedestrian street lined with nightclubs and bars, vendors and street entertainment. One such 'entertainment' was a zealous born-again Christian holding forth to a large, rather bored-looking crowd. The preacher had a life-like blow-up human dummy lying on the ground, part covered by a cloth. Colin said, 'I think I know what he wants, I think he needs the kiss of life!' with which he pushed through the crowd, got down on his hands and knees and started pumping the dummy's chest. Of course, each time he pumped the dummy's chest, the head jumped up and down. The crowd were shrieking with laughter and the self-proclaimed preacher was screaming that he would call the police, that he'd sue. Colin, with a look of pure tequila slammer-aided innocence, finally clambered to his feet and turning to the preacher said, 'I think he'll be all right now, Guv!'

SEVEN

Los Angeles to Cuba

5 - 12 August

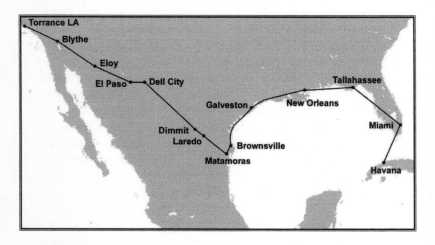

DAY 67

We all hoped to make El Paso, around 700 miles to the east, on the evening of 5 August. I had to add 148 miles to my journey as I was going to backtrack to Santa Maria. (I didn't want to jeopardise my world record attempt by not completing the entire journey in G-MURY.) Colin and I made a really early start, waved off from the factory by Pat Cox and Bud Ames with numerous members of his family. Bud, like Lawrie, had given me much enthusiastic encouragement and advice both before and during both my trips.

Pat Cox said, 'You'll be using Runway 11, then take a left and head for the smokestacks. LAX (Los Angeles International Airport) will want you below 500 feet – their runways are only a couple of hundred yards from the coast.'

I flew back to Santa Maria under cloudless skies, winds were light and variable and the OAT was already reading 26 degrees centigrade at 7.15 a.m. Flying conditions were easy, but I was continually reminded that the race was now against time; to complete, to go the distance and for both of us, Colin and me, to make that northern crossing before the autumn gales. I thought it was possible that there was a cut-off day for allowing VFR flights such as ours to make the attempt, but I didn't even want to ask. We hoped to make El Paso that day, to make up a day. We ended up losing three.

At first I made good time. I made a ten-minute turn around at Santa Maria and then, climbing steeply, headed due east across the High Sierras with peaks reaching over 8,000 feet. Once more I gloried in the solitude, alone with my thoughts and the London Philharmonic Orchestra playing the *New World Symphony*, interrupted only by the necessity of intermittent radio talk. I flew eastwards towards the Mojave Desert then east-south-east past the airfields of Twenty Nine Palms and Desert Centre to Blythe for fuel and to stretch my legs. I had been in the air for nearly five and a half hours and was ready for a break. We had stopped at Blythe in '97 before heading north-west to Oshkosh and Niagara Falls.

Blythe is in the middle of the desert and that day with the hot winds there was a temperature of 47 degrees centigrade. I was only too happy, after refuelling, to take refuge in the small, air conditioned terminal cabin-cum-coffee shop, where I paid my fees and enjoyed a nice cold Pepsi served by a large and seemingly bored gentleman. Then his face broke into a great big grin, suddenly coming alive, and he said, 'Ain't you the gal who came through a coupla years back? Got your snapshot pinned up over there!' He pointed to a small noticeboard above the ice cream chest. After that there was no stopping him. He wanted to know all about the last trip and all about the present one. Half an hour later I regretfully told him that I really had to be on my way. I gave him an updated postcard and made my way back across the baking asphalt to an oven-like G-MURY. I lifted off, getting a friendly wave from the cabin as I turned east once more towards Phoenix and Tucson.

I had heard none of the team on 123.45 or on any of the airport frequencies I had been tuned in to. Heinz had said that he would leave Los Angeles around midday. As for the camera crew, I had no idea. I had told them the night before what time Colin and I would be leaving and Q had said something about catching up with Colin later. Twenty minutes out of Blythe I heard Q on the radio saying, 'Anyone within a hundred miles of El Paso for a relay?' He told me he was going in to Ryan Airfield just to the west of Tucson for fuel. I said I had just refuelled at Blythe and would continue on as I was anxious to know how Colin was doing. The midday heat, hot winds and turbulence had been building. I was having a bumpy time of it and imagined that it must have been extreme for Colin, and that proved to be the case. Shortly after talking to Q, Colin came on the air: 'Oh thank goodness you're there, I'm on the ground at a small airfield called Eloy, the turbulence was horrendous and there's an enormous storm building.' I looked around for a storm. I couldn't see one but Colin always seemed to have a sixth sense for what was just over the horizon. I headed for Eloy and sure enough, shortly after I landed, a mega sandstorm came hurtling across the desert obliterating everything in its path.

Colin had already put his microlight in a hangar, but G-MURY was standing exposed, and Colin wrenched his bad arm putting the tie-downs on the helicopter. Shortly after that first sandstorm went through I tried to get through to Q on the radio and found Heinz. He said he would come and join us, then changed his mind in favour of Q's airfield when we cautioned him about parachutists. The next we heard was that they were all in El Paso!

Colin and I remained stuck in Eloy. We got bunk beds in the airport bunkhouse along with several hundred friendly parachutists from all over the world who had come there for an international parachuting competition. So, we once more ended up in a different place to the others. We were making progress around the world but, as Colin said, 'It's ridiculous, we haven't seen the film crew in days.' I pointed out that today was hardly their fault. 'They could have been at the factory when we took off,' he argued, 'and now here. That sandstorm and all the parachutists . . . such good stuff.'

That was Eloy. Then we hit real trouble in El Paso, or rather 30 miles east of El Paso. Colin and I made an early start, hoping to make a quick stop in El Paso, then continue on to Laredo that night. We prepared the aircraft in darkness and were airborne at first light – 5.35 a.m., arriving in El Paso at 9.05 a.m. By the time we had refuelled, Q and Pat arrived looking clean and well-fed, making us realise how scruffy and hungry we were. Our last food had been hot dogs and several beers the evening before with a group of parachuting enthusiasts, after which we had retired to our dormitory bunk beds with alarms set for 4 a.m.

Colin got away from El Paso at 10.30 a.m. – on camera. (Al and Pat did in fact film us regularly, but not as much as Q.) We were both more or less religiously doing our bat phones, but web-watchers (who were enjoying Al's entertaining daily updates) were frequently asking, 'Where are Colin and Jennifer? We want to see more of Colin and Jennifer.'

Things were looking good. I gave Colin half an hour's start then followed, once more accompanied by a camera crew. Lift-off was slow and heavy. El Paso is more than 4,000 feet above sea level – a vast, high desert plateau. Thirty miles out I tried to get Colin on the radio. He immediately came on, but I could only hear part of what he was saying. 'Readability three, you're very broken,' I said.

'I'm . . . . . . ound, thank . . .ness you are there! Th . . . . you . . . dn't hear me – I'm . . . . . . the ground . . . middle of no . . . near . . . inverted! . . . turbulence is horren . . .'

We somehow got his coordinates, slightly to the north of our track and eight miles south of a small, disused airstrip called Cornudas. We spotted him from a couple of miles away, a small forlorn figure, leaning into the wind, holding onto the wing of his microlight. He was marooned in a red desert, flat and stony with sand and thorn bushes stretching as far as the eye could see. Colin stood on the edge of a track that stretched away in a straight line to nowhere. 'Caution landing,' Q said. 'This is a hell of a spot, it's over 5,000 feet, we've got full fuel and it's 46 degrees centigrade.'

We came in low and slow, but even so the low RPM horn and light were on as we touched down, sending up clouds of dust. We landed some distance away from Colin who was grimly holding onto the wing of his trike, trying to keep it on the ground. The wind must have been gusting up to 30 knots and, with all that square footage of sail, it was all Colin could do to keep it on the ground. 'Come quick, my arm is killing me' were the first words I heard after I shut down. We all ran over to give him a much needed hand.

'Thank goodness you're here,' he said, 'I really thought you might miss me and I'd be stuck. I've never had so much pain in my arm, but I couldn't let go of the wing, I've been hanging on to it for dear life for more than 40 minutes. Wind would have trashed the trike.' We got a grip on the wildly bucking machine. 'You know, as I got out, the wind just lifted it up and dumped it a full metre away, it was a miracle I managed to grab the wing.'

I interrupted saying, 'Why didn't you try and get the wing off?'

'Well, I could have done between gusts but I had to get you on the radio and the aerial is on the wing, I wouldn't have been able to get you, would I?' He was half bent over rubbing his arm and looking up at Pat who had the camera rolling. Shaking his head, he said. 'This turbulence is really dangerous, it's horrendous. There's no way I can fly in this.' He looked glumly up at the sky. 'I always said we should have gone down the west coast of Mexico, this is insane and there's another 200 miles of this high stuff. There's no way I can fly after midday, these thermals are . . .'

I finished the sentence for him – 'Horrendous'.

'I think we've got to find you a new word, Colin,' said Q laughing. We all made suggestions, finally settling for 'diabolical'. But we all felt depressed. It was frustrating for the helicopters as we could cope with the conditions. The only time Colin had the advantage was in cloud, but cloud was not our problem that morning. 'The Cessna might be airborne by now. I think I better try and contact them before they're out of range,' I said, and added, checking my chart, 'There's a small airfield 20 miles north-west that we could all go to.'

I went back to my helicopter, put on my headphones and tried to raise the Cessna. They were airborne and in range. I told James what had happened and that we planned to go to Dell City Municipal. Perhaps Colin would be able to get away early in the evening as the ground cooled?

God, it was hot. I reached for a bottle of water and my black umbrella that I bought in Chittagong and went to join the others, who were dismantling the microlight. As I joined them Q was peering closely at the microlight's prop. 'I've just saved your life!' he said. 'Look at this. You've got a stress fracture in the hub of your prop.' We all crowded round to have a look, then stood there in stunned silence as the full implications sunk in. If that had gone in flight it would have been catastrophic. The shattered hub would have sheered off, shredded the wing and Colin would have plummeted to the ground – terminato! It didn't bear thinking about. Colin had done a thorough check of the machine after we landed at El Paso and he was certain the stress fracture must have happened in the last hour. Perhaps the turbulence, together with Q, had saved his life? But now what were we going to do?

'I must phone Jim Cunliffe at Mainair [his manufacturer and the sponsor of his microlight]. I need to find out where the nearest manufacturer of the prop is,' said Colin, so we left one sad and dismantled little microlight and did a shuttle service over to Dell City Municipal Airport where we met up with the Cessna crew and gave them the bad news about the prop. The airport consisted of nothing much more than an airstrip, an apron and a public telephone with a couple of sheds some distance away. As we were standing around the telephone trying to figure out how to make it work (we could get no network on our mobile phones), a battered and dusty Lincoln Continental appeared at speed from around the sheds and squealed to a halt in a cloud of dust. Out stepped a character wearing jeans with leather braces and a large beer belly. 'Well, howdy folks! What cain ah do for y'all? Ah'm Dale Flach – ree-tired! Ah'm just the city drunk. Welcome to Dell City. Welcome to the middle of *nowhere*,' he said with a great roar of laughter. Dale, we later learnt, had made a fortune in communications – Dell telephones – and his wife was a schoolteacher.

We shook hands and told him our problems. He showed us how to use the phone. Colin managed to get through to Jim Cunliffe at Mainair who was staggered. 'You're prop's got a *stress fracture?* I've never, ever heard of that happening before,' he said. 'I'll check where the nearest manufacturer is. I think Salt Lake City is the nearest. I'll order one right away, and send it to El Paso.'

'Yup,' said Colin. 'Make it care of Superior Aviation. I'll phone you in a couple of hours when we get back to El Paso.'

We described to Dale where we had left the microlight. We wanted to know whose land it was on and could we contact them. He said, 'Well, that sure sounds like Jay Williams' place – the Williams Ranch, though, could be Gunsight Ranch. I guess your best plan would be to pass by May Carson's Diner at Cornudas on Route 62. Jay, that's Jay Williams, he drops in there most days.'

The next two days revolved around May's Place on Route 62/108 – a roadside diner packed with memorabilia. All the tables had red and white check tablecloths with a glass top, and under the glass were thousands of visiting cards and business cards. The legs of the tables were cowboy legs (each curved table leg was inside padded blue jeans in a cowboy boot). It was quite disconcerting to look down and see a man's leg and booted foot between your knees. The ceiling had hats of every description and every inch of wall space was devoted to photographs and documents.

What wonderful people they all were. We were deep in cowboy and Indian (Mescularos) country. Everyone appeared to know everyone and they all wore Stetson hats, cowboy boots and jeans. There was May herself, who happily showed us her brand-new kitchen, brand-new thanks to a gas leak the year before which had blown her kitchen to kingdom come – and almost herself. She introduced us to Debbie Berry and Donny who helped out behind the counter. There was Jerry Ziller who was wearing the tightest of blue jeans and the brightest of smiles and, finally, Jay Williams who said he would check out the microlight and reassured Colin that there were no cattle in that area that might trample on his precious wing. We went out again next day to check that all was well with the microlight and stopped by May's for lunch. I gave several joy rides, including one to Debbie's two children, and May put a jam jar on the counter saying 'Helicopter rides $50 in aid of Operation Smile!' Charles Wooldridge (another local cowboy) produced a hog-nose snake out of his pocket, assuring us it was harmless!

The following day, armed with a new prop (which arrived from Salt Lake City), we made our last visit. We had seen nothing of the camera crew since arriving back in El Paso that first evening. But when the prop arrived and we were preparing once more to go out to the desert I had phoned Al in his room to ask if he wanted to come out. He told me it was 'Pat's call'. I phoned Pat who said he wasn't well, that he thought he had flu, 'and anyway,' he said, 'we're planning to go into Mexico and film some street scenes!' (Half of El Paso is in Mexico). 'Well, we're leaving in 20 minutes, it's up to you,' I said and I left it at that. I phoned Heinz and asked him if he would like to come out and pilot G-JEFA (Heinz is also a helicopter pilot). He jumped at the chance. We met in the lobby, and there was Pat who said he was coming with us. It was only later that Colin told me what had happened.

'I arrived in the lobby and Pat arrived a couple of minutes later looking pretty sour and saying he wanted a short interview of what was going on. "Aren't you coming with us?" I'd said. I was really surprised. "No, we're going into Mexico to film street scenes, get some local colour," he'd said. It was just too much and I said "Look, I don't care what you are doing with this documentary, but I have to tell you I once saw a documentary about some trip and this guy's engine blew up in the desert and he had to replace it and it was the most interesting part of the whole bang shoot. I tell you this has to be a hell of a lot more interesting than any old street scene in Mexico."'

'Whatever did he say to that?' I asked delightedly.

With a wry smile Colin said, 'What do you think? "I can't be arsed!" Just like he always says. But then he says, "Well, I suppose I've fucking well got to come."'

I think Pat was glad he did come. He cheered up and thoroughly enjoyed the drama of trying to extricate an enormous, black, hairy spider that scuttled into the foot compartment of the microlight and couldn't be found. He filmed Colin and Heinz fitting the new prop and tracking and balancing it. I served drinks, generally encouraged, and took photos, including a rather a good one of Pat with my black Chittagong umbrella shielding himself from the glare of the sun as he filmed the others. And then came the excitement of Colin taxiing down Route 62.

Having finally got the prop tracked and balanced to Colin's satisfaction, we had a big debate as to whether Colin should leave the microlight where it was or try and get over to the disused airfield at Cornudas just eight miles away. The cons were that to get to Cornudas would be dangerous as the afternoon thermals were in full swing and there were localised storms brewing; the pros, that a take-off in the dark from a hard surface would be infinitely preferable to a hazardous dirt track with potholes.

Thankfully Colin chose Cornudas as there was the mother of all storms that night. Everything was under water and his microlight wing would have been coated in mud and the track unusable. As it was he made the hairy flight (it was diabolical) to the disused airfield, which had rather higher than expected thorn bushes hanging over both sides of the narrow strip. Much to Colin's dismay, there were also lots of cattle and no fencing. Jerry Ziller suggested that the best move would be to bring the microlight along to the diner. He said Colin could put the wing in the barn for the night and sleep in his caravan.

The airfield was about three miles away from the diner down Route 62. We all drove to the airstrip in Jerry's old Cadillac, bumping over several cattle grids, back to where the microlight sat on the disused runway. We found a reasonable route for the microlight to taxi along as there was no way Colin was going to fly G-NOWW. There was nowhere for him to land it other than on the road and, as he rightly said, the winds had strengthened alarmingly even in the last half hour, plus his arm was killing him. There were lots of good reasons for not flying it, so he was going to taxi it along Route 62.

Just as we were all pushing and pulling the microlight over the final cattle grid, no more than 20 yards from the road, a highway patrol car went by! 'Oh there goes Tod Williams,' said Jerry. 'He'll be stopping by May's, that's for sure. Y'all see him parked there when we arrive. He's OK!'

Okay he might be, but we had our misgivings about his reaction if he saw a microlight speeding down Route 62. We looked cautiously left and right. There was not a vehicle in sight and happily we could see for miles each way – the road was straight as a die. Off we went, Colin batting along Route 62 with us tagging along behind in the Cadillac and Pat half out of the window filming the whole scene. Colin scooted into May's back yard and we managed to have the wing off before Tod emerged from the diner none the wiser.

DAY 71 – 9 AUGUST

Dimmit County, Laredo and on to Matamoras, 697 miles to the south-east, and down to sea level. Colin took off in darkness at 4 a.m. along Route 62 with Jerry in attendance and I left with the camera crew from El Paso at 6 a.m. We met up in Laredo and made it, without mishap, to Mexico. But that was all we were going to see of Mexico. We were deep in the hurricane season and we could see satellite pictures on the television of the storm cells building in Mexico. They were, as Colin said, 'Horren . . . I mean diabolical. I've got a gut feeling. I know we'll get stuck, there's no way any of us can handle those storms, it would be madness and we'd be stuck – no escape route.'

We argued backwards and forwards. The disappointment was huge, we were all so looking forward to our much-planned and eagerly anticipated journey through Mexico, seeing all those magnificent Mayan temples, the jungle through to Belize and the second biggest coral reef in the world. We had then planned to fly onwards to Cuba and Havana, one of the highlights of our trip. Now, agonisingly and reluctantly, it looked as though we would have to route along the Texas coast. We really had no other choice. It seemed such a tame alternative, so ordinary by comparison, but it didn't turn out to be the case. We were in for plenty of excitement and the coastline was infinitely more beautiful than I could ever have imagined. Yet that evening in Matamoras we felt depressed. Lawrence Duffy and Cath MacCaulay from NOW had been due to meet us in Havana, as had Jamie McCallum. Pat said he would let them all know that Havana was 'out'.

We had spent hours doing customs and clearances into Matamoras, Mexico. Next morning we had to reverse the whole proceedings, hopping back into the USA at Brownsville just eleven miles away across the border. Tempers were short. Everyone was fed up and disappointed. Al, being no pilot, had little understanding of 'wise pilot decisions'. He was in a foul mood and pointed the finger at Colin. 'This is ridiculous, this planning is up the creek. NOW don't know whether they are coming or going. How come this decision was made? Colin knew the weather days ago. Everyone was due in Havana and now suddenly Colin says there are storms in Mexico, that he's got this "gut feeling". We're all going by his gut feeling. We've seen storms building on and off for days, what is going on? It's a shambles . . .' Heinz reasoned with him. He had just been to the Met office in Brownsville and had the latest weather report. It supported all Colin's gloomiest predictions. We were doing the wise thing, however much we might wish we were still headed south into Mexico. We just couldn't afford to get stuck in Mexico, time was seriously running out for our northern crossing.

We were a team riddled with dissension as we headed north along the coast towards Corpus Christi under a cloudless sky with the temperature already, at 10 a.m., creeping up to 30 degrees centigrade. The crew filmed Colin coping with lively turbulence as we flew down the channel from Brownsville to Port Isabel on the coast where, happily, the air proved nice and stable. Colin was able to relax and could fly low-level along the beach. Q and Pat soon got bored of level-pegging it with Colin and myself and, having done enough filming, disappeared off into the distance along Padre Island.

Padre Island, San Jose Island, Matagorda and Galveston Islands – a narrow sandy spit of almost unbroken land more than 300 miles long, lying just a few miles off-shore, stretching all the way from the Mexican border to Galveston. It was magical flying. We began to feel better and better by the minute, although Colin was getting hotter and hotter. He had put on his padded flying suit anticipating being up around 10,000 feet with temperatures 20 degrees cooler than at 50 feet. 'Why don't we stop and have a swim?' he suggested.

It sounded like an excellent idea. The film crew were by then some 30 miles ahead of us, and weren't quite so enthusiastic. 'Well – ye-es, but we were sort of thinking of some nice little place where we could all stop for lunch.' I suggested we did both – we were only going as far as Galveston, we had time. But next time I tried to contact them they had gone off the air. 'Well, no reason why we shouldn't stop,' Colin said. 'We'll never find them now, they could have stopped anywhere. I've got to get this suit off, I'm sweating buckets.' I was only too happy to stop. The sea looked inviting and it was very hot in my little glass bubble. 'You land and make sure the sand is good and firm,' Colin said. We chose a large sandy area just behind the dunes, but we should have chosen the beach.

I landed, got out and tested the ground. It was lovely and firm. I should have tested further afield. I radioed Colin that the sand was suitable for him to land. Down he came, and his wheels sank deep into soft sand, bringing him to a sharp and juddering halt! Luckily, no damage done, but he leapt out and came storming over towards me, shouting, 'What do you mean saying the sand is firm? I'm never going to get out of here!' It turned out that I had landed on practically the only firm bit of sand. I should have checked out a full landing strip for him. There we were, miles from anywhere. I would never have thought that coastal area could be so empty. The midday sun was a shimmering white ball high in the heavens and you could see the heat, the mirages, reflecting off the sand. We had a problem.

'We just must find a strip of firmer sand,' I said. 'There has to be some.' Colin got his padded flight suit off and we started a testing search. We finally found a strip, about 100 yards away from the microlight, with very short couch grass sticking through that we hoped would be firm enough to take off from. The next 15 minutes were agony, especially for Colin with his sore arm. We pushed and pulled the microlight across that endless 100 yards. Colin had to walk backwards holding the front wheel up and out of the sand, pulling for all he was worth. I pushed as hard as I could from the rear, and then I got the giggles. I caught an imaginary glimpse of us from outside and we did look pretty ridiculous: intrepid world travellers, stuck in the sands of Texas. I think Colin thought I was cracking up and he started making reassuring noises of encouragement. Drenched in sweat, we finally got to the firmer ground. 'OK, that's it, I'm going for a swim. Let's worry about the take-off later,' I said.

Colin needed no second bidding. We climbed over the burning dunes to the perfect landing spot – miles and miles of the firmest beach. Colin stripped to his underpants while I stopped long enough to kick off my sneakers. I ran in, clothes and all. I remembered doing the same thing in '97 in a river in the jungles of Borneo. It had been heaven, and it was again.

Half an hour later we were back at the microlight with me fast drip-drying. I said, 'You know, it's sad that Pat's not here filming. This would make such great documentary material.' It was true and all I had as I stood poised to record the nerve-racking take-off was my still camera in a none-too-steady hand. Colin climbed on board, started up and took the engine up to full revs. Easing off the throttle, he gave me the thumbs up, then once more rolled on the throttle and slowly, all too slowly it seemed to me, gathered speed down the small, hardish stretch of sand and couch grass. Faster, faster, I found myself standing on tiptoe, raising my shoulders, my hands, willing him off the ground, camera forgotten. Go on! Go on! He wasn't going to make it, he was at the end of the hard strip, and then, just when I thought he was going to sink once more into soft sand, he lifted, he was clear and climbing.

I hurried back to my hot little red helicopter, now looking rather lonely a couple of hundred yards away. My clothes were by then more damp from sweat than seawater. It didn't feel very good, but once airborne with the hot breeze coming through the air vents, I soon cooled down. Colin was sounding hugely relieved. I tried to call the film crew. Still no reply.

Ten minutes later we had Corpus Christi asking us to divert 30 degrees left of track as they had a search pattern in progress. A helicopter had gone down. I asked if they would like us to help. 'Thank you, ma'am, I appreciate that. I think we have a handle on this one,' came the reply. That evening we heard some more news on the television. An H53 army helicopter, a 'Jolly Green Giant', had gone missing. It had apparently taken the combined efforts of three military airbases, all within 50 miles of the accident, to locate the helicopter. It had gone down 30 miles off shore. There were two survivors and two dead, three were missing. It was very sobering. I thought once more about our chances of surviving, of being found if one of us were to go down in the Arctic waters around Greenland. If it took three hours to find an enormous army helicopter that had gone down so close to all those military rescue bases, how long would we have to wait?

Fifteen miles out of Galveston I radioed for joining instructions. No sooner was I through talking with Galveston than Q came on the radio. 'Oh hello. How did you get there?'

'Well, more to the point, where have *you* been. Where are you?' I said.

'Well,' said Q, light-heartedly, 'we've been having a really nice lunch, we're about 20 miles behind you.'

I was fed up. 'What do you think you're playing at? This isn't some sort of a jolly, you're being paid to record Colin's and my trip. You've missed so much. You just went off the air. You never said where you were going and we've had all sorts of dramas. We stopped for a swim, just as we suggested, and Colin got stuck in the sand, then there was this search and rescue going on, and you missed it all.' Q told me that they had got some really good local colour, that they had interviewed some great local characters – and – 'Pat says he's got all the footage he needs of you!'

'What jerks,' was Colin's brief comment on joining me after landing. He then asked me if I'd help locate someone for hangar space for the microlight. I went off to the Civil Aviation Bureau and he went to the hangars. Ten minutes later, while talking with the lady in Civil Aviation, with various other people hanging around, Pat came in looking po-faced and tight-lipped. I gave him a fairly cool nod and continued to write down the name of the man to contact for the hangar. I then looked back towards Pat and all hell let loose. Pat was beside himself, he was so furious. 'How *dare* you speak to me like that? How *dare* you be so rude, you can't tell me my job! If you don't like it the way we're doing it then that's too bad, we're your sponsor, we can't be told . . .'

I interrupted him. I had been standing there in stunned silence, as had all the others in the room. 'First of all stop screaming at me, we'll go outside and talk about this,' I said. I was shaking as I pushed open the door and went back out onto the apron. Pat was still shouting. 'You've been telling me what to do for 72 days. We think we're doing a good job, if we want to get local colour we'll damn well get local colour and we don't give a stuff what you think. This is not just about you and Colin, you're boring! We're your sponsors. You think it's a good story that Colin's on the ground? Stuck in the sand when he should be going for his life trying to get a world record? I think it's fucking stupid, you're meant to be flying, not landing on beaches for a swim . . .'

Again I interrupted. I was trying to stay calm, but was fast losing it. I was shaking. 'How dare you scream at me like this. NOW are not the only sponsors and *you* are not the sponsor, you're the hired cameraman and Tommy Hilfiger are also major sponsors, and we have technical sponsors, and *I* have provided two helicopters . . .'

'You haven't – your husband has!'

I just couldn't believe this was all happening. I looked at this young, 28-year-old cameraman, his face distorted with rage and said, 'I honestly don't think I have *ever* in my whole life had anyone talk to me – scream at me the way you are doing . . .'

'Well, it's about time someone did, it's time someone stood up to you. You're just a spoilt little rich bitch!'

I just said, 'You're out of here.'

To which Pat replied, 'I'd like to see you try' and strutted off.

I walked shakily across the apron to get my bag out of G-MURY and fill in my technical log book, when along came Q. He just stood there there looking grim with his hands on his hips. Where was Colin? Where was my support? I was feeling thoroughly drained, intimidated and traumatised. Had I really sounded so rude? Fed up, yes, but rude? I know I can sound much more abrupt than I intend. And I had been fed up, it needed to be said. But this? I reckoned I was utterly justified in all I'd said – and still do.

Then Q, even more tight-lipped than Pat, said in slow and measured words,

'I – am – so fur-i-ous – I – can – hardly – speak.' He then turned and walked away.

I couldn't cope. We had all had a long day with the disappointments at the beginning of not being able to go on through Mexico, and we had, as Pat had so forcibly pointed out, been together for 72 days. Could we last another 25? How could I ever stand and talk naturally again in front of camera-wielding Pat? I'd told myself, 'never mind the cameras, they are secondary', but now I was a nervous wreck. This was getting dangerous, it wasn't a safe state to be flying in. I needed to be able to make cool judgments in the air, to be in control. If I was ever going to make it safely home I needed all my faculties working well. I had no rights or editorial control over what Al and Pat did or didn't take, they were putting together a good website and NOW, back in London, were very happy with all the material. But NOW in London were not privy to the material Al and Pat were putting together for a documentary.

While I was thinking about all this and fiddling around in my helicopter waiting for Colin, back came Q, still just as grim. He told me that the only solution would be for me to apologise to Pat. And do you know, I did! I like to think that I apologised because I had the maturity to realise that we had both overreacted and that Pat probably regretted his outburst. But I guess I was tired and ready to do anything for peace. I certainly defused the situation and a calmer-looking Pat said, 'I really appreciate that.'

When Colin finally appeared, I told him what had happened. He was naturally unhappy with Pat saying how stupid it was of him to get stuck in the sand. 'I wish I'd been there, I'd have punched them both. And he thinks I should never land outside of an airport? How many times have you landed outside an airport? That was the first time since leaving Brooklands that I have *ever* landed outside of an airfield, other than my landing in China and nearly getting inverted in the desert. I told you, you should never have brought Q. He's nothing but trouble. But you just don't listen to me. I told you about that friend of mine, that pilot, he was free, but he's got another job now. He would have given anything to come and he's really good and he wouldn't have given us any of this bullshit.' And then he said, 'You should send him home, not Pat.' I said that I thought NOW wouldn't go along with that as they needed a camera helicopter pilot and Al and Pat would be deeply unhappy if the hero of their documentary were to go. Colin's solution for a pilot was that we should get my husband Simon out to fly G-JEFA. 'He'll soon sort this lot out,' he said.

'Let's talk about this later with Heinz,' I said. 'We're all tired and over-emotional, I think we need a cold beer. And let's face it,' I added, 'we had a much better time without them today.'

Way back when NOW had agreed to sponsor us and I had discussed cameramen with Rob Bannagan, he had said we should change the camera crew every couple of weeks, that the tiredness and stress would be too much. I had argued that I felt sure whoever came would be bitterly disappointed to be sent back – that they would want to stay the course. (It was also a question of cost – how expensive would it be to ferry camera crew in all directions.) But Rob was right, and much, much later I heard that very experienced military planners try to limit sorties to three weeks because a small team starts to undergo huge pressure after just three weeks.

Colin and I took a taxi to the hotel and all thoughts of changing crews went by the board, as we were immediately confronted by a barrage of questions and decisions. Where had we been? Why were we so late? We were told that Heinz had been checking out distances on his Flight Star programme and had said, 'Do you realise that this route isn't much further to Cuba than the Mexican one? We all think we should go.' Al then turned to me and said, 'This morning you tell me we're not going, that we've all got to stick together. I phoned Lawrence and told him Cuba is out. He'll have cancelled their tickets. Now the vote seems to be that we should go. We've got to make a decision quickly.'

I had always said that Colin and I should stick together but now Colin was pressing for us to go without him. 'Look, I'll just zigzag around here. There's no way I can make it there and back to Cuba, not with this weather. I feel really bad that I'm stopping you from going, and it will give me a chance to rest my arm.' Then, trying to make light of his own disappointment at not going, he laughed and said, 'Well, anyway, why would I want to go to Havana? I'm sure it's a shitty place!' Heinz, Colin and I went along to Heinz's room to check the route and where we would stop overnight and refuel. We left the others with their beers in Al's room, where he and Pat were busying themselves with their editing machines and satellite dishes.

Tallahassee looked like the sensible place for a midway overnight stop. We were 638 miles from Tallahassee and Havana was a further 792. We could all stick together as far as Tallahassee. And then, while we were busy discussing route and details, Colin left the room. I thought he had just gone to the loo, but he didn't come back. When I phoned his room later there was no reply. I wondered whether he was more upset than he had made out. I thought back to all those months ago when Colin and I had been plotting our route, the original route where we had planned to go 300 miles up the Amazon and then to island-hop our way north through all the Caribbean islands. We had laughingly said we would need to spend quite a long time there checking out the islands, and all our friends were opting to come and visit us on either one dream island or another. Now Colin wouldn't be making it to any of them. I had always reassured him we would stick together come hell or high water, and there I was being a real turncoat with no excuse other than wanting to visit Cuba and the need to build up the necessary mileage to qualify for a world record. Of course I could do the zigzagging in the States, but then I convinced myself that Cuba makes a much more exciting story for people to follow on the website, which indeed it was.

Havana, Cuba had been another one of the key places along our route ever since we had found out that we could get clearances to fly in there. It seemed so mysterious and romantic and before our long delay in Japan we were to have met Fidel Castro himself. That had been organised by my good friend David Tang, the Honorary Consul General for Cuba in Hong Kong (the first!) – and the exclusive importer of Cuban cigars to Hong Kong. David is always to be seen with a large fat Cuban cigar in his mouth. He was to have given a party for us, and many friends had made plans to come. Sadly, now, with all of the delays, neither Fidel nor David were available. I said I would send David another fax to tell him we were once more 'on' for Cuba, as he said he would get 'his man' Roberto Pelayo to help us out.

The following morning I turned on my television while I was getting dressed and the headlines were about storms in Mexico. The south-east coast had been devastated and all airports were closed, including Minatitlan where we would have been. Half an hour later at breakfast Colin was saying, 'I told you I'd had a gut feeling.' Al didn't say anything.

The Galveston weather was good, but the forecast was for deteriorating conditions as we neared Florida, where the weather looked as though it wasn't going to be much better than Mexico. The satellite pictures were showing a mass of storm cells, while the rest of the USA was enjoying really good, stable weather. Colin decided to be 'self-sufficient', taking his overnight bag with him instead of leaving it in the Cessna. It was just as well, as he never made it to Tallahassee that night. We all set out together, routing once more along the coast, and we stayed together as far as New Orleans where Q had suggested that we, the helicopters, stop off for lunch, landing on a helipad in the centre of town. This wasn't very friendly to Colin, but he couldn't afford the time to stop as there was still 355 miles to go to Tallahassee. We didn't see Colin again until Charleston, four days later.

We landed on a helipad on top of a multi-storey car park, with a stadium on one side and a spaghetti-junction of super highways on the other, right in the centre of town. It was such a novelty to be able to land on a rooftop in the centre of town. The CAA rules in the UK don't allow single engine helicopters to land in built-up areas. Al, Q and I had a whistle-stop lunch and a tantalising glimpse of New Orleans where none of us had ever been before. I remember Q had a seafood platter, everything deep-fried in batter including a whole crab. The atmosphere between the three of us was reasonably OK. Everyone made an effort, but I didn't feel very relaxed after the scene the night before. Knowing how they felt about me made me uncomfortable. We took a taxi back to the helipad, where Al did some filming and asked me to do an update standing in front of G-MURY. We flew over the old town, routing along the Mississippi with its busy river traffic, and I was happy to see that there were still paddle-boats amongst the more modern traffic of high-speed power boats and container ships.

I tried to contact Colin several times, but for the most part I was kept busy talking to one military airfield after another, requesting permission to transit their zones or having to avoid restricted airspace and danger zones. (The coastal route from New Orleans to Tallahassee is just one mass of controlled airspace and airfields.)

Q and I had taken separate routes and I landed in Tallahassee at 7 p.m., some 15 minutes before them. Colin hadn't arrived. I tried his mobile. He was in Biloxi, just 73 miles from New Orleans. He said he had encountered severe turbulence and his arm was giving him stick so he'd put down there. 'I must have left my credit card in my other bag. Thank goodness you gave me that cash, just hope it will be enough until we meet up.' He then said, sounding pretty fed up, 'I had to hunt all over town for a really inexpensive hotel, this place is packed. I eventually got a room at this motel. I guess it's OK and at least it's cheap.' We chatted some more and I told him about our lunch stop and how he would have a busy time on the radio the following day with all the airfields. He laughed and said, 'Oh, you know me, I'll either be at sea level or 13,000 feet and probably won't have to talk to anyone.' I found the rest of the team relaxing over a beer in the hotel bar and suggested we have dinner together: 'How about we all meet up at the steak bar down the road?' Heinz and I waited, but none of the others came. Once again we hadn't discussed departure time and – another omission – I didn't have Q and Pat's room numbers.

At 7.30 the following morning I phoned the front desk and asked the concierge to put me through to their rooms. The phones rang and rang with no reply. I had a shower and tried to phone again but there was still no reply from either room. Once more I contacted the front desk and they said they would send the housekeeper to wake them up. She apparently had to shake Q before he woke up.

I went to the lobby, ordered a taxi, and waited. There was still no sign of anyone, by which time I was getting twitchy. Again I went to the desk, the concierge phoned Q's room, no reply. This time I went with the housekeeper. I also had to shake him to wake him up. And then I went back to the lobby where the concierge told me he had managed to get Mr Doyle on the phone. I had a second cup of coffee, and waited, getting more and more stressed out. Finally Q sauntered in. 'C'mon, c'mon!' he said with a smile and gave me a big hug. 'Relax, I promise you we won't be late, you've got to relax. Have you had breakfast? Must have some breakfast.'

So we had breakfast (the breakfast room was right in the lobby), and I tried to relax. But why should I have to have the added task of getting these guys moving in the morning? So I told Q as much. He turned on all the charm – and he can be very charming. I relaxed a little and Pat finally arrived with a cheerful 'Hi! Am I late?' The last laugh was on me, though. We were halfway to the airport when I realised I had left my bumbag on the chair where we had breakfast. The final delay was of my making. Happily some nice honest person handed in my bag, which had *everything* in it.

At the airport we checked the Met. There was a belt of storm cells to the north of Miami but we thought we could probably weave our way through. Heinz phoned from the hotel. He thought otherwise, that the weather looked too tough for the Cessna. I told him that Colin was going to attempt to push further south and that would leave them the furthest north, but it was their call. We could always put down in a field and the Cessna couldn't.

We took off, intending to route down Florida's west coast. We flew over the Okefenokee Swamp, which looked dark and forbidding in the rain with storms all around. I shuddered at the possibility, however remote, of having to do a forced landing in those mangrove swamps, and could picture all too vividly all the hungry alligators. The weather was deteriorating rapidly. Tallahassee advised us that the weather was better on the east coast and so we turned east and re-routed north of Orlando where we were confronted by a black wall of storms – total obliteration. There appeared to be what looked like the tiniest of gaps through the middle, just a glimmer of light, and we went for it, getting thoroughly bounced around, but only for a few moments and then we were through. From there on we were in the clear and had a good flight south down the east coast over the luxurious homes lining the shore for hundreds of miles.

The Cessna had decided to give it a try and had made it – just. According to Al it had been absolutely terrifying. They had been thrown all over the place and he never, ever wanted to experience anything like it again. Colin only got as far as Tallahassee. Avoiding storms he had covered a distance of 535 miles – instead of the straight-line distance of 282 miles from Biloxi to Tallahassee. Once again he had to hunt all over the place for a room.

We arrived in Miami before G-EELS at 3.20 p.m., with more than enough time to get to Cuba before dark. We parked at Signature Aviation, our ground handlers. Air Traffic Control were very sceptical as to whether we had clearance to fly to Cuba – they don't get too many private flights going there as Americans still cannot get visas for Cuba. We patiently explained that we were British and so were our aircraft. All was finally settled, but then we found we had left all our Jeppesen Airways charts in the Cessna and we were once more back on airways for the flight to Cuba. How quickly we had forgotten all that hassle after the freedom of flying through North America.

The flight plan required that we list all the reporting points. I had to go out to my helicopter and get them off my GPS. Next we needed the Met, which we were advised we could pull up ourselves off the TV monitors; Signature Flight Support were not very supportive. Months later I received an invoice from them for $120 for the Met.

Q, relaxing in a chair, said, 'No hurry, no hurry, it will take them ages to process our flight plan – no point hanging around the helicopters in this heat.' I was all for pushing on as soon as possible, we still had over 300 miles to go to Havana. Then G-EELS arrived and we all exchanged hairy experiences. Suddenly Q was all go, 'Come on! Come on! Time to go! Got to go!' and was out the door. This was a habit of his that I was all too familiar with.

I climbed quickly aboard G-MURY, started up and tried to get Q on 123.45 – nothing. I tried listening in on various airport ground frequencies to see if I could hear Q – nothing. I was in the middle of putting my flight plan in the GPS when I saw Q taxiing off out of the parking bay, without saying a word to me. We always check to see that the other one is ready before take off. Had he got his sound turned down? Miami is a very busy international airport, so all I could do was follow and assume he had asked for clearance for take-off for 'a formation of two'. I was going to look pretty stupid if I started asking for separate instructions. I was not happy and I was only half ready, my flight plan still not installed. We took off. I kept on trying to get him on 123.45 and tried several of the airport frequencies (there were many) but had no success. It wasn't until we were five miles out that he finally came through, asking if I was there.

'Why didn't you tell me you were taking off?' I asked him.

'It's all a question of priorities, it's all priorities, you'll just have to accept that,' he said with supreme arrogance. I then said something about his priorities and he replied, 'Just shut up and calm down!'

Under normal circumstances neither of us would have talked or behaved like this to each other, it was all just getting crazy. A few minutes later he started making ultra-friendly remarks like, 'Jeffa, do you see that police car stuck in the mud?' The last thing I wanted to do was talk to him. Then, 'Jeffa, do you read me? Jeffa, are you there?' So I would have to make some non-committal response. He kept up the odd jokey remarks as we headed south towards the Florida Keys and Havana. We were late.

An hour and a half out and just over halfway we could see storms building at a rather alarming rate. I tried to concentrate on how stunning the light effects were and what wonderful paintings they would make, rather than on the potential danger. I took a number of photos. With half an hour to go, we were at reporting point Golfo, just off the coast of Cuba to the east of Havana and had started our descent from 6,000 feet (the Cuban authorities had insisted that we fly IFR). The storm clouds that had been illuminated with heavenly light were now black and menacing, night was closing and it looked as though an almighty storm was trying to race us to Havana.

I pulled full power, as did Q, and we dashed towards Jose Marti International Airport. We asked for permission to fly direct in to the apron. The Tower, rather surprisingly, asked us if we would do a fly past! 'Uh, tomorrow,' Q said. We landed as the first huge drops of rain splashed on to the dry asphalt and then the wind hit like a sledgehammer. Roberto Pelayo, holding a rather ineffectual umbrella against the horizontal onslaught, welcomed us. He told us that it rains most evenings but 'today is very bad'. (The following day he told us that it had been the worst storm of the year.) G-EELS had landed half an hour ahead of us and had made it to the Melia Cohiba Hotel without getting wet. We were soaked to the skin.

Roberto introduced us to Jorge and Raul. He had organised for Jorge Lopez Mendez and Raul Perez, representatives of the Minister of Tourism – two charming and good-looking young men – to look after us. They would take us around town the following day. Everything was laid on: cars at our disposal, hotel, scenic tours of the city and even a night at 'Tropicana', a show-biz cabaret spectacular.

Havana was better than any of us could have imagined. It was hard to believe that this was the oppressed country of Fidel Castro that we had read so much about over the years. The Havana we saw, Ernest Hemingway's Havana, was a city of sunshine and music, a city steeped in culture. We drank in the old Spanish-style architecture and the more recent old colonial buildings, the wide avenues and narrow cobbled streets, and the biggest collection of working 1950s American cars in the world.

Jorge and Raul did us proud. We went to Revolution Square, which can hold a million people and where Fidel Castro had made so many impassioned speeches, as had the country's national hero Jose Marti, perhaps Cuba's most revered patriot, I suppose not only because he wanted independence from the Spaniards, but also because he was determined that the country would not become a territory or a puppet of the United States. Furthermore, he was convinced that the revolution must be fought by a revolutionary army controlled by civilian leaders so that, on independence, there would be economic and political justice for all citizens – not control by military leaders. His legend started at the early age of 17 when he was deported from Cuba for criticising the Spanish military and he spent most of his life abroad writing passionate poems and prose. But alas, he was one of the earliest victims of the revolution, dying in 1895 before seeing independence itself.

Jorge and Raul showed us with pride the boat that had carried Castro and his boys to Cuba (now high and dry in the grounds of the government buildings). They proudly told us how, in 1957, Castro and Che Guevara had launched their revolution, how they had trained 80 young men in Mexico and then sailed across in their small boat to Las Coloradas in Cuba. We heard how they had landed and hidden in the swamps and mud, where the army bombed them. They had split up into three groups, Castro's group was reduced to twelve men and six guns and then Castro said, 'This is the end. Now we win the war!'

We visited the most famous cigar factory in Havana, Partagas, on the side of Capitolio (Cuba's copy of Capitol Hill). We went into the inner courtyard, with its cool archways and the all-pervading smell of tobacco, where we bought cigars. (Later we found out that it was strictly forbidden to take cigars from Cuba into the USA.) Jorge said, 'Now I will take you to La Bodeguita where we will drink mojitos.' He went on to explain 'Mojitos is our national drink, very refreshing, we make it with lime and rum and lots of mint, Ernest Hemingway, he drank mojitos every day at La Bodeguita.' They were very proud of Ernest Hemingway.

So, we went to La Bodeguita, a tiny packed restaurant on about four levels, consisting of practically nothing more than a stairwell with a few tables squeezed around it and graffiti on every square inch of the once-white plaster walls, every customer having left a message. There was an excellent bar at the top where we sat on high stools drinking our first delicious mojitos, which tasted deceptively non-alcoholic.

Next we went to Ambas Mundas, the hotel where Hemingway lived before buying his farm. We went up on to the roof garden and had more mojitos under the cool awnings looking out over the rooftops of Havana, while a three-man band played lively Latin American music. And then we went to La Mina restaurant in the Playa des Armas where there was yet another wonderful band playing. Half the tables were outdoors in the tree-shaded courtyard with peacocks and regular farmyard hens and cockerels wandering around.

It seemed like the streets were filled with laughter and music and in one square there was a troupe of acrobats, clowns and men walking on stilts. The team were all having a good time. We more or less stayed together. I felt that there was some warmth and friendship, but this was no doubt helped by the mojitos. Late in the day we returned to the Melia Cohiba and saw a newly-wed couple just departing in a bright red, 1950s convertible Cadillac, bedecked with ribbons and balloons. To round off a perfect day we went to Tropicana, as the guests of Rogelio Rodriguez de la Torre, the director. 'Welcome to the Eighth Wonder of the World!' he said and he wasn't far off. It was an extravaganza to end all extravaganzas: the music, the lighting, the outdoor setting (the performance the night before had been rained off), the costumes and the near-naked girls dressed in not much more than G strings, tassels and feather boa headdresses, dancing on the circular stage, on platforms in the trees and amongst the audience. We learnt that it was Fidel Castro's birthday. My only sadness was that Colin had not been there. By all accounts he was having a dreary time at the Holiday Inn in Tallahassee.

EIGHT

Cuba to Montreal

14 - 21 August

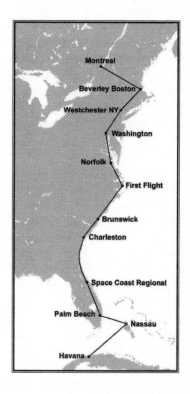

Montreal
Beverley Boston
Westchester NY
Washington
Norfolk
First Flight
Brunswick
Charleston
Space Coast Regional
Palm Beach
Nassau
Havana

DAY 76

Back to the realities of a team divided. This time it was Al. Not a big deal, but upsetting nonetheless, especially when I thought that the day before had done so much to improve relations.

The night before, I asked the team to be ready for an 8.45 a.m. departure but, after everyone left the lobby, Jorge said that the cars couldn't be at the hotel before 9 a.m. I didn't bother to give anyone the revised time as it always takes a little while to pay bills etc., and the airport authorities wanted us to all leave together, including the Cessna crew.

I got up the following morning at 6 a.m., had a shower and phoned James Barker and Jo Jo in England. They needed the time updates and changes. James was trying to update our fuel suppliers, EAFS, as to when and which airfields we would be coming into. He also asked me if I could do a quick piece on the bat phone for our technical sponsors. He wanted a minute for each as he was optimistically trying to put together pages on them for our 'Return Home' press pack. James told me that NOW had finally agreed to put an Operation Smile link on the opening page of their website, something I had been asking for since before we ever left England. Jo Jo told me that Jason Brake (who worked for Nick Harris, our PR man) would be coming to Nassau and was arranging a press conference. 'It's just a small island,' I said, 'I can't think that Nassau warrants a press conference.' Anyhow, it was too late for changes, he was already on his way.

The next thing I knew it was 9 a.m. I grabbed my bag and rushed downstairs where I was confronted by a thunderous-looking Al who said in cold and measured tones, 'I would appreciate it, that if we are leaving at nine, you tell me it is nine and not a quarter to nine. I'm always punctual.'

I apologised. 'Al, I'm sorry.' I was going to explain some more, but he had already turned on his heel and walked away. There was no sign of Q, and it turned out he had left for the airport an hour earlier. To make the situation worse, the cars then didn't show, we had to wait for a further half an hour for them to arrive. When we got to the airport Q was prancing around saying, 'I've done everything. I've done the flight plans, refuelled the helicopters, I've been ready to go for hours. Why are you so late?' Thankfully, however, the day got better.

Having said farewell and a million thanks to Jorge and Raul – who said that we must come back again and that we should have stayed at least one more night as 'dinner at El Floridita is a must, it is known as the "Cradle of the Daiquiris."' – we headed, low-level, north-east to Nassau, 341 miles away across the Caribbean Sea. What a contrast to our crossing of two days before, where we had been dodging thunderstorms with glimpses of an angry, grey sea 6,000 feet below. Now we were skimming the waters, which ranged from the deepest blue to the purest of translucent turquoise, with white sands, coral reefs and coral islands. We even landed on one coral outcrop. For much of the journey we were able to see the seabed, it was so shallow and so clear.

Jason's press conference had an attendance of one! There were, rather surprisingly, three newspapers in Nassau – but only one turned up. So did the British High Commissioner, whom I mistook for a reporter. Jason had organised rows of chairs, a microphone and our 'NOW Challenge' backdrop with all the sponsors' names on. Heinz put in a loyal appearance, the journalist got an exclusive, the High Commissioner congratulated us and we all had a cup of tea. We thanked them for coming. That was that.

Jason, Heinz and I went out onto the swimming pool terrace overlooking the bay and enjoyed ice cold beers, watching Pat, in the distance, doing a lengthy interview with Pascal. I phoned Colin, now at the Space Centre. He had done little flying, his arm was feeling much better but he sounded down in the dumps. I decided it was not the moment to mention how much we had enjoyed Havana and so just said, 'See you in Charleston. We should be there around four.'

'Have a good flight,' he said.

Shortly after leaving Nassau at 8.30 a.m. the next morning, with storms already building, we spotted water spouts, the first I had ever seen. I circled one of them with Pat filming G-MURY, but was quite relieved when Q said Pat had got enough footage and I was able to move further away. The thing was, you could see the water spouts very clearly from certain angles and then suddenly they weren't there. I wasn't keen to fly into one. I got away unscathed, however, and we had a safe onwards flight.

We landed and did customs at Palm Beach and then flew onwards to Charleston. We overflew Cape Canaveral and were given permission to do a low fly-past along the immense Space Shuttle runway. I was flying behind Q and longed to say, 'Don't you want to film me?' One little red helicopter on that vast runway would have looked so good. Other than that the day went well. The ETA of 4 p.m. that I had given Colin was not far out – we landed at 3.55 p.m. Colin had already landed and the Cessna, we were told, was due in shortly. Even the aggro side of things had been OK. That was until, driving into town, Q and I got into a stupid argument about an unpaid HeliAir account and him using my mobile phone. It ended with him saying, 'And I'm still waiting for an apology from you for being one hour late at Jose Marti Airport!' . . . we all needed a change.

When we arrived at the hotel, the first thing I did when I got to my room was to phone Colin, and the moment I saw him I overreacted, I just burst into tears. Colin looked alarmed, sympathetic, confused and wanted to know what had happened. I was in the middle of blurting out all my woes and how I couldn't take any more, when Heinz arrived saying, 'I am not going to have that man Al in my aeroplane any longer!' Things were going from bad to disastrous.

Heinz had been in a hurry to get away from Nassau before the storms. He urged all the team to be quick. There was a big storm heading directly towards the airfield, and once it hit there would be the inevitable delays. First of all Pascal announced that she had to make an urgent phone call, which couldn't have had anything to do with the next few hotel bookings as these had all been taken care of by Operation Smile, whose home base was Norfolk, Virginia, our next stop after Charleston. In Washington the following night, Heinz's friend Tom Krauz was giving us all a wonderful freebie at his Hay Adams Hotel. Then Al had said that he too had to make a phone call. Heinz argued that they had to get away otherwise they could be in for an indefinite delay. Al was adamant he had to make his call and sauntered off across the apron. The net result was that the storm came romping in, all VFR flights were cancelled, so they had to re-file for an IFR flight and had been stuck in the plane on the ground for an hour and a half. Heinz was furious and said to Al: 'In future, when, as captain of this plane, I say we have got to leave, I expect you to comply – now look what's happened.' Al got on his NOW high horse and told Heinz that he couldn't tell him what he could and couldn't do, and was very rude.

We were all wishing the camera crew out of our lives. I felt badly that Heinz was being given a bad time. I had invited him to come on this trip, and he had come along for the fun and the great adventure, but this was no fun. Heinz and Colin were keen for Q to go home, and to bring in Simon. I had my reservations, partly out of fear about the scene it would cause, partly because of the problems that it would create with HeliAir and, well, Q and I went back a long way. We had shared so many adventures and, ridiculous though it may seem, at the end of the day, despite all the arrogance and lateness and chippiness, I am genuinely fond of him.

Having Simon in his stead? The thought of having him along to lean on and to sort everyone out was so very tempting. I was sure he would soon have everyone united and working together. But I had to consider the risks. How sensible would it be to bring him in for what was the toughest leg of the whole trip? Good pilot though he was, he only had 300 flying hours to his credit. He would have no back-up co-pilot. Could I risk that? Could I live with myself if anything were to happen to him? Could I face my family and life without Simon? It just didn't bear thinking about.

Heinz and Colin both had full confidence in Simon. 'He's a good pilot, he'll manage,' Heinz said. I thought about the potential hazards we could be confronted with on that northern crossing. I was concerned enough about how I would manage if the going got rough. It would be a nightmare if I had to worry about Simon too as he had no experience of extreme weather and was unfamiliar with many of the instruments we had on board. But by far the biggest worry was that he doesn't know the meaning of fear.

I phoned Simon and, of course, he loved the idea of joining us. But he said there was no way he could, certainly not immediately. He was up to his eyebrows in work. 'Why don't you send Q home and have the helicopter crated up and sent back to England? I'll pay,' he said. I reminded him that a camera helicopter was part of the deal, part of the contract with NOW. 'Well, look, I'll have a word with Michael Johnson [the boss at NOW] and see what he has to say. At the very least he can talk with your cameramen.' Later that evening Heinz came and told me, with a rueful smile, 'Al just came and apologised, so I can hardly boot him out now.' Had Simon already spoken with Michael Johnson? I left a message for the camera crew telling them that Colin and I planned to leave the hotel at 6.45 a.m. I reminded them that we were all due in Norfolk at 3.30 p.m., where Operation Smile would be greeting us.

Colin and I departed the next morning, just before seven, but there was no sign of the others. I was both relieved and irritated. We couldn't hang around as head winds were forecast, and we were really keen to visit Kitty Hawk.

Kitty Hawk – just the name was magical. Kitty Hawk was where Wilbur and Orville Wright had made the first ever manned motorised flight. The airfield, First Flight, was 337 miles away, and just 67 miles from Norfolk, Virginia. The chances were that the camera crew would catch up with us in due course as I was planning to level-peg it with Colin. Colin said, 'It would be really good if we could drop in at Brunswick County Airport, there are a bunch of microlight pilots there. This bloke, the Airport Manager Howie Franklin, contacted me the other day and I said I'd try and visit if we had time.'

Brunswick was practically on our direct path and then we found that we had three knots of tail wind. It looked as though we had time, so in we went, and were given a very enthusiastic welcome. Lots of photographs were taken, and Howie, now retired, gave us a book of matches and lifesavers from Air Force One on which he had been chief pilot. We were only there for 15 minutes, the tail winds had increased to 15 knots, we were making excellent time and visibility was good.

Just before 1 p.m. we made our final approach for Runway 20 at First Flight, one mile to the west of Kill Devil Hills. We could see the monument on the slight rise of ground where the Wright brothers had launched themselves on that epic day back in 1903. The winds had strengthened still further and were gusting up to 30 knots from the west. The runway was lined with tall fir trees. I followed Colin in, and then it all happened so fast. One moment Colin was making a steady approach, the next he had hit massive wind sheer and was hurtling, tumbling towards the runway. There was no way he was going to pull out! G-NOWW was virtually standing on its right wing tip when it hit the runway at 60 miles an hour. The right wheel somehow touched first, then tipped crazily to the left before bouncing back to the right and careering off the runway into the long grass, heading straight for the trees. Colin managed to correct the wildly careening craft at the very last moment, and, still moving at an appallingly fast rate, succeeded in getting back onto the runway, where he regained full control and taxied to the grass parking area at the far end of the runway. 'That was by far the worst landing I've ever had' was his first comment. 'I thought I was a goner. That was dangerous.' I agreed.

'I made the mistake of trying to fly down that long runway. I'd have been all right if I'd landed short on the threshold.' He shook his head. I thought once again how even the greatest and most experienced pilots can make a wrong judgment, a near-catastrophic wrong judgment.

First Flight Airport was nothing more than the asphalt runway 02-20 with a grass parking area and a car park by the 02 threshold of the runway. We left our aircraft and joined the other visitors walking up the hill to the monument. Colin said, 'There's no way I can take off down that runway with that crosswind and that wind shear. I'd be a dead man.'

'Well, you nearly were,' I said. 'What can we do?'

'Let's take a look at the other end of the runway after we've seen the monument. Perhaps there is room to take off across the threshold.'

We climbed the hill and looked out across the fields, imagining how it must have been for the two brothers, Wilbur and Orville Wright, who, at precisely 10.35 a.m. on 17 December 1903, had made that first flight lasting only 12 seconds. The first flight in the history of the world in which a machine carrying a man had raised itself by its own power into the air in free flight, had sailed forward on a level course without a reduction of speed, and had finally landed without being wrecked.

They were the sons of a church bishop. Both bachelors who never finished school, they had a shared childhood fascination for flight, sparked, I'm delighted to say by a toy 'helicopter' driven by rubber bands brought home by their father. Their fascination became a hobby and finally an obsessive desire to achieve human flight.

They made three flights on that momentous day in 1903 and several hundred yards away we could see the stones marking the distances flown, each one just that little bit further than the last. To the right of them was the museum.

We decided to go and check out Colin's flight – to see whether it would be possible for him to take off at right angles from the existing runway – and then visit the museum if we had time. Down the hill we went, past the stones marking the flights, we passed the second stone marking Orville's 15 seconds of flight covering a distance of 200 feet and finally reached the third marker of Wilbur's flight of 59 seconds and 852 feet. We then made our way over to the 02 threshold of the runway, a hundred yards away. The fir trees on the nearside ended just before the threshold, but the trees on the far side formed a solid wall rising to over 50 feet, and it was all slightly sloping uphill. We then paced out the distance and checked that there were no holes, perimeter wires or ditches from the runway back towards Wilbur's furthest hop, which was at right angles to the runway and into wind. The ground was rough, covered in short, tough and extremely prickly thistles, but it was unbroken, more or less flat and free of obstacles.

Colin needed about 160 metres to be able to confidently clear the trees. We paced 80 metres, 100 metres; at 120 metres we crossed over the path leading to the final marker, 140 metres and there was a ditch. 'That will just have to do,' Colin said. 'I'm light enough on fuel – should be OK.'

We went and had the quickest of looks at the museum, but were unable to concentrate as our focus was on Colin's take-off. We felt divorced and apart from the other visitors. 'I'll go down by the path and hold back any visitors. What a shame Al's not here to film this,' I said. We had heard nothing from them.

'OK. I just hope I can time it so that that other plane doesn't see me,' Colin said with a grin before heading off back to the microlight. (There was a small plane giving joy rides of the area.)

Colin set off across the prickly fields. I could see why everyone was keeping to the paths as the thistles were so tough they went through the soles of my sneakers. I made my way along the path towards my 'crowd control' position. Colin had quite a way to go. When he was halfway back, in came G-JEFA. 'Well, at least Al will be able to film the take-off, even if he missed the landing,' I thought.

I wandered along the path and passed the second stone where a guide was holding forth to a large group of eager Japanese tourists. I wondered if they would make it as far as the third and final marker and what they would think if they did! I didn't have to wonder for long. Up until then I had seen few people venture as far as the furthest marker as the midday heat was intense. But, just as Colin appeared at the end of the taxiway and turned to cross the field, the tour group moved on towards the third marker stone. What was the guide going to say?

I went forward, blocking their path, and said, 'Uh, would you mind just waiting here a minute?' I went on hurriedly. 'You see that microlight over there, he's flying around the world, the first microlight to ever fly solo around the world.' They were now all looking interested. I quickly explained the situation and finished by saying, 'You are about to witness real live aviation history in the making!' By now quite a crowd had gathered with their cameras poised. Colin had crossed the path and was lining up for take-off. There was no sign of Al and Q, where were they? Surely Colin had told them what he was going to do?

Colin gave me the thumbs up and started to move across the grass. Video cameras went on and cameras started clicking. I cast a quick look at the guide, who thankfully looked as excited and tense as everyone else. Faster, faster, Colin was bouncing along the uneven ground, quickly gaining speed. Had he got enough room to clear the trees that were looming closer and closer and suddenly looked incredibly tall? Faster and faster, now bouncing alarmingly. Was the ground just too rough? Were the trees too tall? He lifted, and once airborne, rose steeply, clearing the trees by no more than a couple of feet. Everyone clapped and cheered. I thanked them all and headed back to G-MURY. Halfway back to my helicopter, G-EELS arrived.

Q and Al had joined up with the G-EELS crew when I met them all as they were headed towards the monument. I said hello to Al and Q who were nearest and gave a friendly wave in Heinz's direction. I didn't ask them why they hadn't come along to film Colin's take-off. I knew the answer I would get. I just said, 'Well, you missed Colin nearly killing himself.' Al, rather surprisingly, said he would like to do a short interview in front of the monument which was 200 yards away at the top of the hill. I told him that I'd promised Colin I would join him right away. 'A pity,' Al said. There were *so* many responses I could have made to that. Instead I just repeated that I'd told Colin I would join him and that I didn't want to be late for Operation Smile and that I hoped they would be on time. If only they had been on time.

Once airborne I quickly made contact with Colin and asked him how things were going. 'Oh the take-off, no problem, bit bumpy. I had to laugh when I saw you holding back that mob.' I told him what I had said to them and how they were watching history in the making, and asked 'Where are you now?'

'I've got 47 miles to run, I'm just about ten miles south of Currituck County Airfield, I'm up at 9,000 feet, tracking 330 degrees, engine's misfiring a bit.' As usual he was right on track. I pulled a little more power and started climbing. I wasn't unduly worried, Colin was always having problems with his engine. He kept me regularly updated as I slowly caught up with him.

Twenty-five miles out from Norfolk's International Airfield, Colin's engine was misfiring badly. 'Every time I try and pull more power the engine cuts out.' he said. Nineteen miles out: 'Keeps misfiring – wonder if I ought to land?' he said.

'Your call, Colin,' I said. I really couldn't advise him and of course we were both thinking of the reception awaiting us at Norfolk. Bill and Kathy Magee (the founder directors of Operation Smile) had advised us that the press would be there in force. I thought of the pressure I had been under with my magneto failure in California with all the press waiting.

Fifteen miles to run: 'I'll keep going. Keeps cutting, wish I could keep my height, but think I'll make it.' I had had Colin in sight for some miles and had come up on his left side. We were now down at 5,000 feet. At ten miles I told Colin I would call Norfolk for joining instructions. 'Norfolk, good afternoon, Golf Mike Uniform Romeo Yankee formation.' I gave them all our information and the Tower said that we were number one for a straight in on Runway 05.

Seven miles to go, we were down at 3,000 feet and then, with just five miles to run and cleared to land, Colin came on the air. 'Engine's gone! Can't re-start, I'm going for that playing field.' He only had two choices, there was a golf course, but there were people on it, and a playing field, which was empty but surrounded by trees. Both looked horribly far away, but there was nothing underneath us, it was all built up, no open areas. I got on the radio to Norfolk. 'Golf Mike Uniform Romeo Yankee – May Day! May Day! May Day for Golf November Oscar Whisky Whisky – the microlight has an engine failure – making an emergency landing – am following him down!' The airfield acknowledged, and said something, but I was just too busy watching and praying that Colin was going to make it over the trees. Could he do it? The trees were alarmingly high, one especially. He swooped to the left of the biggest tree and missed the top of the one beside it by inches, dropped fast to the ground and stood on the brakes, hauling on the wing, the high mesh perimeter fence rushing towards him. From my position it looked as though he was going to go hurtling into the wires. I didn't see how he could stop in time. But he did. At the last moment he veered to the right and finally came to a halt with the left wing tip a couple of feet from the fence.

I came to a hover at about a hundred feet. I told Norfolk that the microlight was safely on the ground and that I was landing. I shut down as quickly as I could and rushed over to Colin who was clambering out of his microlight looking rather relaxed! I just ran over and gave him a big hug – I think I was more shaken than he was.

'That was a bit of a close one,' he said as we looked around at our surroundings. The playing field and school buildings were surrounded by trees and more houses. We could see no one and there was an uncanny silence – then we heard a siren in the distance, and another and another and then there was a helicopter circling overhead. The fire brigade were the first to arrive, closely followed by the media, two ambulances and several police cars. The police quickly cordoned off both our aircraft with yellow tape saying 'scene of the crime'! Next came the highway patrol and a whole mass of more TV crews and press. And last of all, of course, were our very own camera crew who had missed everything. I saw them circling overhead: what idiots they must have felt, how they must have kicked themselves. To add to their injury, they were refused clearance to land. So, after circling overhead for some time, they continued on to the airfield, and finally arrived at the 'scene of the crime' just as Colin and I were being made to give separate statements in separate cars.

Kathy Magee, with Missy DiBona and the Operation Smile contingent, arrived around the same time as our crew. I'd had endless correspondence with Missy over the last year and finally we got to meet. Kathy said the first they knew that something was going on was when all the media who had come to meet us at the airfield started disappearing at speed. Operation Smile were delighted by the end result, the publicity was beyond their wildest dreams. Kathy did say to Colin that she really appreciated all he had done, but please don't go to such lengths on their behalf again! That evening Bill and Kathy gave a big reception in our honour at their lovely home. Colin, the hero of the day, arrived rather late as the police would not let him fly to the airfield (I was given permission). He had to completely dismantle his microlight, including taking the wing to pieces, with all the many wires on top securing his aerials. He then had to load it all onto a truck and take it to the airport. But he was looking happy, he was alive and being given a helping hand by the lovely Janine from Operation Smile. He said with a laugh, 'I nearly died twice today, I'm ready to party!' We had a lovely party, Bill made a moving speech and talked about Operation Smile. Colin and I said a few words of thanks.

Colin reckoned he needed to spend six hours overhauling his engine, but it was only 141 miles to Washington so the chances looked good that he would make it the following day. But he never did. After partying the night before, celebrating being alive, he was moving rather slowly the next morning, so it was 10 a.m. before he started work. Then he came with us to look at the 'flying hospital' aeroplane – the enormous L-1011 that Operation Smile had used on their 'World Journey of Hope' in '99, which just happened to be at the airfield – and this delayed him still further.

The World Journey of Hope '99 was a nine-week global tour designed to raise attention and awareness about Operation Smile. Medical volunteers travelled aboard the L-1011, supporting Operation Smile's efforts at local hospitals. During those nine weeks, thousands of volunteers performed facial and reconstructive surgery on more than 5,300 disfigured children, just as they do during annual missions to 18 countries each year to correct cleft palates and other facial deformities on children and young adults – all free of charge. I had seen Operation Smile in action during the World Journey of Hope in Kenya, and what an emotional experience that was. I was so moved by the poignant sight of a long line of mothers and fathers, clutching their small babies or holding the hands of young children. Resignation, suffering, despair, you could see it all. Many of them had walked for days to get there, having got word on the bush telegraph. They had heard of miracles and they got one. To see the incredible joy on a mother's face when her precious baby is handed back to her, whole and perfect and knowing that child would now be able to have a life, a normal life – well, I was in tears most of the time. In developing countries there is so often a stigma attached to deformities, they are considered to be 'bad luck'. The child would be considered bad luck and the family too in some cases. The children would often be hidden indoors. Many babies with hare lips would have cleft palates, meaning that they were unable to suckle. The chances of them surviving are virtually nil.

I think it was only when Bill Magee talked to us, followed by that visit to the Journey of Hope, that the full importance of what Operation Smile does came home to our team. What a dedicated team Bill and Kathy have; what great work they do. I'm only sorry that Bill has to spend so much of his precious time on fund-raising when he could be operating. At least all monies go direct to source with the minimum spent on administration.

We all felt good for our brief stay in Norfolk. It did us all good to step outside our small, fractured team world, even if only momentarily, to be with Bill and Kathy and their dedicated team and to be happy that we were also trying to raise awareness and funds for such a worthy cause. I was anxious to continue on to Washington where the helicopters were having their 50-hour service. Adrian James from HeliAir was waiting. Everyone was looking forward to two nights in Washington DC. We left Colin working on the microlight.

He stripped the engine down, rebuilt it, and by 5 p.m. was ready to do a test flight. Norfolk gave him permission to climb and circle directly over the airfield. Janine went too. Two hours later he phoned me to say he wouldn't be making Washington that night. After the test flight, he had landed, made a few adjustments, said his goodbyes and thanks and taken off for Washington. He said, 'The engine still wasn't really right. I realised it would be dark by the time I reached Washington, there was that much head wind, and I couldn't risk it so I returned to the airfield. The funny thing was that all the Operation Smile team had left, but Kathy was driving home and just happened to look up and saw me heading back to the airfield. So she came back to get me.'

'Well, that was a bit of luck, but what a bummer that you're still there.'

'Yes, and I think I've got to get a new engine. This one's had it. I stripped it down and it's still running rough. I don't think I can risk this engine for getting across to Greenland and Iceland. I have talked to Jim Cunliffe and Jim says that the Rotax engines are made in Canada and the agents won't ship them over the border or some such nonsense. Anyhow, I think I can make it to Montreal, so Jim says he can come out and help me install it if that's all right with you.' I told him that of course it was all right and hoped NOW would foot the bill. 'But how confident do you feel about making it to Montreal?' I asked.

'Well, I'll just go nice and gentle, not lean it off and not run full power and with a bit of luck it should be OK.' I said something to the effect of what a relief it would be when we got to Canada and Colin asked how Washington was. 'Well, this hotel is fabulous and Heinz's friend, Tom Crouse, the general manager, is doing us proud. We've all got lovely rooms and I've got a stunning view of the White House and you'll miss out on the banquet Tom is giving us this evening. Do you know I just had a feeling you weren't going to make it and you know the weather forecast for tomorrow is really lousy. Jamie McCallum, Lawrence Duffy and Dave Ullman are all here, and as you know, we are going to have the long-overdue "rallying meeting" tomorrow morning. I could have done with your support. But of course you have to do the safe thing.'

'Yes, I really had no choice. I wish I could be there to support you, but Heinz will be with you, and Jamie. I always seem to miss out on the nice places – first Havana and now Washington.'

'It's really bad luck. So, what now?' I said.

'Oh, Operation Smile are being really lovely and Janine is taking me to the Amusement Park.' I began to feel less sorry for Colin and more so for me. I hadn't told Colin that Heinz would not be around in the morning to support me. He and Tom Kraus were having a game of golf.

Jamie McCallum had come out from England to look after our PR in Washington, New York and Boston and Lawrence Duffy to go through film details with his crew. Dave Ullman was now back with us and would be staying with us all the way to England, to give the camera crew some more technical support. Tom Kraus laid on a magnificent feast in his elegant banquet room covered in murals depicting historical scenes. Dave somewhat blotted his copybook by apparently telling Tom Kraus that the murals were 'all wrong' and that the furniture in the front hall was a disaster, too old fashioned! Tom laughingly recounted this to Heinz the following day over their game of golf.

The next morning the weather was dreadful – low cloud, wind and rain. We had the meeting in my room. I tried to hide my nervousness and tried to sound cheerful and encouraging, giving a rallying talk to that roomful of men. I said how I had made many mistakes and that with the wisdom of hindsight there was much that I would have done differently. I knew everyone had been under lots of stress, and we had all said things at times that we didn't mean. We were often tired and we all had had to put up with each other's company for a long time. And then I said, 'But we only have two more weeks to go, I hope, so let's make a great big effort. What we are doing is pretty darned fantastic and it would be a shame to spoil it all now.' I then said a few more things about appreciating everyone and finished by asking if anyone else had anything to say. No one did, just a few murmurs of appreciation and everyone departed.

Jamie and I went out to the airport to see Adrian James who was working on the helicopters, and to do an interview with the *Washington Post*. Jamie thought that the meeting had gone well. I said that it would have been nice if a few of the others had said something, but he thought that it hadn't been necessary or particularly appropriate. He said, 'You know they're all good guys, you've all been together a long time and it's not easy.' And to that I had to agree.

Adrian said he wouldn't be finished on the helicopters before midday, and then, on doing a final check on the magnetos, he noticed one tiny filament sticking out of the casing joining the cable to the magneto. There was one single thread holding the cable together. The cable in question was the one leading to the thrice-replaced right magneto. The wire had been bent this way and that so many times that threads must have been quietly separating for some time and hidden from sight inside the casing. It had only been thanks to Adrian's eagle-eye and making such a thorough final check that I had been saved from a fourth magneto failure.

Colin arrived at our next stop, Westchester, before we ever took off. He phoned me on my mobile, seconds before we were leaving, rotors running, and said: 'I'm on the ground.' I thought he had made yet another emergency landing: 'Christ! Are you all right?' He replied that he had already arrived, but had no idea what hotel we were staying in. Neither did I. I tried to get Q on the radio, but he was chatting to Al and despite endless hand waving and more tries on the radio, I failed to get him. I had to shut down and run across the apron to where he was parked. He didn't know either. But he did have Pascal's phone number and when he managed to get through to her she told him that Operation Smile had booked us all in the Sheraton Hotel. What he hadn't heard was the 'Stamford' part. There was no Sheraton in Westchester where Colin was.

I had a great flight. Ronald Reagan Airport is slap bang in the middle of Washington DC. The camera crew and I took off, getting stunning views of the city, the skies washed clean and clear after the previous day of wind and rain. We flew along the Potomac River past the White House and the Cenotaph monument. Then, half an hour later, when we reached an equally haze-free, crystal-clear New York, we were given permission to fly up the East River, across Central Park, around 'The Lady' (the Statue of Liberty) as many times as we wanted, at 300 feet, and then once more up the Hudson, passing the twin towers of the World Trade Centre, taking lots of photos. I was so pleased with the one in this book, which captured G-JEFA, centrally placed, passing the towers. Now, as I write this, it's 23 September 2001 and when I look at that photo I say a prayer for all those who died on 11 September and their loved ones. While watching the events unfold I was consumed by shock, disbelief, sorrow, anger and then pride in the stories of heroism emerging. The world as we knew it has changed forever.

Stamford, Connecticut, was miles from Westchester Airport where we landed and, much to the unhappiness of all those wanting a night out, New York was in the opposite direction. It took our taxi driver an hour and a half to find our hotel. We took 40 minutes to get to Stamford, the rest of the time was spent driving round and round in circles (our taxi turned out to be a New York City registered cab and had never been to Stamford) trying to find the wretched Sheraton Hotel. Nobody else seemed to know where it was either. The Sheraton had recently been bought by the Western Hotel Group and we kept being directed back to the same place – and Stamford is all one-way streets. I phoned Colin a couple of times, but his directions were not too good and finally he put me on to Pascal, who proved her team worth by giving us immaculate directions. This was Pascal's swansong, though, as she would leave us in Boston.

Over dinner, Colin told Heinz and me (the others had gone in to New York City) that he had a big send-off from Norfolk. Janine had driven him to the airport at 6 a.m. where all the local press and TV crews were waiting expectantly, no doubt in the hope of more entertainment. He was Norfolk's 'man of the hour', everyone turned up to see him take off and tools were downed. Happily for Colin, all had gone well. He climbed to 8,000 feet and set off towards New York, staying high. 'But the engine was rough and when I was coming in here it cut out at 2,500 feet but I managed to restart it. I'll be glad when we get to Montreal and get that new engine.' I asked him how he had managed to find the hotel. He told us he ended up waiting for the Cessna: 'I just went to sleep in the grass until they arrived.'

Colin and I were in the hotel lobby at 8.30 a.m. the following morning. There was no sign of the New York City goers. We were all invited to lunch with my friends Fred and Susie Winthrop at their beach house in Ipswich and the weather was beautiful. We took the direct route because of Colin's engine, sadly missing out on the coastal route over Nantucket, Martha's Vineyard and the Boston Lighthouse.

Rhode Island, Connecticut and Boston are home country for me. I was born in Providence, Rhode Island, on 11 June 1940, the same day and same year as Fred Winthrop, just up the road in Boston. War had broken out and my parents decided it would be best for my pregnant American mother to take my sister Gillian and stay with her parents in Providence where my grandfather was a professor at Brown University. My thoughts naturally turned to my family and I recalled how, in 1910, my great-grandfather had taken my grandmother to Squantum Field near Boston to watch Graham White's attempt to win the $10,000 Boston Globe Award by flying around the Boston lighthouse and across the harbour. Thousands were gathered to watch this unheard-of spectacle; few if any had ever seen a flying machine (it was only seven years earlier that the Wright brothers had made those first historic flights). The crowd were utterly silent, many were praying, but when he lifted off and headed out across the harbour there was thunderous applause, everyone leaping up and down and hugging each other. There was even more applause when, after two circuits of the harbour, he touched down safely to win the Boston Globe Award. My grandmother told me that as a little girl in the 1890s her father had said, 'I want you always to remember that your father believes that someday man will conquer the air. I am laughed at by my friends who think it is impossible to put a machine carrying a man in the air.' But he lived to see the impossible and his sons Burton and Lawrie were both to become early aviators. I sort of hoped that, as I approached Boston, he was looking down and cheering.

We had head winds and Colin was going extra slow, conserving his engine, enlivening the journey with its hiccups, which got ever more frequent as we approached Beverley Airfield to the north of Boston. I requested direct in on Runway 09 (we had to route to the west of Boston) but Beverley insisted on Runway 34 – we were number three and they wanted us low-level at 1,000 feet due to the proximity of Boston's International Logan Airport, just 15 miles away. There were few suitable landing spots on the approach (we had both been checking out possibles ever since taking off from Westchester) and yet again we had a cliffhanger. I should have asked for priority clearance; the other two planes, a Cessna 240 and a Piper Saratoga were just doing circuits, and they went agonisingly slow. Finally, it was our turn, we were cleared to land. Colin did the shortest final approach and landed diagonally on the runway, but he was safely down. We still had another 248 miles to go before we reached Montreal and his new engine.

Victor Capossi and his team at General Aviation Services couldn't have been more charming. He immediately offered space in his hangar, and when I asked if CBS television might come to film us early the following morning for their *Early Morning Show*, he was delighted. CBS had wanted to film us at Westchester, asking us to wait an extra day. We had reluctantly been forced to say we had to press on, explaining how late we already were and how critical our northern crossing was. CBS nationwide would of course be wonderful for both our sponsors and Operation Smile. We had been loath to say no and had been delighted and amazed when they said they would drive up to Boston from New York and film us there.

The Cessna and film crew arrived not long after and then Fred and Susie arrived and we went to their beach house. We had delicious lobster sandwiches and ice cold beer. Freddy and Suzie generously invited us all to stay but everyone bar Heinz and I opted to go to the hotel and see the sights of Boston. I said goodbye to Pascal and wished her well and lots of happiness in the years ahead. Then, as we were all leaving, Colin took me aside and said, 'That Al, he's unbelievable. I just asked him if I'd done something to upset him because he was looking so sourly at me. And do you know what he said? He said, "I'm just fucking fed up with this whole thing. I can't wait for it to be over. I can't wait to get home."'

'I can't believe it,' I said, 'I know he's been looking glum, but . . .' Colin interrupted and said, 'I thought your meeting went well, that everyone was going to make an effort. It doesn't seem to be working if you ask me.' For me that was the straw that broke the camel's back.

'As far as I'm concerned, he can go. If he wants to go, we should let him go. It's not fair on him and it's not fair on us.' By the time we got to the

Winthrops' house I had calmed down. I told Heinz and the Winthrops what Al had said to Colin, and Heinz said something to the effect of, 'Well, if he really feels that way then let him go.' Fred and Susie both said that they thought the whole atmosphere had seemed a little strained, and how tough it must be, and they hoped we would all be able to hang in there.

Simon phoned shortly after we got to the Winthrops' house and the first thing he wanted to know was how the team spirit was. I told him the latest and he flipped. 'I told you you should have a fresh camera crew.' I agreed, but repeated what Freddy had said about hanging in there, and only having two weeks to go. Simon said he was going to talk to Michael Johnson. 'I'm going to tell him that this stress is downright dangerous. What you are doing requires a cool head on your shoulders. How can you possibly perform to your best and make sound judgments with this sort of aggro going on? It's unacceptable.' I said I would also try and get through to Michael Johnson, to see if he couldn't rally the team spirit where I had failed.

Simon and I had first met Fred Winthrop in Thailand in 1967 before he was married. It was great to be with him and Susie, and once again to be in a home that I had visited many times. Heinz and I had such a good time. Fred took us off for a ride on his mountain bikes as darkness was falling. The exercise was great and cycling along those woodland paths, bouncing over tree roots and watching the Canada geese coming in to land on the lake was a brief and lovely respite.

CBS had said that they would be at the airfield at 5 a.m. and asked if we could be there by 6.30 a.m. for their live programme at 8 a.m. Fred and Susie nobly volunteered to drive me out. Fred's cousin Dotty would bring Heinz out later. We took large cups of coffee with us and arrived at the airfield just as the sun peaked over the cloudless horizon. The still air was crisp, with a hint of autumn, a perfect day. Autumn – a salutary reminder that the summer was drawing to a close in Boston, and Boston was more than 1,000 miles south of our most northerly point in Greenland. From now on airfields would be getting fewer and we would be moving away from the comforting security of help near at hand. But I loved the wild places, the infinite horizons, the untamed world where nature still held sway. I also had a very healthy respect for it, and my heart always beat a little faster. I knew only too well how small and vulnerable we were and to what limits we might be tested.

Jamie was at the airfield and CBS was busy setting up cameras and equipment around G-MURY. Colin arrived and was anxious to have a little talk with his engine, and be on his way as soon as possible. The 248 miles to Montreal would take Colin a maximum of five hours. Jim Cunliffe was due to arrive at 5.30 p.m. We did our five minute snip for CBS and then we were on our way. What a long way for the film crew to come and what a performance for just a few minutes, but 'everyone' saw it.

There was no sign of our film crew so we left without them. Still air gave way to a brisk north-westerly and got steadily stronger and stronger. Colin was considering turning back: he had a ground speed of 28 knots, and said the winds for Montreal were forecast to be even stronger, and his engine was still running rough. I asked Boston approach if they could give us the Montreal winds. '250 degrees at three knots!' came the reply. We would have tail winds by the time we got to Montreal.

We pushed onwards, Colin up at 8,000 feet while I flew low under the broken stratus layer of cloud, through forested valleys, over hills and around mountains. For me it was glorious flying, but there was the constant worry over Colin's engine. He reported that it wasn't getting any better and I decided that I had better climb, go up and join him. It is just rather nice to know that someone's got their eye on you and can follow you down if the worst comes to the worst.

Three and a half hours out, and I was beginning to dare to think we were going to be able to get Colin to his new engine, rather than having to smuggle it to him over the Canadian border, when he said, 'It's running really rough – I don't think I'm going to make it!' After the Norfolk failure I was far less sanguine about rough engines. I checked my chart. 'The nearest airfield is a little place called Morrisville, it's about ten miles north-west of us, do you want to head over that way?' He did.

I thought about how panicked I'd been when my engine coughed in California with the dud magneto, and how matter-of-fact Colin was being with yet another potential emergency landing on his hands. But he's had so much practice, he told me he'd had 23 engines fail on him over the years!

We turned 30 degrees west and said a few prayers – I certainly did. We were only 65 miles from Montreal's Saint Hubert Airfield on the east bank of the Saint Lawrence River and a tantalising 30 miles from the American/Canadian border. We also had the Green Mountains to cross. 'Come on, Colin, come on,' I silently willed him onwards. Someone heard our prayers. Colin announced that it seemed to be running a bit smoother. 'OK, let's risk it – if I can just get over this ridge of mountains it looks pretty flat on the other side – should be all right there.'

We pushed on, crossed the Green Mountains – he still had an engine – and the foothills gradually gave way to the flat plains around Lake Champlain. Colin said the engine was still rough but not critically rough. I said goodbye to Burlington Airfield with whom I'd been in radio contact for the last hour. I silently said goodbye to America, as we crossed the border into Canada, and called Saint Hubert approach, 25 miles out.

The film crew caught up with us just before we arrived at Saint Hubert and were able to film Colin and me coming in together – a rare happening, the last time we had been filmed landing in formation had been in far away Anadyr. Heinz drove the hire car into town and everyone vowed never ever to allow him near the wheel again. He drove like a madman.

Colin and I went to collect Jim Cunliffe at Dorval, the main international airfield – and missed him. We went to the international terminal and he came into the domestic, having changed flights in Toronto. I was then too late to have a drink with Lawrence Stroll, my friend, sponsor and chairman of Tommy Hilfiger, and running late for dinner with Brian and Mila Mulroney. I quickly changed, grabbed a taxi and left. I wished I had something a little more elegant than my black trousers and little red top that I was heartily sick of. Mila was wearing a glorious flowing creation, looking cool and beautiful. But it was *so* good to be with friends, relaxing on their terrace with a glass of cold wine, enjoying an unseasonably warm late summer evening.

DAY 84 – 22 AUGUST

Colin went out early to the airport with Jim to fit the new engine, which didn't arrive until 11 a.m. as the factory sent it to Toronto by mistake. The film crew went with them. I stayed in town as I had been asked to do a *Good Morning Canada* TV show. Then I went off to find some cold weather gear for Colin, who had announced in Boston that he had nothing for the cold ahead other than his new, untried, electrically-heated suit, which probably would work as it was designed for deep sea divers in Arctic waters, professionally made by a company called Typhoon who had given us a bit of a discount. The gloves, however, I was less sure of. They had been made by Michelle and wired up by Colin. The idea was that he would plug them in and run them off his electrics. I had visions of an electrified Colin.

I hunted around without much success as winter stocks weren't due in the shops for a couple of weeks. Luckily, Fred Winthrop had lent Colin his ski gloves with silk liners in case he could find nothing better, and they were to prove ideal. I finally found him a fleece hat and neck warmer. Heinz and I met up for lunch in a little Italian sidewalk café, and then Heinz went off on a bike ride and I went for a walk. Then my mobile phone rang. It was Colin, 'All hell has let loose here! Al's been given his walking papers. Everyone is up in arms.'

'Oh my God! How? I mean, who phoned? What did they say?'

'Lawrence Duffy phoned Al and told him that he had been told from "on high" that Al was to return to England. That Dave Ullman could handle Al's share of things and that Al was booked on the British Airways flight that night to London. They are all livid. They want a meeting this evening at 5 p.m.' I said I would be there.

I began to feel sorry that Al was going, and started thinking of all the good things about him. He could be very entertaining, with a dry sense of humour, and he loved the wild places. I remembered how he had been practically moved to tears crossing the flat calm sea to Corfu and then standing on a beach in Russia where we had landed just for the hell of it on our way from Magadan to Markovo. He had stood there at the water's edge just lost in the beauty of it all. Finally turning, he had walked back across the pebbles and said, quietly, with a catch to his voice, 'It doesn't come much better than this.' Now he was going home and he was going to miss out on some of the most spectacular, some of the most remote and glorious scenery of our entire trip. Then I hardened my heart: 'Well, it's his own fault, he's only got himself to blame – they've made my life a misery.' But I wished it hadn't been him.

Heinz got back around 5 p.m. and I told him the latest. 'Well, this should knock a bit of sense into them all,' he said, 'but it's too bad it had to be Al.' I looked rather surprised at that, remembering when he had declared that he didn't want Al in his plane any more. Heinz grinned and said, 'I know, he was a real pain, but he had the decency to apologise and we've all been operating under a lot of strain.'

We met in an elegant room with deep brocade armchairs set more or less in a circle. Heinz was on my left and the film crew opposite. Al was not there and there was no sign of Colin – installing the engine must have taken longer than anticipated.

Pat had been nominated the spokesman. He had a rumpled piece of paper in his hand with a list of questions and statements. What did he say? What did we talk about? I truly remember little more than Pat's opening words. He looked up from his crumpled paper with a look in his eyes of pure loathing. Hatred? Fury? Perhaps a mixture of all three. He said through clenched teeth and pursed mouth, 'Can I talk without risking the danger of being fired too?'

I looked at all those accusing eyes and said, 'Of course.'

I listened as Pat went through his list, ending by saying, 'We will continue filming and editing for NOW, we will finish the job, but don't expect anything more from us.'

I was such a wimp, I said little other than muttering something about unacceptable levels of stress, and that Al had wanted out in any case, but that I was so sad and sorry it had come to this. Heinz was Swiss to the core, very diplomatic and reasonable, taking no sides, and I think he managed to defuse much of the situation. Q then took it upon himself to do a sort of summing up, arguing for both camps.

Colin arrived back minutes after we came out of our meeting. I saw Al on the other side of the lobby, his back towards me. He was checking out. Heinz told Colin about the meeting, I was still too numb. Colin listened, made a few comments and then said to me, 'After I spoke to you on the phone, James Davey, he comes up to me and says, "I'm taking my plane back to England, I've had enough of this, I'm getting out. I've spoken with Peter Wood and he says I can leave any time I want."' What would NOW say to that? The Cessna was part and parcel of the contract. I began to focus, I had to pull myself together. I went up to my room and phoned Peter Wood, who was very suprised to hear from me. James had never phoned him, he knew nothing about what was going on and certainly hadn't given James any authority to fly the plane home. 'Do you want me to come out there and knock a few heads together?' he asked. I also phoned Simon and told him everything. He thought the action was long overdue and if he had his way he would have fired the lot! 'How dare he [Pat] dictate to you – who the hell does he think he is? I'll tell you – he's just a cameraman, an employee, being paid by NOW, he's not your sponsor – how old did you say he was?'

'Twenty-eight,' I said. 'Well, he's under thirty.'

'Christ, I can't believe I'm hearing all this. And as for Q . . . if he'd been loyal to you from the start none of this would have happened. When I think what you have done for that guy, two trips around the world, trips around Europe and he repays you like this, it's inexcusable.' We talked for some time, and I felt a little better. Simon, I know, was being fiercely defensive. It is difficult if you're not there to appreciate the tensions, tiredness and general irritation with each other. But Simon was right, Q had denigrated me from the start.

I lay in bed that night unable to sleep, thinking with little joy about the tough days to come, all the weeks gone by, where we had all gone wrong and why. Perhaps being the only woman, and a woman in the chauvinistic world of aviation, didn't help. I thought of Al and how he must be feeling. I tried to think more positively, assessing our situation – we had got as far as Montreal, Colin had a new engine and we had won through endless heart-stopping moments. The other aircraft were in good shape. Dave Ullman was with us and I liked Dave. I had managed to pilot my helicopter three-quarters of the way around the world. We were getting masses of e-mails and messages of encouragement and enthusiasm on the web and for all the team tensions there were great moments every day. For example, just the day before, soaring over the treetops and through the valleys, life had been so good. Looking back, tense and scary moments become great moments, times when you've overcome the odds and lived to tell the tale, and they are all part of the great adventure. I fell asleep hoping that we could all now pull together. We needed to have our wits about us. We had over 2,000 miles of icy water to cross before we reached home.

NINE

Montreal to Brooklands

23 August – 6 September

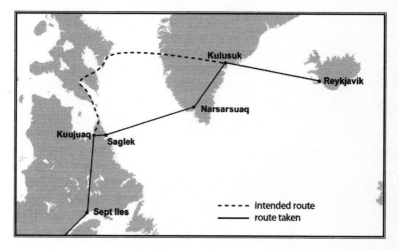

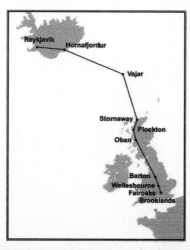

'There's a cold front coming in,' Jim Cunliffe told Colin and me when we arrived at the airfield at 7 a.m. the following morning. Jim had already been there for an hour, doing a final check of Colin's new engine.

'That should get you there,' he said, giving the engine a pat, as Colin hauled on his fleece-lined jacket, looked up at the sky and said, 'I wonder if I ought to wear my waterproofs, looks as though it's going to pour with rain.' It wasn't looking good, the cloud was low and grey with lower and greyer-looking cloud coming in from the west. 'Well, at least we've got a tail wind. If you're quick I think you'll be OK,' I said. 'No time for breakfast.' (Which was where Jim and I were headed). I thought I would hang around, give Colin a start and half-hoping (half-dreading) that Q and whoever was flying with him would arrive before I left.

They didn't show by the time Jim had had his full bacon and eggs and I had picked at some toast (trauma plays havoc with my stomach). It started to rain. 'I best be gone, Jim, and I'm so sorry that you had to put up with all our dramas, you were a lovely sane element.' He laughed and said, 'Well, don't you worry any more, it'll all sort itself out. You two are doing great, just concentrate on what it's really all about. And Colin's got the new engine. That other one had had it. As Colin admitted, he'd been leaning the fuel off too much getting the mileage.'

I flew along the south bank of the Saint Lawrence to the city of Quebec, where I got permission to fly low-level, getting a great view of the city. A watery sun was just beginning to peak through the grey cloud, casting slivers of silver light on the Heights of Abraham, the towering cliffs that the old city and fort of Quebec stand on.

The last time I'd seen Quebec City was in 1955, aged 15, when I had sailed up the Saint Lawrence with my family to Montreal from England. We were going to spend the summer holidays with my Aunt Kathy in New Hampshire, getting to know our American cousins. It is strange how random moments stand out in one's memory. We all stood at the rail of the ship, gazing up at the high cliffs. I had been wearing a blue and white check dress with a strawberry embroidered on the pocket, white socks and sandals. This time I was gazing down.

Ten miles past Quebec, I crossed over the Saint Lawrence to the north side and caught up with Colin who had taken his usual direct course and had passed to the north of the city. He was a difficult-to-spot dot in the sky, way up at 11,000 feet. 'Why don't you come down a bit? There's no turbulence, it's lovely,' I said.

'I've heard that one before and nearly been inverted,' he said with a laugh.

However, he did come down to 8,000 feet and for a while we flew together, but it was so beautiful lower down and I could meander around and still keep up with Colin. After half an hour I went back down to a fun 500 feet. The skies were now completely clear and the wind had veered to the north-west, giving us 12 knots of tail wind. The awfulness of the day before was on a back burner. 'This is what it is all about,' I said to myself, and then said as much to Colin. (I was forever ooing and aahing over the wonders we saw, of sunlight and storms over land and sea, while Colin would point out that that was a storm building or a front moving in or the beginnings of sea fog.) He laughed and agreed and said, 'If the wind stays like this we're going to have head winds after Sept Iles.'

We heard Q and Pat on the radio when we were about an hour out from Sept Iles. Their ETA was 14 minutes after ours. Q asked if we could slow down a bit so that they could catch up and film us going in to the airfield? Rather reluctantly we agreed. 'Hurry up though,' Colin said. 'I'm dying for a pee.' (I'd done a pit stop earlier). Ten minutes later Colin said, 'My arm's giving me stick', which was our secret code for changing frequencies. I switched over from 123.45 to 'our' frequency. 'Why are we slowing down for those idiots? It's their fault. If they want to film us they need to get up earlier,' he said. I agreed. I am glad we didn't slow down because when I contacted Q again to find out where they were, he said with a laugh, 'Oh sorry, we went to see some whales.'

This was great country. At 2,000 feet (I'd climbed a bit) I could see the mountains off to the north, the mighty Saint Lawrence now looking more like a sea than a river to the south, and ahead of me the bay and the small fishing town of Sept Iles with its 'sept iles' sprinkled around the mouth of the bay. Four miles beyond the town on the open plains was the surprisingly large airfield with three runways. The air was fresh, small scattered cumulus scudding across the bluest of skies; this was hunting and fishing country, the big outdoors. We had left suburban life and would see no more until we crossed the water. We landed, I got out of G-MURY, gave a big stretch and laughed to see Colin haring across the apron in search of a loo.

We had landed at 1.30 p.m., the weather was great. Q and Pat arrived 20 minutes later and the Cessna shortly after. The original plan was to stay the night there, but the weather was good and the forecast for the following day was bad. We decided to push on to Wabush 190 miles to the north and if we felt up to it we might even make Schefferville, 130 miles yet further north. In still air, that would be a good six hours for Colin.

I hadn't seen Pat and co. since the night before and didn't feel too comfortable. While we were refuelling, Dave came over and took a whole lot of still digital photos, smiling and friendly. Q wandered over, but I didn't rush into conversation. He said, 'You're being very quiet.' And then, in a rather kind voice said, 'Do you want to talk?' Still feeling hurt and uncomfortable with him I said. 'No, no.' To which he replied in a very matter-of-fact voice, 'I'm not surprised. You've just ruined a young man's career,' and walked away.

Colin, feeling better, quickly refuelled and took off . . . and was back half an hour later. 'I got 14 miles out, the turbulence was getting bad, really dangerous and I had 28 knots of head wind. And the cumulus were towering up to 13,500 feet so I couldn't see myself getting above that lot, but I feel really bad holding you all up like this.' He was apologetically shaking his head. We tried to hide our disappointment, some better than others. There was a fair amount of grumblings and mumblings, 'We're never going to make it at this rate,' 'Weather's bound to be worse further north,' 'I'm sure he could have gone.'

The weather the following morning was miserable: low cloud, wind and rain. I phoned Colin at 6 a.m. and he told me he had already been out. 'I've looked at the mountains and they're completely covered in cloud and I've seen the television and there's a 25-knot head wind.' I got out of bed and opened the curtains on to a dreary world – what little I could see of it. It had looked so lovely the night before in the setting sun. Our bedrooms at the hotel were all on the upper level of the two-storey wooden building with a long balcony connecting all the rooms. We overlooked a small harbour full of fishing boats of every shape and size. There was a boardwalk in front with the harbour wall behind, complete with helipad. Beyond was the open water of the Saint Lawrence with several of the islands in view. That morning I could barely see the harbour wall.

At 8 a.m. I joined Colin for breakfast. James Davey came striding in and said in a very abrupt, peremptory fashion, 'Why aren't you at the airport? Q went ages ago.' Colin told him that we didn't have flying conditions, 'Well, I suppose I will have to go and phone Q,' he said, sounding as though he didn't believe a word of it, and stomped out of the room. Shortly after, they all came in to breakfast and tempers flared. Q wanted to know why we hadn't been at the airfield. 'We had a window,' he said, 'But of course it's gone now.' Pat said something dismissive. Q was shaking his head behind Colin's back and pointing to the Met forecast that he had got, implying that Colin had got it all wrong. Colin was fast losing his cool. The other hotel guests were taking a lively interest in proceedings. Pat was saying, 'Yeah, calm him down. Calm him down.' I thought we were heading for a punch-up. I jumped up and made placatory noises in all directions and said, 'It's all too easy for us to sit in judgment, we aren't flying the microlight, and anyway – look out the window, there's no way any of us can fly in that.' The cloud was down to the ground and the seven islands had disappeared.

Colin wanted to adjust his prop, so I went out to the airport with him. He had managed to get the microlight under cover in Petro Air Services' hangar. Karen, Bob, Daniel, Martin and Jeannot ran the show and what a great bunch they were. I think it was Karen's family business with Bob in charge, a good-looking hunk of a man. Karen suggested I bring the helicopters over to the parking area by their hangar as we would be charged a fairly hefty amount if we left them on the apron. In the pouring rain I trudged several hundred yards down the taxiway and across the apron and taxied them over one by one. It was the first time I had flown G-JEFA since leaving England and I had forgotten how light and easy it was to fly, how immediate the controls are. I shot up off the ground. What a huge difference the hydraulics make.

Daniel kindly drove us back into town and he and Karen joined us for a drink that evening and told us a little about themselves and the town. Sept Iles made a living from tourism, hunting, shooting and fishing. They had all opted for the country life, none of them wanted the big cities and although the winters were long and cold, the short summers were beautiful – this was the first rain in a month! We asked them to join us for dinner. They couldn't, but suggested we went to Les Terrasses du Capitaine, a hundred yards away. 'You can't miss it, it's made of two old boats,' Karen said.

Heinz, Colin and I trooped along there and found ourselves involved in a 'family do'. Two young girls were putting on a show, one singing, the other playing the guitar, with all their family and friends there to cheer them on. They were very good. Our waiter told us proudly that Sabrina Levesque (the singer) was going to London in a couple of weeks to sing in *Phantom of the Opera*. Just as Heinz and I were finishing our deliciously fresh cod and Colin his scampi, the others happened to pitch up. Colin saw them outside and said, 'James, he spotted us and they started to turn away but realised I had seen them, so I guess they thought they better come in.' It was an uneasy truce. No one was really comfortable.

Next morning we woke to equally appalling weather. Colin and I once more went to the airport to see if we could get some more charts of Canada and get the Met. We were met by a steaming Karen, waving papers at us. 'I looked up your website. Who is this Dave Ullman? How can he say all these terrible things about Sept Iles?'

Of course we hadn't been privy to what Dave had put on the website, but we already knew that he was not the most tactful of souls. According to Dave, Sept Iles was a dump, he advised everyone to avoid the place, and said it had nothing to recommend it. And here were these lovely people who had done so much to help us, giving us endless coffees and snacks in their pilots' lounge, rides into town, free Met service and a hangar for Colin.

Tourism was their life blood, and they had accessed our website to find this!

We did our best to placate them. I told her that that was just Dave's view, that he must be a townie, that we thought Sept Iles was wonderful (which we did – even though we were desperate to get out). 'But half a million people are accessing your website every day you said. And they'll all be reading this.' At that moment Dave had the misfortune to arrive and we all blasted him. He looked suitably appalled, I genuinely think he hadn't thought it through. He said he would do another piece on the merits of the delicious seafood and how the big open spaces weren't for him personally and he wasn't into hunting and fishing . . . Karen took us off to pick blueberries that afternoon.

That evening Q announced he had booked a fishing boat. 'Come on, everyone, let's all go!' he said. He ended up going on his own and caught several fish. I still feel bad that I never went.

On the third day we woke to better conditions. There was still a lot of cloud around, but the TV was showing an improvement and I could see the islands. I told the others I would call them from the airport if Colin was able to take off. Bob was there to open the hangar and gave us a hand and at 6.45 a.m. I told Q that we were on our way.

We had a great day. Other than a slight hiccup when approaching Wabush when Colin had said the cumulus were building so fast he didn't think he would be able to get over them and would have to land there. But he pressed on, dodging great puffy clouds which slowly became more scattered. He stayed high, chugging along at 9,000–12,000 feet, eyes focused on Kuujuaq. I climbed up to 8,000 feet a couple of times, principally to talk to Goose Bay and Wabush. It was beautiful, with an utterly different perspective to the low-level flying. You could see forever, the air was so clear, the sky so blue and clouds as white as white, and it was great fun to dance through the tunnels and skim the misting edges. Below was a world of forests, dark lakes and rivers. I preferred, though, to smell the pines and returned to spend much of the time at tree level.

Heinz came on the radio suggesting we all go into Goose Bay, refuel and head for Greenland. 'We've got a weather window, we've got 28 knots of tail wind, we could make it.' The only trouble was that Colin and I were by then 250 miles north-west of Goose Bay so would have had to battle with a head wind to get back there. It just wasn't on. I then checked the distances on my GPS. Goose Bay to Narsarsuaq in southern Greenland was 776 miles. I told Heinz that he might make it, but the margins were tighter than I was prepared to risk. Even with 28 knots of tail wind that was going to take nine hours. The helicopters didn't have the endurance to level-peg it with Colin for that long and we had all agreed we would stay together over the Arctic water. Also, I wondered whether Goose Bay would have allowed us to sally forth.

North of Schefferville I came across a vast herd of moose, all on the move, travelling west, crossing a hundred rivers that all ran north–south. I first spotted a group of about 15 swimming across one river and then lost them in the trees, only to spot another much larger group in the next river. The more I looked, the more I saw, river after river. I must have seen well over a hundred, mile after mile, and they looked wonderful, their proud heads held high, swimming one behind the other. Seeing them in the wild like that was a sight I will never forget. I called Q, who was by then only half an hour behind me, and gave him the coordinates so Dave could film them. Sadly, they were gone by the time they got there.

In '97, Q and I had spent a freezing cold night in a cabin at Fort Mackenzie and got out my chart to see if I was anywhere near or if I had gone past it. There it was, Fort Mackenzie on the shores of Lake Canichito. Some 70 miles off to the north-west, I decided to divert. The weather had deteriorated, a low front was fast coming in from the west and the high, white puffy clouds were now low with scuds of rain. I saw a low cloud of spray, but it wasn't the rain, it was the waterfall where on our last trip we had spotted two Frenchmen on a fishing holiday and they had given us one of the fish they had caught for our supper. They had spent the last two weeks kayaking and fishing their way down the Caniapiscau River from Kuujuaq. We were the first people they'd seen and were even more surprised to see us than we were to see them. They were from Clermont Ferrand in France.

I never got to the cabin to see if it was still there. The sky to the west was black as the ace of spades, the world no longer looked so friendly and I didn't want another night in Fort Mackenzie, even though I did have my sleeping bag this time. The only reason I had carried it under my seat three-quarters of the way round the world was the memory of that freezing cold night right there in Fort Mackenzie.

Bad weather chased me in to Kuujuaq, a small Inuit town of brightly painted cabins on the shores of the River Koksoak, which fed into Ungava Bay, the great sea passage leading to Hudson Bay. This separated us by over 200 miles of water from Baffin Island and another 150 north of that southern shore was Iqaluit, our next intended stop.

Colin had another 'diabolically horrendous' landing with a crosswind that had once more nearly inverted him. But he was getting there, we were getting there, closer and closer. It was 25 August, we were hoping to be home in ten days, on 4 September. Yet never had England seemed so far away. We tucked Colin's microlight safely away in a hangar and made our way to the small hotel where last time Q and I had had the most wonderful hot breakfast after our night at Fort Mackenzie. My memories of Kuujuaq were rose-tinted, a haven after 'that night' and we had only stayed long enough for the hot meal and refuelling. The realities of a longer stay proved different. The restaurant hadn't changed – the same bunch of Inuits sitting their over their coffees, beers and cigarettes – but it all looked drab. They told us they stopped serving dinner at 6 p.m., and it was by then 7 p.m. They half-relented and made some sandwiches for us, we were starving, especially Colin and I as we had missed out on breakfast and hadn't eaten since the night before. The hotel bedrooms I was seeing for the first time. They were basic and mine hadn't been cleaned. There was an ashtray piled high with cigarette ends on the bedside table, and the bed, although made, was dirty. Welcome to the Inuit town of Kuujuaq.

Next morning at 5 a.m. the weather was awful. There was a strong wind with cloud down to the ground. We were hoping to get all the way to Iqaluit that day. The plan was to fly east along the coast, then continue coastal, north up the Labrador Peninsula, which gave us the shortest crossing to Baffin Island, passing over Resolution Island (where last time we'd seen a polar bear), then up Frobisher Bay to Iqaluit.

At 6 a.m. Colin and I and the camera crew set off for the airport. We walked as there was no one at the front desk and no taxis and the airfield was nearly a mile away along a gravel road. It started to drizzle with rain. By the time we were halfway there it was raining in earnest, with a bitingly cold wind, and we had no umbrellas. I thought how just a couple of degrees more and this would be snow. I tried to hold my windcheater half over my head, but we were soaked by the time we got to the hangar where the microlight was stored. We tugged and heaved Colin into his electric suit, his fleece suit, his moon boots, neck fleece, electric gloves, ski gloves and waterproofs; he looked like the Michelin Man gone mad and was sweating buckets. The cloud was still very low, we waited an hour but there was little improvement.

'I think we can go. We can follow the coast, there are no obstacles, no trees, just a few icebergs as you get further north,' Q said. Colin wasn't reassured. 'It's fine for you, but where are my options?' We helped Colin reverse the dressing procedure, then trooped once more back to the hotel to join the others who were having breakfast. They were very disappointed but not surprised to see us. I thought of what Frank Robinson had said to me on my first ever meeting with him, when I had tried to persuade him to come on side. 'I'm concerned that you will make the right decision, that you will be prepared to wait for days if necessary, that you will have the patience . . .'

This was one of those times. We were frustrated, our patience was running thin and we were up against the clock. We couldn't afford to wait for the clock to tick much further if we were going to make it to Iceland before the winter.

We held a power meeting in Heinz's room. I brought along my charts. Everyone was there, slumped in various attitudes, the picture of dejection. The camera crew were discussing commercial flights to Montreal. The forecast for Iqaluit was lousy, with the area of low pressure looking as though it could be hanging around for days. What other options did we have? Could we make southern Greenland direct from Kuujuaq? That was over 800 miles and the last 600 miles were over water. That was the absolute limit of our range but the biggest problem was that the direct route would take us first across the high Labrador plateau, over the Torngat Mountains with peaks rising to over 5,500 feet. What if there was early morning fog?

I still liked the idea of Iqaluit, it gave us the shortest sea crossing to Greenland, and I had had too long to think about this coming leg and the consequences if I had to ditch in those freezing waters. My thoughts were interrupted by Heinz saying, 'Just look at this.' It was a message on our website, printed on the diary page. It read:

A Stern Warning On What The Team Still Have To Face
Jonathon Herbert, an experienced helicopter pilot currently in Romania, contacted us to express his reservations about the next leg of the trip:

I am happy if I can give some advice to Colin and the chopper pilots but I think they are all grown up people and I hope also responsible pilots. Determination is sometimes in contradiction to the meteorological circumstances.

My aviation background:
Around 3,600 flight hours since 1977; past (and future) turbine helicopter owner; crossed Atlantic twice (west to east) in a Bell 206 L111 under VFR conditions; experienced (approximately 760 hours) in bush environment (hot and cold).

My advice to Colin:
Stop this dangerous attempt now and get a hitch in Q's R44. It will be exciting enough – trust me. I cannot emphasise enough that the approaching environment at this time of year can be lethal for any microlight! You are not only risking your own hide, but putting the SAR crews at risk too.

My advice to Jeffa and Q:
Take your thermals with you and after Fort Chimo get used to the
'squeeze' of your survival suits.

Have enough chocolate with you and a special insulated bag (for your
battery) in case you are forced into a camping break. Learn how to
remove the battery (don't forget the tools!) and take the battery with
you into your sleeping bag. The battery is your best friend over there!
This is no joke.

Leaving Sondrestrom, head south to Nuuk and further to Narsarsuaq.
Hazards: Freezing rain (stay close to the sea) and sea fog, but you
should be able to avoid these terrible turbulences.

Important:
Leaving Narsarsuaq, head south-east to approx Latitude 60 deg 11min
North/Longitude 43 deg 19 min West, then head north towards
Kulusuk. Do not try and cross the ice cap, do not cut corners . . .

Colin looked suitably outraged and said, 'Pack it in? He's got to be kidding.'
The camera crew looked as though they agreed with everything Jonathon
Herbert said. Heinz asked, 'Where's Fort Chimo?' No one knew!

Jonathon Herbert's words of caution and warning momentarily had
everyone in a lighthearted mood. There were lots of comments about Colin
packing it all in and Heinz squeezing the microlight in the Cessna. We did
a bit of an inventory check which had everyone laughing. We had two
sleeping bags, no one had thermals. Colin had tools, Q and I had Swiss army
penknives and Leathermans (tools) and we had lots of chocolate. 'My
battery could be a problem,' said Q (the new R44s have the battery under
the instrument panel).

'Well, he obviously hasn't done his homework on us,' I said. 'I guess he
doesn't know that Q and I have already flown over 400 miles straight over the
ice cap from Sondrestrom direct to Kulusuk.' But we all knew that Jonathon
Herbert was talking a lot of sense and, of course, we did have the basics. We
all had survival suits, life jackets, life rafts and several EPIRB's. God knows I
had read the CAA booklet on the Do's and Don'ts and what to expect north
of 60 degrees latitude enough times.

Colin and I were looking at the charts and, half jokingly, I said, 'Well,
there's always this little disused airfield,' pointing to a place called Saglek, 210
miles away to the east of us on the Labrador coast and just slightly to the south

of Kuujuaq, which is probably why we had never noticed it. 'That – could – be – it,' Colin said slowly, thinking through the possibilities. 'Yup, I really think that could be the answer!'

I was beginning to wish I hadn't pointed it out.

'We can fly over there, spend the night there, then make an early start the next morning,' Colin said. 'Even if there is early morning low cloud we don't have to worry about mountains, we can just head straight out over the water to Greenland.'

Q came over and took a look. 'Mmm . . . interesting.' We started to discuss it seriously. 'What if the runway is totally unserviceable for Colin?' I said.

'Well, I would just have to come back again then, wouldn't I? I'd have enough fuel.' And Colin's old gut feeling came into play. 'I've just got a gut feeling about Iqaluit. I just know we'll get stuck there, we could be there for days and days. I think we should give this place Saga, whatever its name is, a go.'

At that point I heard the phone ringing in my bedroom across the corridor and rushed out of the room. It was Simon. I brought him up to date. He asked about everything and how everyone was getting on and I said that we were stuck with bad weather but team-wise it all seemed to be reasonably OK. I spoke too soon. While talking with Simon, Q sauntered into my room, and sat down in the moth-eaten old armchair. I said goodbye to Simon and turned enquiringly to Q and asked what was going on. 'Oh well, Colin's having a real old fight with that lot.'

'What about?' I said jumping up off the side of my bed.

Q just shrugged his shoulders and said, 'Mmm well . . . this and that – I don't know.'

'Well, I want to know,' I said and hurried back into the other room.

Colin looked as though he was about to hit Pat. Pat had his eyes raised to the ceiling and his mouth pursed tight, and he looked about to explode. James looked interestingly defiant. 'Oh dear! Now what?' I said. It turned out that as soon as I was out of the room Pat said that there was no way that he was going to any disused airfield with no accommodation. He said, 'This is your challenge, not mine!' James had then added, 'And I'm not taking *my* plane into any disused airfield.' Colin had got back onto 'gut feelings'.

'Well, we may not have much choice,' I said. 'Let's see how the weather is looking this evening. It's obvious we're going nowhere today. But perhaps it would be a good idea to go to the airfield and see if any of the bush pilots know anything about Saglek.' That got a few nods. We continued discussing options and then around midday the weather did improve fractionally so

Heinz, Q, Colin and I went to the airfield looking for bush pilots to ask about Saglek and perhaps go for a local flight in the R44s.

There were a couple of pilots at the airfield but neither of them seemed to know anything specific about Saglek. One said he thought that Saglek might be the place that someone had said was an unmanned radar station. The other said, by way of an apology, 'No one goes out much that way, there's nuthin' there after George River – just a whole lot of nuthin'.' Not very encouraging, but we were all beginning to warm to a new adventure. It was, after all, 'our challenge'.

We went for a local flight and had a fun afternoon dodging rainstorms and chasing rainbows. Colin spotted some musk ox – lovely big creatures. They look a little like bison with the longest, shaggiest coat that would put even the best of Scotland's Highland cattle to shame. We landed on a small rocky island and ate bars of chocolate and when we got back to the airfield Q suggested that this would be a good moment to test our 'sea rescue system'! Q had 'fitted' the two helicopters with 25-foot long ropes with a carabiner clip on the end, which could be clipped onto our life jackets. The idea was that we could hoist each other out of the water. That was the theory anyway. Heinz, always practical, had done some mountaineering, and worn harnesses and said that the life jacket would be excruciating within minutes. Lovely though the idea was, he said, no one would be able to haul themselves up a rope, especially with numb fingers in Arctic waters. 'How in heaven's name did you think you would be able to hold the helicopter in a hover close to the water? There'd probably be a big swell and you would end up in the water too,' he'd said.

We tried out the rope. We hung Heinz, the biggest and heaviest off the side of an oil storage tank. Even using a pulley system he only managed to get a foot off the ground. We couldn't stop laughing, he looked so ridiculous and of course it was a disaster. But we kept the ropes.

We arrived back at the hotel in time for our 6 p.m. supper and once more discussed and argued about the route. The forecast was not good. The low-pressure system at Iqaluit had barely moved and another low was waiting to come in. One option was to go to Kangiqsualujjuak – no one could pronounce the name, everyone was having a go and sort of getting stuck in the middle, and then one of the locals at the next table said, 'People call it George River, easier for some to say.' George River was 90 miles to the east along the coast. We would all reassemble there. The Cessna would bring a barrel of fuel which we would share out and then, depending on the Met and local weather, we could choose between Iqaluit, going direct to Greenland, or try Saglek. The final decision was that we wouldn't make a final decision until the morning.

I went to bed, watched a little television and then lay there thinking about the next day, praying the weather would be good enough to go and wondering which way. I went over the pros and cons and I thought about the camera crews and James's reaction to the idea of Saglek. I could understand James, whose first priority was to see the Cessna home safe and sound, but Pat saying 'It's your challenge, not mine', that needed a little thought. I finally fell asleep thinking about loyalty and mutiny, leadership and adventurers, the spirit of adventure and how some people had it and others didn't.

Alarms were set for 5 a.m. I leapt out of bed and opened the thin curtain – the same low sea fog, I looked over towards the airfield where the ground rose slightly across the scrubby field. The Tower was just in the clear, it had been hidden the day before. The phone rang. It was Colin, who rather surprisingly thought it looked better. 'Let's get up to the airfield.'

We hadn't made the mistake of the day before, we had booked the local taxi. Colin, Q and I set off for the airfield. Pat and Dave decided they would be going in the Cessna until further notice!

The weather showed no sign of improvement. We went over to the Tower and got the Met which wasn't very encouraging. As expected, the first low was moving gradually east with an even larger area of low pressure closing in behind. Iqaluit was looking less of an option. On the way back from the Tower we talked to a pilot refuelling his Twin Otter plane, and he thought there was a good chance the fog would lift around midday. We asked him about Saglek. He scratched his head and said, 'I don't go that way myself, my run's over to the west, but I met a guy – he went in there. Let me see, must'a been a coupla years back. Said it was some sort of radar station, unmanned most of the year.' We chatted a little – he wanted to know what we were doing and wished us luck as he headed off to herd his small group of passengers into his bright yellow plane. The conditions we had that day were not a problem for him, he was just heading up to Kangirsuk, 140 miles up the coast to the west and, like G-EELS, he could fly on instruments.

We stowed our kit and went back for breakfast. The three of us decided that we'd go for Saglek. Colin was adamant and we all agreed that if we couldn't take off till midday, there was no way we could make Iqaluit – it was much further north and a longer route. The only plus point for Iqaluit, quite a big one, was the shorter sea crossing.

We hoped the news that another plane had been in to Saglek would persuade the others to feel more inclined to join us. They could bring along that precious barrel of fuel. It was 833 miles from Kuujuaq to Greenland, via Saglek. The margins were tight but the wind forecast was good – north-westerly veering to south-westerly, 25–35 knots at 5,000 feet.

Heinz would have come but the others were adamant. They were having none of it. James repeated his words of the day before, 'I'm not taking my plane in there.' I was surprised that Heinz didn't say something as he was the captain, but I suppose he thought there was nothing to be gained. James went on to say, 'We can route direct from here to Greenland, we've got the range.' They had no problem flying over cloud-covered mountains and no freezing conditions were forecast.

We thought the chances were good that there would be some sort of building by the airstrip at Saglek, and that we would be able to somehow get inside it for the night. If not, we would have to sleep in the helicopters. James was happy to lend us his little gas cooker and gave us the rest of his freeze-dried scrambled eggs and one packet of chow mein. We scrounged tea bags and instant coffee from the kitchen plus a couple of packets of biscuits and the remains of Yuri's vodka and decided that would have to do. The weather had improved a little. Saglek was action and the unknown. It was all rather exciting *and* we were about to be on the move once more. Kuujuaq was a dump, and the dreary weather made it all the more so.

Heinz and the mutineers came out to the airfield to see us off. I bought two five-gallon red plastic jerry cans that we filled with Avgas. There was another pilot by the fuel pumps and I asked him if he knew anything about Saglek. 'Nope, can't say I do. But I think that's the place that one of my mates tried to go in to, but the Americans wouldn't give him permission.' We wedged the jerry cans upright on the floor in the front of each of the helicopters. We needed every ounce possible.

There was a cloud base of 500 feet but the sky looked brighter to the east. Spirits were high. Colin set off taking a coastal route in case he had to put down at George River, which was about 20 degrees left of track. I followed half and hour later and Q, who suddenly had to go to the loo, followed a half hour behind me.

The further east we went the better the weather got and the scenery more and more dramatic. The ground rose steadily and what little rough, low-lying vegetation there had been slowly disappeared, as did all the cloud. Forty minutes out and I was in a different world, gone was the fog and greyness of Kuujuaq, gone the days of waiting, the skies were the most incredible blue. I decided a little music was called for and that *Legends of the Fall* would suit the great open spaces and my happiness. The world below was one of old granite worn smooth by the glaciers and winds of tens of millions of years. Small pockets of crystal-clear water trapped in rocky pools and crevices, little streams flowed towards the sea from glacial lakes. And then, as the plateau rose ever higher, odd patches of snow began to appear. A majesty of desolation and I was alone at the uttermost part of the earth, just me and God's world and I laughed for the sheer joy of it all.

Colin was off to my left somewhere and quite a long way behind me, having done his initial coastal route. Q was also in the air. Should I wait for them? I could always land, but even that would use up precious fuel. We had all leaned off the fuel mixture as much as we dared. The winds had been northerly rather than westerly and I was getting more crosswind than tail wind. Saglek was now 80 miles distant. What were we going to find? Would the airstrip be OK for Colin? Might it be manned? For some reason, I wasn't worried. Perhaps that was just my normal optimism hurtling to the fore, but everything seemed so right. I was loving the adventure of it all. This was living. This was what made it all worthwhile. And as on so many of the great moments I would find myself quoting a few lines of John Gillespie Magee's poem:

> Up, up the long, delirious, burning blue
> I top the windswept heights with easy grace
> Where never lark or ever eagle flew . . .

Sixty miles out and I could see the Labrador Sea, the North Atlantic Ocean. The great barren landscape below me was over 4,000 feet above sea level. I was at 5,000 feet and I could see the massive fjords ahead where the high plateau plunged sheer to sea level into the Arn River that flowed into Saglek fjord. The sheer scale of everything was beyond belief. I gloried in it, but not without a little nervousness. Was I going to get turbulence once I reached those great fjords? There must have been a good 35 knots of wind at 330 degrees. Was I going to get the sort of turbulence Q and I had when we came off the ice cap near Kulusuk? The winds then had been much stronger and the ice cap over 9,000 feet. But mountains are mountains and winds and mountains . . .

I could see a cluster of white blobs, satellite dishes on the furthest point – a radar station. I checked my chart. The airfield was shown to be just to the west of that highest point, hidden by a 3,000-foot mountain.

I told Colin and Q that I could see a radar station and icebergs. I climbed another thousand feet as I approached Saglek fjord, hoping to stay clear of any turbulence. There was practically none so I was able to enjoy that magnificent Labrador coast with the high plateau falling sheer to a green valley floor and the Arn River. There seemed to be a golden light with the green, then the river met the sea where all was rock once more and the light was cold and there was pack ice and icebergs. I flew down Saglek fjord, still 30 miles to go, and started my descent, reporting back to Colin and Q. I flew past Hans Havan Island and the smaller Rose Island beside it. Could they be named after a husband and wife? What a cold and forbidding namesake. Five miles to go, I was down to 500 feet and there was still no sign of the airfield. Then I rounded the final point, two miles from the position marked on my chart, and there it was. What a surprise! This was no disused airfield. Saglek was a hive of activity. My immediate reaction was to slow down – what sort of a reception were we going to get? I quickly called the others, Colin was high enough to hear me. 'Blimey!' was Colin's comment. 'Well, I guess I've got a runway then.' He laughed and said, 'Good luck!'

The runway ended about a hundred yards from the water's edge then ran slightly uphill through a short open valley which led once more to the sea. To the left of the runway was a large apron with a row of sheds on the far side. Several groups of men stopped whatever they were doing and were watching my progress, no doubt with keen interest. Of course I had no radio frequency with which to say 'Hi, I'm friendly', or check if there was any other traffic. I thought I better look good. I came in on right base, hovered, looked left and right, then cautiously taxied across the runway to the apron and landed in the corner furthest from the buildings. I shut down trying to think positive thoughts about what fun this must be for them.

No one made a move in my direction. I got out and gave a friendly wave, and then a jeep came tearing round the corner of the dirt road that led up to the distant radar station and screeched to a halt a few yards away from me. A man jumped out and stood for a moment just looking at G-MURY, shaking his head. He walked over, smiled and said 'Well, hello there! Welcome to Saglek, I'm Phil Chubb – and who might you be?' I didn't know quite how to begin. 'Uh, well, hi, I'm Jennifer Murray, I'm – we're – there are two more coming – we're flying around the world . . .'

Phil interrupted me, saying, 'You're WHAT?! In that machine? You must be mad.' Then I saw him looking over my shoulder and shaking his head with a look of total and utter disbelief. 'Well – I'll – be – darned!' he said, 'that sure beats everything.'

He just stood there lost for words, watching Colin chugging down the bay. Then suddenly he turned towards one of the groups of men on the far side of the apron and shouted, 'Hey, you guys, get the runway clear!' They were already running towards their jeep, and then I saw why. There were several caribou halfway up the runway (I learnt later that this was routine). Q landed several minutes later. Phil kept shaking his head and saying 'I'll be darned.'

Then he said, 'Well, you know you guys sure kept us guessing. We've had you on our radar for hours. We just had no idea what those three slow-moving little specs could be coming towards us.' He then went on to tell us that we had arrived at US Air Force Defence Command Surveillance Station (Labrador), that it was strictly off limits and that if we had applied for prior permission to land it would not have been given!

'You'll have to wait down here while I go back up to the station [5 miles away up the mountain]. I'll have to clear this with Goose Bay.' He cheerfully added, 'Worst case, we'll take you up and feed you and give you a shower, but you might all have to sleep in those sheds,' pointing to the row on the far side of the apron. Then he said, 'Oh we have a B748 [twin turbine plane – rather larger than G-EELS] coming in any minute now – lucky you arrived when you did.' We agreed. We gave him our pilot's licences, passports and our website address and off he went.

It was pleasant sitting on the grass at the edge of the apron. We had landed shortly after 3 p.m. and it was a hot 18 degrees centigrade. We thought of the others sitting in foggy Kuujjuaq and felt good. Colin was saying 'I told you so. I just knew my gut feeling was right.' I wondered what Goose Bay would say and, more especially, whether they might not like us flying to Greenland from Saglek. There was more action as the jeep was once again rushing out onto the runway (1,460 metres of paved runway with overruns at either end) to clear off the caribou for the incoming flight. Caribou were duly cleared just as the plane came into view from the south.

An hour later Phil was back and said there had been a bit of flak from Goose Bay as 'they like to know about these things' but we were cleared to stay and we didn't have to spend the night on the shed floor. We assumed they had made no comment about our onward intentions.

Colin of course wanted to get his microlight into one of the sheds. None of the doors looked quite large enough, but Phil said it would have to wait until later unless we wanted to stay there for the next three hours as the jeep was needed. 'Why don't you come on up now? Supper starts at five o'clock.' We piled in the jeep and as we bumped and bounced up the road made up of fairly large rocks he told us that if we had arrived three days later we would have found the station unmanned. 'We shut down during the winter. We'll be getting the first snow any day now.'

Halfway up the mountain Phil halted on one of the bends overlooking the runway. 'Do you see the wrecked plane down there?'

There, far below us, were the remains of a plane that Phil told us had crashed in 1942. He told us that there had been seven on board, the captain's name was Grover Hodge Junior. They were on a ferry flight, they got their navigation wrong and thought that they were south of Goose Bay when they were actually to the north. Too late they realised their mistake. They turned south, fuel ran low and they crash-landed at Saglek. All survived, only one was slightly injured. But this was before there was ever an airstrip or anything there. They were all under the age of 24, it was December and none of them had any idea about survival in the wilderness. They survived for a little over two months, but eventually all died, never knowing there was an Eskimo village four miles away. 'The Captain kept a diary, we have it up at the Base if you'd like to read it,' he said and kindly let me have a copy.

DIARY OF ONE NOW DEAD

No more than 50 yards from the runway of the Air Defense Command's Saglek Air Station (Labrador) lie the weathered remains of a B-26 medium bomber of World War II vintage. Here, on December 10, 1942, below Saglek's 1,800-foot cliff which overlooks the North Atlantic Ocean and Saglek Bay, was the site that fate had chosen for the bomber crew to exist for nearly two months in subzero temperatures and die . . . still believing that help would arrive.

Although only a few miles from an Eskimo village, none of the crew walked out. On December 23rd, three of the crew started south in a boat that was a part of the B-26's emergency equipment. They were never seen again. The remains of the crewmen that stayed with their downed plane were found in March after death had taken each brave member of this little team. Today, in 1968, an Air Defense Command surveillance station, manned by USAF officers and enlisted technicians of another generation, maintains a constant alert as a fitting memorial to these and other brave Air Force men.

The diary of the B-26 pilot has been retained in its original text. The last entry in the diary is February 3, 1943. We pick up the pilot's commentary while the ill-fated crew is awaiting departure from BW-1, Greenland, en route to Goose Bay, Labrador.

NOVEMBER 12, 1942
We've less than six hours of daylight between sunrise and sunset now. Had about two inches of snow last night and everything was really pretty. Spent most of the morning sweeping it off the plane. They said that there's a chance of leaving tomorrow but this place seems so much like home that it doesn't seem like we should leave.

NOVEMBER 16 ,1942
This place is full of changes. Yesterday afternoon Jansen and I walked

down to the river. There was a solid sheet of ice resting on the rocks, and it was covered with almost two inches of snow. Every once in a while, we would break through up to our knees, but there was nothing under the ice. Last night we had rain with a warm wind with gusts up to better than 60 miles per hour. So this morning there was only isolated patches of ice left. Today was the first time in two weeks that we have been able to walk on bare ground. We've had all kinds of weather, most of the days were fairly warm. But one day it was six degrees. We've seen days when not a breath of air stirred.

NOVEMBER 26, 1942
I still say this is screwy weather. We were alerted this morning at 0330. There was a ***** overcast. We killed time until 0600 then we got briefed. It was still overcast and seemed to be getting worse. The A-10's and the B-25's started kicking off, but about then, it started to rain and the ceiling looked like it was very low. About 10 minutes later it stopped raining and an A-20 came over at 600 feet with room to spare. By 0830, the sun was shining and everything looked as nice as we could ask for, but it was too late to take off.

NOVEMBER 30, 1942
Took off at last for Goose Bay. About 1315, we ran into some clouds and I turned around and called for the formation?? to turn around also. One plane dropped out. I think I saw the two P-40's later. I lost the others while letting down below the clouds. We saw an opening to the south at about 2,000 feet and after flying in that direction we broke out. We finally had to go back up to 13,500 feet, but it was clear sailing, so we kept on. Lt. Josephson gave us a new heading to get back on course, but we know now it was too much of a correction. About halfway I picked up Goose beam, but the set went dead after a few minutes. It was too late to turn back then, so we tried to get it on the compass, but couldn't. We finally hit the coast. We decided we were south of Goose Bay, so we turned north until we finally realized we were north. We were almost out of gas, so I started looking for a place to land. I wanted to get back to where there were trees, but the engines started missing, so we came back down. The crew never batted an eye when they were told that we were going to have to make a crash landing. Even if I do say so myself, it was a good landing and Lt. Josephson did a good job of cutting the switch. We hit a rock that tore the bombay open and one

prop tip went through the fuselage behind me. Outside of that, the ship was intact. It swung around almost 90 degrees without stopping, but made a good wind break that way; it was almost dark so after eating a cold ration we went to bed inside the ship; we had 17 blankets; a comforter and bedroll, but we slept very well. Lt. Josephson took a star shot and decided we were 300 minutes from Goose.

DECEMBER 11, 1942

Lt. Josephson walked to the ford to the west and Golm the one to the east. We spent most of the day clearing up the ship and pooling rations in the afternoon. I climbed the mountain in front of us [where Saglek Air Station is now located], but didn't learn much. Nolan worked on the output all day without results. We cranked the dingy radio. It was pretty windy so we spent the night in the ship.

DECEMBER 12, 1942

Made three big improvements in our situation. Lt. Jansen and Golm discovered a lake close to our ship and saw a fox. Waywrench and I saw 50 seals; we know that there is food there. We made a lean-to out of tarps under the wing and slept there. It was much better.

DECEMBER 13, 1942

When the star shots were figured out it showed us to be close to the town of Hebron. Worked on the put-put all day with no success, so we tried to work the liaison set on the batteries but they were too weak. We pooled our covers and slept together.

DECEMBER 14, 1942

Wind blew all day with increasing velocity and snow. Our lake went dry so we are back to melting snow. We went to bed early.

DECEMBER 15, 1942

Had to eat a cold breakfast because the wind blew too much snow in our fire. Nolan changed the voltage regulators and got 25 volts, long enough for me to get a couple of stations on the liaison receiver. The put-put stopped, but we hope we know what is wrong with it. So we hope to get a message out soon.

DECEMBER 17, 1942

The put-put went out, but we did try the batteries. They, too, were dead.

DECEMBER 19, 1942

More snow last night. Nolan and Mangins tried to work on the put-put but it was too cold. We built a fire in the lean-to and thawed out.

DECEMBER 20, 1942

It was so windy we stayed in bed all day.

DECEMBER 21, 1942

Everything was really snowed in so we spent the day eating and thawing out blankets and planning a trip south. Lt. Josephson, Lt. Jansen, and Sgt. Nolan plan to head south in the boat the first clear day.

DECEMBER 22, 1942

Had a perfect day, the first clear day in over a week. We worked on the boat and cleaned snow away from the lean-to all day. We ate a pretty big meal with the three boat men eating a little extra.

DECEMBER 23, 1942

Got up at 0715, got the boat ready and started carrying it. The wind was pretty strong and the boat was heavy, so we had a pretty hard time of it. We didn't get to the water until noon, and then it took quite a while to find a place to put it in the water. We intended to put them off shore, but they appeared to be making slow headway to the south. That was the last time we saw them. We had a hard time coming back across the snow. We had some peanuts and caramels and went to bed.

DECEMBER 24, 1942

Christmas Eve and we've been here two weeks today. It was lonesome with just the four of us, but we got up pretty early and dug out the gas strainer so we could make a fire. It was so windy we couldn't work outside so we dried out the blankets. Golm got blistered pretty bad and swollen hands which have to be doctored. We stretched out our eating to cover most of the day. We had a sardine sized can of herring with crackers, a spoon full of peanuts apiece, a black cough drop, and a caramel, a cup of grape drink, and plenty of coffee, using the same grounds over and over. It's really a surprise how much one can get from a small thing like a caramel, but we looked forward to it with anticipation each day.

DECEMBER 25, 1942

What a Christmas. Mangins' feet pained him so much we had to get up at 0330. He was in agony before that, but was better after, although his arches pain him pretty bad. Got up again at 0900. Golm went exploring, I massaged Mangins' feet, and Waywrench started fixing up the floor, which was in pretty bad condition from the fire. Later we had to dig out the rear entrance to the ship to fix the window up. After that, we had a first aid lesson. The only one who doesn't have anything wrong is me. We are about to eat our Christmas dinner and go to bed.

DECEMBER 26, 1942

Had another swell day. The weather was perfect. Waywrench cleaned up the back of the ship, while Golm dug around in the rear of the bombay, uncovering a can of fruit cocktail and a can of Chicken a la king. I worked on Mangins' feet and did some odd jobs. Everyone is feeling better, and I hope that Mangins will be up in a few days. We aren't starving by any means, but the conversations are mostly about food. One surely can remember some tasty food.

DECEMBER 27, 1942

Started today as usual by treating the casualties. Mangins' feet are better, but we found a big blister on each foot. Golm and Mangins spent the day drying blankets. Waywrench finished cleaning out the back of the ship, and I climbed the mountain to see if I could see anything out to sea. I also took a roll of film. The enforced diet is beginning to tell on us, but we'll eat a little more tomorrow.

DECEMBER 28, 1942

This has been a terrible day. The wind started early in the morning and has kept us inside all day. We had two fires which took the rest of the day to repair. Mangin's feet are quite a bit better, and he will start working on the put-put soon. We may get the liaison set going yet. In the meantime, we can feel the effect of the short rations more every day. We pray almost every minute that they boys in the boat will get through and get help soon.

DECEMBER 29, 1942

Today has been just average. The wind started up early again, but not too hard. Mangin's feet are almost back to normal.

DECEMBER 30, 1942

Today was overcast with snow showers. Spent most of the day working on the inside. Golm lost a fingernail and may lose another. I'm just thankful that his hand doesn't pain him. Worked a little on the put-put and made some progress, but it was too dark to work much. Got up a game of 500 Rummy which everyone seemed to enjoy. The boys have been gone a week today. God grant they are still going.

JANUARY 1, 1943

Happy New Year. It snowed and blew all night and kept it up all day. So since we had no fire we stayed in bed all day.

JANUARY 2, 1943

More wind and snow today. It slacked up a little around noon, so we got up with the aid of a fire in a peanut can. Waywrench got the prop and ceiver tank out with a gallon of alcohol and glycerin, and I dug out the oil drain. After that, we had a couple of hot fires and plenty of hot coffee and had a lemon powder and cup of bouillon. Our main dish was the last can of datenut roll with jelly, and it was very good. We didn't finish with the eating and drinking until almost noon. Then I worked on Mangins' feet and we went to bed. There was quite a bit of loose snow outside but the very shape of the ship keeps it fairly clean. It actually rained today and I don't know what effect that's going to have on our situation. The boys have been gone ten days today, which is the time we figured it would take them to make the trip. We hope they made it and can bring help soon.

JANUARY 3, 1943

There wasn't much wind last night so we thought we would have a good day, but the wind picked up, and it snowed all day. The ship has a sheet of ice on it and is covered with snow. Besides that, the drifts are higher and closer than they have ever been before. We hooked up the hand fuel transfer pump, and I'm positive we pumped some gas over to his side, but we couldn't get it to drain out, so we had to use the alcohol to cook with. I got into a big hurry once and caused a fire in which I got burned but not badly. Now we are all wearing bandages. I found two bouillon cubes in the radio operator's desk. Spent a lot of time putting snow under our bed. It must be raining outside now. It couldn't be melting ice on the wing. We keep praying for clear weather and hope that the boys got through. Also to try out a new theory to where Hebron is.

JANUARY 4, 1943

Had a blue sky when we got up, but it stayed overcast all day. There wasn't much wind, however, so we got up and went to work. Waywrench and I got quite a bit of gas out of the other wing, so we are pretty well fixed on that. Mangins has the put-put almost ready to try again. We are just praying for good weather both in hopes of a rescue plane (if the boys got through). I am cutting down still on the rations.

JANUARY 5, 1943

It started off like a beautiful day, but turned to a light low overcast. Waywrench and I cleaned the plane of snow and Mangins finished the put-put, which seems to be in pretty good shape. It started clearing late this afternoon.

JANUARY 6, 1943

This is the eighth day of bad weather. The entrance is blocked, and it doesn't do any good to dig it out. It has been two weeks since the boys have left and spirits are still high in spite of the bad weather.

JANUARY 7, 1943

We've been here four weeks today. The entrance was blocked up this morning. As I was going into the ship, I saw a little bird. We caught him and boiled him for a couple of hours. Then made a stew by adding a bouillon powder. It was really delicious. Golm started to go looking for Hebron, but the snow was too soft. Mangins got outside for the first time in 13 days. If we can't find a town or get the put-put going in three days, we are going to have to sit and wait until the weather clears and pray that the boys got through because we are too low on food to do anything else. God help us get out of here safely.

JANUARY 8, 1943

Today was the most strenuous for me since we got here. I tried to get to Hebron, and I still think I know where it is, but there are two mountains in the way. I can feel myself growing weaker and we have less to eat every day. I don't know what we would do if we didn't have that three pounds of coffee. We sit around and drink that and talk about all kinds of food, but I think we all crave chocolate candy more than anything else. The boys have dug out the back of the ship so if tomorrow is clear, we still have one last try with the put-put radio.

JANUARY 9, 1943

Well, we put the put-put back in its place, and it jammed again so that leaves us with one possibility, that the boys got through.

JANUARY 10, 1943

We have been here one month today, 30 days. Spent most of the day, which was perfect as far as the weather was concerned, looking for the plane and fixing up bandages. The boys' spirits were much higher today, after our little church service. Our only food today was a slice of pineapple and two spoonfuls of juice.

JANUARY 11, 1943

Our third day of perfect weather, also the coldest day since right after we got here. Spent the day watching for the plane which didn't come. The oil gave out on this side, which brings about another problem. The short rations are beginning to tell on us, but we are still in high spirits. If we don't live to eat some of the food we talked about, we've mentally eaten one of the best meals in the world.

JANUARY 12, 1943

Today was the boys' 20th day, our 33rd, and was overcast, but was calm. We got the oil almost dug out but are all so weak that we can hardly work. The boys' spirits are still high though, and we had a couple of lively bull sessions on our one topic, food. Our ration today was a slice of pineapple.

JANUARY 13, 1943

Another calm overcast day. We dug up the oil, dried out the blankets, made a new bed on snow, and ate our last food, a slice of spam and a soda cracker apiece. All we have left is a half pound of chocolates and three drink powders, but we talk like rescue was certainly tomorrow. It cleared off late this afternoon, so maybe there is hope for tomorrow.

JANUARY 14, 1943
Clear day, but with wind. We cleared off the plane and waited, but nothing happened. Late this afternoon we were playing cards, when . . . oiled the gas too fast and caused an explosion which burned both his and my face, hair, and hands. Our rations were four chocolates, but we are still working out pretty well. After a devotional, we went to bed.

JANUARY 15, 1943
A perfect day as to the weather, but the coldest since we got here. Spent most of the day trying to keep warm and listening for a plane. Also made big plans for a couple of days in New York when we get our furloughs. Rations were two chocolates and a bouillon powder. No one is particularly hungry yet, but we are getting weaker and colder because our bodies aren't putting out enough heat.

JANUARY 16, 1943
Another calm clear day, but the coldest we have yet had. The oil froze up, so we had to end up by burning nothing but gas. The only thing we have left is one bouillon powder and two sticks of gum. The strain is beginning to tell, but we still have good bull sessions about food and the furlough in New York.

JANUARY 17, 1943
Couldn't have asked for a better day except that it is so cold that the oil is frozen and won't burn. So our gas is going pretty fast. Had our last food, bouillon powder, so unless rescue comes in a few days . . . The boys have been gone 25 days which is a long time, but they are our only hope. Our families will really miss some swell dishes and menus.

JANUARY 18, 1943
Cold and clear. My watch stopped, so we didn't get up until noon. Must be a little warmer because we got a little oil. Today was our first complete day without any food, but spirits are still pretty high. It's surprising how much punishment the body and mind can take when necessary. We are still in pretty good condition but rather weak. Not much hope left.

JANUARY 20, 1943

It snowed and blew all night, but we all slept pretty well, and we were much more cheerful today. We stayed up longer than we should have though, and are pretty tired. That snow has been blowing pretty hard all day and is piling up in front of the door, so I don't know what we will do if it doesn't stop pretty soon.

JANUARY 21, 1943

Six weeks today and rough night with snow and rain, so everything was soaked when we got up. Only Waywrench and I got up and then only long enough to melt snow for water. Things could be worse.

JANUARY 22, 1943

Got up around noon, and was up until about 6. I cleared up the entrance and made the bed. We could stand some good weather.

JANUARY 23, 1943

Spent a miserable night. Everyone got crowded and nobody could get comfortable. Had a good day, but everybody is pretty discouraged, although the conversation was pretty good. We haven't really felt famished but we are really weak. It really gets me to see these boys start to do something and have to stop from the lack of power to go on. Waywrench has developed a case of piles and is really suffering.

JANUARY 24, 1943

Had a miserable night. Everybody got up at 0130, shot the bull and drew gas, and went to bed at 0730.

JANUARY 25, 1943

Overcast but fairly calm. Each day we don't see how we can last another day, but each time we manage to go on. We all smoked a pipe of tobacco this morning and Golm really got sick, and I felt pretty bad. But we came out pretty well.

FEBRUARY 3, 1943

Slept a solid week in bed. Today Waywrench died after being mentally ill for several days. We are all pretty weak, but should be able to last several more days.

NOTE: This is the last entry in the diary. The men were found in the first part of March by Eskimos from Hebron and were only about three and one-half hours' walk from Hebron.

LIST OF FOOD WHEN LANDED: 7 cns of spam, 3 cns of peanuts, 8 cns of chicken, 2 cns of pineapple, 3 cns of fruit cocktail, 2 cns of datenut roll, 1cn of brown bread, 3 bxs of chocolates, 28 Hershey bars, 4 pkgs of dates, 1 lb of crackers, 4 bxs of fig newtons, 1 lb of cheese crackers, 1 cs of coke, 2 cns of salmon, 3 lbs of coffee and 20 pkgs of caramels.

What a sad yet uplifting story of stoicism, courage and bravery, with the tragic poignancy of help so near to hand and never found.

The base was like something from a 007 movie. We were on the remote coast of Labrador, 200 miles from anywhere, surrounded by sea and barren mountains, yet here was a state-of-the-art, no-expenses-spared US Air Force humming, throbbing base with offices, storerooms, machinery rooms and excellent living quarters. We were ushered in to a huge open-plan mess room complete with billiard table, TV section, sitting area and restaurant with a hatch to a large stainless steel kitchen where 'Cookie', a large and smiling Inuit cook was busy cooking up a storm of T-bone steaks and chips. How glad we were to be there.

In true American style there were soft drinks, muffins, doughnuts and cookies, just there and waiting and all for free. The only downside was that the base was dry. 'No Alcohol on the Base.' I thought guiltily of our vodka bottle. A nip would have been nice, a cold beer even better. Q and Colin had a game of billiards, and then I played the winner – Colin. Q announced that he was going for a 'breath of fresh air'. Colin quickly beat me at billiards and we decided to join Q, who, to our surprise, we found deep in conversation on the satellite phone. Why couldn't he have said he was going to try and touch base with Pat?

The car did not come back from its work detail until darkness was falling. Phil introduced us to Mike Cross, the new Site Supervisor and handed him a gun. On seeing us looking rather surprised he said, 'Bear patrol!' and explained that they always had a 'bear detail'. Any working party going out had one man armed with a gun whose sole job was to keep watch. There were apparently lots of bears and they were attracted to the food around the camp. A man had been mauled the year before.

We bumped back down the road. By now it was bitterly cold. The microlight wouldn't fit through the shed door and we had to get the wing out of reach of the caribou. We shoved and hauled and tried to angle the microlight in and then, not seeing in the dark, the tip of the wing had caught the edge of the door, snapping the end batten. Colin started blaming me because I had been over at the other side of the apron sorting out some stuff in my helicopter at the moment of 'snap' and apparently I was meant to be guarding that end. We finally had to take the wing off the trike and put the pieces in separately. That meant we would have all the business the next morning of hauling and squeezing full fuel tanks back into place.

Mark said he felt sure they would have something in the storeroom that would do to replace or repair the batten. We went back up the mountain to the enormous warehouse storeroom. It held everything, from a vast snow plough and enormous earth-moving machines to the tiniest nut, with a fork-lift truck to get things off top shelves. Mark found a length of aluminium that was virtually identical to the broken batten and, incredibly, had the identical thread. 'Now what else do you need?' he said.

'You don't by any chance have any car fuel?' I asked.

Mark thought they might have an unopened barrel down at the airfield, but their equipment all ran on diesel fuel. 'We'll check it out in the morning but we might as well find you a length of hose to siphon it with in any case,' he said.

The bedrooms at the base were clean and simple, all natural pine wood and white painted walls and ceilings. From my window I could see a million stars, the ghostly shape of the mountains and the blackness of the sea – I gave an involuntary shiver of anticipation, excitement tinged with fear about the long-awaited Arctic crossing.

I woke at 5 a.m. to a cold enchanted world. We were above the clouds. The seas and valleys were blanketed and the mountain tops were dark shapes and silhouettes against the dawn sky, a few stars still lingering. While I was getting dressed the first colour suffused the heavens, indigo replaced by the purest of pale aquamarine, the skies above the low cloud were clear. I looked over towards the American and Canadian flags fluttering gently in the light breeze. The wind still looked to be from the north-west. I hoped we would find some fuel.

I had already checked that the other two were awake. I quickly packed my bag, stripped my bed and folded the duvet. No one, we were told, would be using the rooms before the spring. We had been shown where the laundry room was the night before so on the way downstairs I put my sheets and towel in the machine and headed on to the dining room, Cookie was already at work and a couple of men were tucking into their waffles and bacon. Mark kindly volunteered to phone Goose Bay for the Met forecast for the region, and for Greenland. Greenland, today we were going to Greenland!

There was an area of high pressure over Greenland. The en route weather looked stable with no freezing conditions. We could expect scattered cloud at 10,000 feet with occasional rain. Winds were the only problem – 320 degrees at 10 knots. It looked as though we would be getting head winds.

At 6 a.m. Mark took us down to the airfield deep in fog, but assured us that the low sea fog would clear within the next two hours. There was one 50-gallon barrel of fuel sitting unopened by one of the sheds. Mark thought it hadn't been there for more than a year. He then said he had to go, that the car was needed, and he wished us the very best of luck and refused any suggestion of payment for anything. 'The Forces are delighted to have been of service!' he said with a laugh. We all shook hands and he headed once more back up the hill, disappearing quickly into the swirling fog.

What with reassembling the microlight, adding the extra barrel of fuel into our various machines, doing all the checks and getting into our survival suits, it was two and a half hours before we were ready to depart. First we carefully shared out the good fuel in the red jerry cans. Then we prised open the barrel and smelled what we hoped was regular car fuel – it was definitely not diesel. We siphoned off a cupful and held it up to the light. It was a rather disconcerting orange colour but otherwise looked OK. We siphoned the fuel into our red jerry cans and carried them over to the aircraft, topping the microlight up first. We were halfway through doing the helicopters when we noticed that the jerry can had an alarming amount of rust and what looked like water in it. We poured off a sample, it was a mess. Colin got really upset. His ratio of good fuel to bad was quite a lot higher than the helicopters, but his Rotax engine can run on just about anything.

I had taken ten gallons of the bad stuff and Q had five. We dipped our tanks. I had 90 gallons, Q had 89 (G-JEFA, being more fuel efficient, had used a few gallons less than G-MURY on the journey from Kuujuaq). We had 623 miles to go to Narsarsuaq Airfield. I did a few sums and I could see the others doing the same. 'Five hundred and forty-two nautical miles, average speed 60 knots, pulling 17–18 inches of manifold power (to level-peg it with the microlight), leaning off the fuel should give a burn rate of around 9 gallons an hour, 81 gallons used, 13 gallons in hand.' That was not much of a reserve even in still wind, and head winds were forecast. What if we had to go around bad weather? What if there was fog in Narsarsuaq like we had right now in Saglek? I remembered that the CAA booklet advised that all aircraft crossing the North Atlantic carry half as much again fuel as required to make the flight.

We weighed up the odds, dodgy fuel versus narrow margins. Narrow margins won. Having seen the muck in that fuel I was already nervous enough about it swilling around amongst my lovely clean, blue Avgas. I argued that there was no freezing rain forecast and if we flew high enough then I could lean the fuel off even more. But then what if the head winds strengthened? We would have to fly low . . . The final decision was to leave the last 15 gallons behind.

Checks done, we helped each other into our survival suits, and, just as in Okha, I immediately wanted to have a pee. I scrambled down this sort of gully to the side the apron and had a huge struggle, getting half out of my survival suit and then trying to hold the suit and go to the loo without falling over. Mission accomplished, I clambered back up to G-MURY. Colin was already in G-NOWW with motor running.

The fog, as Mark had predicted, had dispersed. There was a strong wind blowing from the west and the skies were clear as Colin taxied towards the runway before lifting quickly, battling the stiff crosswind. The helicopters followed a couple of minutes later. The time was 9 a.m. We circled over Saglek Base, I took a last look at the remains of the ill-fated B26 bomber and thought sadly of those young lives lost, praying that we would have sufficient fuel, then turned north-east across the Labrador Sea and climbed slowly to 5,000 feet. I kept looking back towards the land until it was only the faintest line on the horizon – goodbye to the great North American Continent. I experienced a mixture of emotions as I took a long last look at the Labrador coast but the most prevalent one was fear. It was time for some stirring music and I settled for Tschaikovsky's *1812* and began to feel much braver.

Q came on the air. 'Umm, did anyone file a flight plan?' We had all clean forgotten. We then hoped that we would hear someone else on frequency before we got too far from land and be able to get them to file one for us. There we were, embarking on the longest and potentially most hazardous leg of our entire journey with no flight plan. No one knew we were there, no one was monitoring us.

Our luck was in, though, as ten minutes later we heard a bush pilot on 123.45 chatting to someone. He sounded rather startled when Q asked him if he could file a flight plan for a formation of three aircraft that were on their way from Saglek. Q had to confirm twice that he had heard Saglek correctly to Greenland and he needed yet more confirmation that we were indeed going to take nine hours to get to there. 'Just a minute, let me get a pencil.' He took the details and said he would try and get through to Goose Bay (he obviously had HF radio, as most pilots in the area did) and would come back to us. Ten minutes later he told us he had got through to Goose Bay and had filed our flight plans. He gave us a squawk frequency and told us to try and do a relay with an airliner to Narsarsuaq every hour. At least everyone now knew we were there.

One hour out and I knew I was in trouble. I needed another pee. I made the big mistake of announcing my problem to the other two, who then kept asking for a progress report! We had eight hours to go – I was never going to make it. Anyhow, it was a sort of uncomfortable diversion from watching the endless blue, listening for any possible hint of an engine hiccup and checking the skies for distant storms. On the good side I found I was only burning eight gallons of fuel an hour with an air speed of 55 knots. On the bad side we had the predicted ten knots of head wind at 5,000 feet. It was no better at 1,000 feet and worse at 8,000 feet where there was 15 knots.

Two more hours passed and I was dying to go to the loo! There was nothing else for it – I was going to have to pee in my pants. But the funny thing is, it's quite difficult to actually go – all those years of potty training come to the fore, and then there was the thought of having to own up to the others. But I rose to the occasion and oh, the infinite relief! A lovely warm feeling, which didn't last too long, and of course the others thought it was wonderful. Half an hour later, when G-EELS came on the air, it was the first bit of news to be relayed.

The Cessna crew had spent another dreary night in Kuujuaq. The weather had remained grey and overcast and they had taken off into cloud. Pat asked Colin and me to say a few words for the camera – specifically asking for a few comments on my damp situation. We remained in radio contact with them for the next hour. Then they were once more out of range and we continued on our lonely way.

Time passed infinitely slowly. We did relays with two British Airways flights, one inbound to New York, one to Boston and a United Airlines flight bound for London. Surprisingly, none sounded intrigued or asked a question.

The wind veered. We now had a spanking 20 knots of tail wind and everyone was feeling much more relaxed about the fuel situation. I was playing my usual over-water game, trying not to look at the dot of my helicopter on the moving map on my GPS too often, so that I would hopefully see some progress when I did look. I always seemed to look too soon and there appeared virtually no change, until finally past the halfway mark and the point of no return it seemed to speed up a little. We were committed to Greenland.

We all heard or thought we heard our engines running rough at odd moments, ears over-sensitive to the slightest change of pitch, vibration or rhythm. On these occasions I would be hit by a whoosh of adrenalin, my heartbeat going crazy, all senses on red alert, listening, listening, checking instruments, checking yet again that the life raft was at the ready, and whipping once more through the whole ditching routine in my mind. And longing to be anywhere other than 5,000 feet over the North Atlantic Ocean. Finally I would relax again – until the next suspected change in noise.

I wished that I had some new CDs as I had played them all so many times before. Certain music was right for one setting or mood and not for another. Some I had to stop playing entirely, like *The Mission* (from the film). It has a couple of places that sound like engine problems and had scared the daylights out of me several times. I settled for an old favourite – *New World Symphony*.

Colin looked as though he was having rather a relaxed time of it for once. Cruising along, straight and level. For the time being there was no turbulence, so he could be more or less 'hands-off', his arms just resting on the bar. I had a little more to do as I kept having to slow down, which meant pulling carb heat to prevent carb icing. R44s don't like flying continuously at 55 knots. But once we got the tail winds and I no longer had to worry unduly about fuel, I felt I could circle from time to time which made a change and I could increase the power. It was our longest stretch of open-water crossing (out of sight of land) and it seemed to go on forever. Perhaps if we had had to fight the elements – turbulence, storms, icing, cloud – it would have gone faster. As it was, we only had to worry about possible engine- and fuel-related problems.

Five, six, seven hours: we saw nothing but sea, other than one container ship an hour out of Saglek, and each other. We had talked to G-EELS and done our relays and heard the odd radio talk of airliners at 34,000 feet, talking to some far away station. Other than that we were very much alone by modern day standards. I thought about the early aviators and how incredibly tough and how truly alone they had been. It didn't make me feel any braver or less lonely, though.

I thought of our British pilots, Alcock and Brown, in their Vickers Vimy, the first pilots to successfully fly across the Atlantic Ocean. They conquered the Atlantic, but spent practically the entire journey in fog. Their radio broke down shortly after take off and it was so noisy they had to communicate with each other by writing notes – and there was I with my Bose noise reduction headphones and glorious music. Alcock nearly lost it at one point when he went into a spiral and only just pulled out before hitting the water. They finally made it to Ireland, landing in a bog. It is incredible to think that Alcock and Brown conquered the Atlantic a mere 16 years after the Wright brothers made those first epic flights in 1903.

I appreciated how incredibly lucky we were to have such good weather, especially after all the doom and gloom and warnings with the worries of Arctic snows, gales and icing. The earlier aviators had been less lucky. Seven years after Alcock and Brown, Charles Lindbergh, on his epic solo flight, had major weather problems too. He had ice-build on the wings of his little 'Spirit of St Louis' and was pushed down to sea level, where luckily the air warmed up enough for the ice to melt, coming off in great chunks and lightening his aircraft enough so that he was able to stop his perilous downward descent into a watery grave and could once more climb, cautiously. The journey from New York to Paris non-stop took him 33 and a half hours to complete and, with virtually no sleep for hours before take-off, he fell asleep and he too nearly hit the water. It was only the sun reflecting off a little mirror onto his eyes that woke him, just in time. Five years later, to the day, Amelia Earhart, in her modified Lockheed Vega, was the first woman to fly across the Atlantic, from Nova Scotia to Ireland. She also encountered low cloud on her flight.

Seventy miles from Greenland, I was endlessly peering for my first glimpse of land. Low cloud on the horizon so often looks like land and then, like a mirage, takes a new and insubstantial shape and disappears entirely. Finally, there, much higher up than I had been looking, were snowy peaks. 'I'm going to make it,' I said to myself, and then, out loud, 'Here's one for the ladies!' I was reminded of the little note that Sarah Ferguson (the Duchess of York) had given me with a little St Christopher medallion (which I was wearing), before my first trip. She wrote on it, 'On behalf of the women of the world –YES! YES! YES!'

One hour later Q and I landed on an enormous iceberg and got out to stretch our legs and take photographs. We still had over 60 miles to go. Low stratus cloud hugged the coast and filled the fjords. Once more airborne, my GPS told me I was flying up the Skov fjord, and I had lost sight of the others. I think everyone was enjoying being over land, even though we could only see the mountain tops, with occasional breaks in the cloud revealing black water below. Then I came to an open valley with green, grassy fields and a small crofter's stone house. It was the only grass I ever saw on Greenland.

Narsarsuaq was clear of cloud and turbulence. I landed with almost a sense of anti-climax. We were in long-awaited Greenland. Now we just had to get out. And I had to get out of my rather damp clothes.

Narsarsuaq consisted of an airfield, a hotel and not much else. The runway ran alongside the top of the fjord with the great glaciers beyond rising steeply to the mighty ice cap. There were a couple of large hangars with one enormous Air Sea Rescue helicopter, and a small terminal building, neat and clean and tidy, built in pine. The hotel was also pine, and full of a group of Japanese hikers. It didn't surprise me. Trekking in Bhutan once, with a group of friends, we were six days travel from anywhere, trying to cross a 14,000-foot pass in a snowstorm, and who should we meet but a group of Japanese ladies who had just come over the pass from the opposite direction.

The light in Greenland is like nowhere else I have ever been. It is thin and clear with a translucent quality, and we were seeing it at its best – how lucky we were with the weather. We woke the following morning to clear skies and still air. The hotel manager, Mogens Colberger, told us it had been an appalling summer, that the whole of the previous week had been dreadful, and the day before was the first decent day they had had in weeks. We were in the middle of an area of high pressure, and with a bit of luck we hoped we could travel east together.

Back at the airport we got the Met for the region. The front over the west coast was moving north, while a ridge of high pressure was stationary over the south and central part of Greenland. Freezing level was 8,000 feet with nil icing below that height. Winds in the fjords were variable: 3–12 knots, and along the east coast 5–15 knots with risk of fog patches. The weather from Iqaluit to the west coast of Greenland, our original route, was appalling with stong to gale force winds – head winds.

Colin, Q and I all took off within minutes of each other. Q was on his own with Pat and Dave opting once more for the security of the Cessna. They had taken Jonathon Herbert's warnings on the Internet seriously, he had also said: 'Do not try to head 090 after Narsarsuaq. The wind is still too dangerous over the ice cap. Be patient, head south, and don't cut corners.' In another message he pointed out that 'the usual, but not guaranteed, window for VFR/non de-icing equipped craft is from the first week of June to the last week of July.' It was now 30 August!

We had over 400 miles to go to Kulusuk airfield, lying up the east coast. With winds so light and the weather looking good, we decided to ignore the well-meant advice of Jonathon Herbert and set off north-east for Kulusuk.

Colin took off down Runway 25, out over the fjord, then turned left. Q followed him. I took off last and turned to the right. I wanted to be on my own. Perhaps it was not the safest thing to do, but I just wanted to be alone in that great vastness, enjoying the power and the glory of it all. I headed slowly up the valley, heavy with fuel, to the north of the airfield, the grey, stony rubble quickly giving way to ice and snow – the inexorable path of the glacier flowing south from the ice cap.

Heights and gradients are very deceptive in the snow. The glacier didn't look as though it was anything more than a gentle slope, but I climbed from sea level to eight thousand feet within 15 miles. There was a friendliness, even a sense of security in the bare, smooth rocks of the mountains to either side of the glacier, and some flattish areas, possible landing spots. The glacier itself was split with thousands of deep crevasses.

And then there was the great expanse of white as far as the eye could see.

The ice cap was awe-inspiring, a never-to-be-forgotten sight. I was at 9,000 feet, the charts showing the highest ground at 8,000 feet. It was impossible to judge how high I was above the ground. There was no reference and there were high cirrus clouds giving an overall whiteness to the world. I began to feel not quite so happy at being all alone, and I was getting a lot of vibration due to height and weight, but even when you know what the cause is, it is not relaxing. Colin came on the radio saying that he was getting bad vibrations and his were obviously much more serious than mine, 'I'm getting really bad vibrations – feels as though I'm shaking to bits.' Minutes later he located the problem – one of his wheels was loose. He dealt with that by putting the brake on and seemed pretty relaxed at the prospect of having to land with a loose wheel.

Seventy miles of ice cap, it didn't seem so far. The last time it had been four hundred from Sondrestrom on the east coast to Kulusuk. Judging my height above the ice cap remained a problem. Q told me later that it was the one and only time when he had no sense of height clearance, a weird, disorientating feeling, and how he was glad of his radar altimeter. I asked Q what height he was at and what separation his radar altimeter was getting. He was at 8,300 feet on a QNH of 1021 and had a 400-foot separation. I decided I better stay up where I was until I had something non-white to focus on. Then, of course, the next concern was whether there was going to be turbulence coming off the cap. I knew it wouldn't be as bad as last time, nothing could be as bad as that: we had had a 100-knot tail wind, and the catabatic winds coming off the ice cap had nearly finished us off. I thought the helicopter would be torn apart and when we finally made it to Kulusuk, they told us they had recorded winds gusting up to 130 knots!

This time the winds were a fraction of the strength. I could see the tips of bare mountain tops, a land filled with snow, the only indication that the ice cap had started to slope downhill. I headed for the more open of the two glaciers that I could see, and all went well, with only mild turbulence. Colin, up at 13,000 feet, was feeling almost cosy in his electric suit, which was working well, and said he was clear of turbulence.

We all remarked on how lucky we were and how Pat would be kicking himself for not coming in the helicopter with Q to capture the breathtaking panoramas. All we had was Colin's small front-mounted video camera on the microlight, and Q attempting to fly and film with Pat's small camera. I was just taking still pictures.

What a day that was. We saw icebergs of every shape and description, spouting whales, glaciers, and Q saw two polar bears. We had both been polar bear spotting along the coast. It was such fun weaving in and out among the inlets, coves and icebergs, looking for what we thought might be perfect polar bear country. I even landed at one point to get out and take a photo of G-MURY and stretch my legs. I kept the rotors running and only went a short distance from the helicopter, though, for fear a polar bear might wander around the corner.

Four hours out of Narsarsuaq, two to go to Kulusuk, and I hadn't seen either of the other two. Colin was flying 25 miles off the coast, keeping clear of turbulence, and Q was somewhere up ahead of me. Then Colin came on the air saying 'I thought we agreed that we would all stay together over these Arctic waters?' I tried unsuccessfully, to persuade him to come closer to land. Reluctantly I said I would go and join him. Q offered, but he had opted not to wear his survival suit that day, so it didn't seem like a very good idea. Out I went and no sooner had I met up with Colin than Q, much to my envy, spotted two polar bears. Colin and I did, however, see an incredible number of humpback whales spouting away, and the icebergs were spectacular. I landed on a couple of them.

Six and a half hours after taking off from Narsarsuaq, and Colin and I were on our final approach for Kulusuk's gravel runway. The airfield and small hotel were on an offshore island, free of snow and clear of the worst of the catabatic winds flowing off the ice cap, but the island sported its own small mountain that climbed sharply from the edge of the sea-level runway, rising to over 1,000 feet. Colin had been justifiably concerned as to what that might do to him. The late afternoon winds were gusting up to 35 knots. He had a bit of a tussle, but his wheel stayed on and the landing was nothing like some of his other hairy touchdowns.

We were soon surrounded by numerous Danish pilots and ground staff, all curious to know who and what we were. The pilots were flying helicopters or 30-seater fixed-wing planes up and down the small, scattered communities along the east coast. They all lived in Iceland or Denmark and came for two months, then returned home for the next month. They told us that the entire population of Greenland was a mere 55,000, that they were a mixture of Inuits and Icelanders, and that 20 per cent of them were born outside Greenland. Tourism was apparently on the rise, with helicopter and boat tours, trekking, kayaking and skiing. The only deterrent that I could see was the bitter cold. Later, Colin and I went for a ten-minute walk along the harbour. It was very beautiful, and very cold. When we got back to the hotel, Heinz and the rest of the Cessna crew were there and they told us how Heinz had persuaded them to go out in a boat to see the icebergs. They were still shaking from the cold, but were thrilled with the experience and couldn't stop talking about the sculpture park of icebergs in every shape and form and size, and the amazing turquoise hues you get of the ice just below the sea's surface.

Our hotel was clean and neat with bright blue shutters on the windows. Dinner was a no-choice set menu of vegetable soup followed by beef stew, beans and mashed potatoes. There was no dessert, the chef telling us that he only made a dessert every other day. But then he relented and gave us each a bar of chocolate. The wind died as the sun set behind the mountains.

DAY 93 – 31 AUGUST

Another glorious day, the only downside being the wind. At Kulusuk it was 060 degrees at 8 knots and the forecast for Reykjavik, 454 miles away across our next long stretch of the North Atlantic Ocean, was for 360 degrees at 10 knots. We could expect no tail winds for the long sea crossing, but Reykjavik was saying CAVOK, which basically means the skies are clear. The difference in tail winds to head winds is enormous when you're talking about an aircraft with an air speed of 60 knots. It is not difficult to work out. With a tail wind of 20 knots, Colin would have a ground speed of 80 knots. With 20 knots of head wind it would be half that, a mere 40 knots.

Once again we were minus our intrepid cameraman. The Arctic waters were not for him. Colin, Q and I set off on our seven-hour crossing.

We took off at 9 a.m. The sky was the most incredible blue, the icebergs sparkling in the sunshine, they got fewer and fewer the farther we went from the coast. There was a huge berg 40 miles out which I landed on and Q got some pictures. Contrary to forecast, the head wind disappeared and we soon found ourselves picking up a tail wind. The wind veered to 310 degrees and increased in strength. The gods were with us, we ended up with 20–30 knots of tail wind which only dropped off in the last 30 miles to a gentle 6 knots.

Land in sight – Iceland – and the two longest legs of the Atlantic Ocean were nearly over. The worst of the Arctic conditions were behind us. We just needed a little more luck to see us safely home.

As I write this, I'm constantly interrupted with thoughts for Gwen Bloomingdale and Barbara Gard, who, in March of 2001, went down in the waters off Reykjavik. They were on their way from the USA to England to compete in the London to Sydney Air Race that Colin and I took part in, in G-JEFA. Gwen and Barb were two very experienced pilots. I was told that they went off the air some ten minutes after take-off from Reykjavik. The chances are that it was icing. No one will ever know what exactly happened. They were two brave and courageous ladies who had done much to promote the joy of flying. They died doing what they loved to do.

Iceland was green and civilised by comparison to Greenland and everywhere else we had been since leaving Sept Iles. Reykjavik, on Iceland's west coast, looked warm and inviting with its gaily-painted houses and roofs.

Late that afternoon most of us headed out to the hot springs to enjoy the natural sulphur benefits. The only down side with the hot springs was that it was a 40-minute bus ride each way and I had a sore arm. I don't how I did it, but it had started to feel sore a couple of days earlier, and was now giving me quite a lot of pain. I could only think it must have come from sitting in the same position for many hours, repeating the same movements. I became a lot more sympathetic to Colin, but his arm seemed to be finally on the mend.

Iceland heaves and bubbles with hot springs, glaciers and volcanoes. It is a young island and the largest volcanic island in the world. It was only 58 million years ago that Iceland shrugged off Scotland. Volcanic eruptions are the norm. The Hekla volcano has erupted more than 20 times since the twelfth century and the huge eruption in 1947 was one of the greatest in the twentieth century. We didn't see any eruptions, but we saw lots of geysers puffing clouds of white smoke heavenwards. We flew over the black lava sand beaches and high over the glaciers. We saw herds of wild ponies in rich green valleys between snow-capped mountains, and the rivers where you can enjoy some of the best salmon fishing in the world. I added Iceland to the long list of countries I want to go back to.

Halfway to Hörnafjordur airfield on the south-eastern tip of the island, I found I had solid cloud cover below me. I had been happily flying at 5,000 feet over the Myrdale glacier, which covers the whole of the top of a mountain range on the southern shores of Iceland and was very beautiful. The glacier was above the cloud. Colin, further east, found himself in the same situation over another glacier. He decided to stay high and continue on in the hope that the airfield would be clear. We had good tail winds and it would have taken him ages to go back to the clear skies to the west and come back underneath the clouds.

I decided not to risk it. I turned round, headed out over the sea and started looking for holes in the cloud. Ten miles back I found a place where the cloud looked less dense, I got a glimpse of grey sea below and quickly put the helicopter into autorotation and dropped through into a murky world that contrasted so sharply with moments before when I'd been in glorious sunshine and snow. I was now flying over a windswept sea with foam-flecked waves crashing onto black sands. I continued east at low level and had fun flying at ten feet above the ground along the beach. At that height you can really appreciate the fact that you are going along at over a hundred miles per hour. Colin came on the air saying he was up at 9,000 feet with half an hour to go to Hörnafjordur and could still see no break in the clouds. He said he would hang around until I got there, so I could give him the cloud base.

The cloud remained low. I saw open flat lands to the north, then the mountains once more pressed in. I passed the occasional herd of sheep and cattle and a couple of settlements, small, white-painted buildings with the odd splash of colour, sheltering in the lee of the mountains. Ten minutes later Colin said that the clouds were broken. He had 20 miles to run and was descending into Hörnafjordur. I could see the skies brightening in the distance. The camera crew had followed me and we all made it in to Hörnafjordur. Of the Cessna there was no sign.

It was only 12.30 p.m. We felt we should push on. We were only just clear of another cold front that was moving in from the south-west and we still had a lot of water to cover. The Faeroe Islands were another 300 miles to the south-east. We would be crazy not to continue. We talked it over and were all equally anxious to go on. I went up to the Tower, where Carsten, the same Air Traffic Controller who had been there in '97, greeted me. He remembered Q and myself well and didn't seem in the least surprised to see us. I told him that we wanted to continue on to Vagar (the airfield in the Faeroe Islands). He looked at his watch and told me that they closed at 5 p.m. Could we make that? I thought possibly not, but told him 'yes' and filed flight plans for arrival at 4.45 p.m. Carsten then said we were making the right decision, that the forecast for the next 24 hours was for sharply deteriorating conditions.

'Help yourselves to coffee and biscuits – you remember where they are? Just down the stairs,' he said. And just at that moment we heard Heinz on the air asking for joining instructions. That was a relief, as I had been afraid they might have made an even later start as they, of course, thought we were all spending the night in the small town of Hofn.

As it was, we had an extra delay waiting for the customs/immigration officer who was also the postman. Colin needed to be on his way, so we asked Carsten if he could go and leave his passport with me. Carsten had looked a little dubious, but then shrugged his shoulders, smiled and said OK. So Colin hurried off to put on his survival suit and I went along to take some photos. Jo Jo had been asking for some time for pictures for our sponsors. Bose wanted 'headset' photos, Spare Air wanted spare air canisters and H.R. Smith wanted the EPIRBs. Twenty minutes after Colin departed, the postman-cum-customs-officer arrived. We handed him the pile of passports. He never did a head count and wasn't interested in inspecting the aircraft.

We caught up with Colin halfway to Vagar. Everyone was feeling good. We were ahead of our (heavily revised) schedule and we had 25–30 knots of tail wind all the way. 'It's gong to be rough into Vagar,' Colin said. Only then did I remember that Vagar is renowned for wind shear. Ten minutes later, Heinz, in the Cessna, reported that they were two-way with Vagar who had cautioned wind shear.

Colin got more and more concerned the closer we got. Ten minutes out we were still picking up a good 28 knots of tail wind from the south-west and the runway ran north-west to south-east along a valley with high mountains on either side. He would have a crosswind landing. 'Why did you ever plan a stop in the Faeroes? Why couldn't we have routed direct to Scotland?' Colin asked. I reminded him that it was over 550 miles from Iceland to Scotland and it had seemed sensible to schedule a stop in the Faeroes. I added, 'They are an incredibly beautiful group of islands and well worth a visit.' He wasn't very impressed with the latter reason and reckoned that the Faeroes could have been kept as an alternative. 'You helped select the route,' I reminded him.

Colin decided that there was only one possible way of getting in to the airfield and that was to make one of his spiralling descents. He asked ATC if he could stay high (he'd climbed to 7,000 feet) until overhead the field. Vagar agreed. I moved slightly to the south at 4,000 feet. The camera crew stayed high to record the whole thing. I was nervous and felt responsible for having chosen Vagar in the first place. Colin started his descent, spiralling down at 2,000 feet per minute. From my position it looked terrifying, my heart was in my mouth and from my angle of perspective I honestly thought he had turned over. But Heinz told me later that from the ground he had looked good. Colin was a very relieved man to be on the ground. He said that it had been one of the toughest landings he had ever had to make.

The bad news was that there were no hotel rooms available. It turned out that there was a 'strong man' competition and a football match the following day – the Faeroes versus Moldavia, who were ranked forty-third in the world, the Faeroes being one hundred and sixtieth. It was all go in the Faeroes. Johan Mortensen, the Honorary British Consul, said he would see what he could do about rooms. He managed to find two double ones in Torshavn (the capital town) on the neighbouring island of Esturoy. He said the rest of the team would have to stay at the youth hostel, where he managed to secure the last three beds.

Pat, Dave and James, during all the negotiations and phone calls, had been sitting in the arrivals hall looking resigned and not a little fed up. They were immediately voted into the youth hostel. (I have to say, not without a certain satisfaction on Colin's and my part – memories of the Saglek mutiny still fresh.) The rest of us high-tailed it in the two helicopters over to the capital town of Torshavn on the next-door island, where we landed beside some warehouses in the harbour and where Q had negotiated for us to leave the helicopters overnight. We took a taxi and were driven for miles up a long and twisty road. Twenty minutes later we arrived at the hotel, overflowing with enormous muscle-bound men in singlets and shorts, and footballers all in team colours. Our two rooms had been reduced to one. Reception was looking thoroughly harassed and apologetically told us our room had three beds, they would put in one more and in the meantime would we like to have some dinner? We were famished. We had eaten nothing since Carsten's biscuits at lunchtime.

The hotel was not used to catering for so many, or maybe the strong men had devoured all the food and they had had to go and get more, but we had to wait two hours for food. Even getting a beer took half an hour. The compensation was a telephone call from Pat. They were having a perfectly horrible time. There was nothing to eat, there were no blankets (or sheets) and they had no money. Halfway through dinner, a girl from reception came to our table and told us that we could have a second room after all. I grabbed it.

I lay in bed that night thinking about the next day. Our journey was nearly over, we would soon be home. Tomorrow we were going to be in Scotland, at my sister's house. It was hard to believe and, while half of me was thrilled, the other half was unable to accept that it was nearly all over. Everything I had focused on for the last two years would end, be finished. I was elated and depressed. It was all so strange. I would be returning to a normal life. While thinking all these thoughts I finally fell into a dreamless sleep.

The three men had an interrupted night. Colin and Q had gone into town. Colin returned some time before Q and had decided that he ought to leave the light on in the bathroom, leaving the door open, just a crack. Sometime later, Heinz woke up and wanted a pee, but saw the light under the bathroom door. He could just make out that one bed was empty. So he assumed someone was in the bathroom. He waited and waited. Finally he got out of bed and started pacing up and down. Colin had half woken up and couldn't think what was going on. Heinz continued to pace. He could stand it no longer and decided to pee out the window, and of course at that moment Q returned!

Breakfast – a buffet – was a revelation in the amount of food that it was possible for a body to consume. The strong men's trays were piled high with bottles of milk, loaves of bread, bananas, ham, cheese and eggs, and then they were going back for more. When we went out to the car park to get our taxi, we found that the contest was underway, right there in the car park. Men with great ropes in their teeth were attempting to pull army trucks and a sizeable crowd was cheering them on.

Back at the airfield we found our hungry and unhappy crew. I apologised, then said, 'But cheer up, with a bit of luck we will all be in Scotland tonight.' I received sour looks and Pat asked if I would do a piece for the camera. That done, I hurried off to see about refuelling all the aircraft (everything had been closed the night before). A flight had arrived from Copenhagen, and curious passengers streamed across the apron, looking at our motley aircraft. We had to wait while their plane refuelled and Colin, as usual, was anxious to be on his way, forecasting diabolical turbulence and head winds. It was already 9.30 a.m. and the wind was beginning to pick up.

We donned our survival suits for the last time and Colin got away without mishap. I followed half an hour later accompanied by Q. Pat was in the Cessna. We headed south towards the islands of Sandoy, Sudoroy and the smallest inhabited island in the Faeroes, Stora Dimun where Ola Jakup ur Dimun lives with his family. They are the sole inhabitants. We had visited them the last time and I was hoping we would find them at home and be able to say a quick hello. Ola Jakup is known as 'the intellectual' – the best read man in the Faeroes and incidentally in the *Guinness Book of Records* for having the smallest school house in the world (for his 4 children).

The Dimuns have been there for seven generations. It is a tough life by any standards but not as tough as before. Now they have electricity (a generator), a telephone and a helicopter comes once a week with supplies. Not so long ago they had none of these things and their only contact with the outside world was a boat that came once a month and often during the winter months the boat could not get through. The island has sheer cliffs on all sides, so provisions used to be hoisted up by wooden pulleys which are still there. Ola Jakup makes his living from his sheep and selling puffins to Torshavn.

There are millions and millions of puffins in the Faeroes and during the season they catch them in large nets that look like overgrown butterfly nets. When the wind is right Ola lies on the ground at the edge of the cliffs and catches the puffins as they swoop in. In '97, they had invited us to have lunch with them, and we had puffin (it tastes a bit like grouse), home-made cheese, butter and milk from their six cows, home-made bread and salad from the garden. While we sat eating all their delicious home-made fare, Ola Jakup told us about the islands and of one of the legends of Stora Dimun. He said that many years before, the wife of the then owner had a fierce argument with her husband and killed him. The authorities from Torshavn tried in vain for ten years to arrest her and bring her to justice, but she managed to defend herself and her island against all comers. Finally they captured her and condemned her to death by drowning. But her hair was so long, she floated. So all her hair was chopped off and she finally drowned. 'Was that your ancestor?' I asked. 'Probably!' he said, laughing.

As we approached Stora Dimun I could see the Dimuns' house and the ponies and sheep, and then a small figure appeared from the house. It was Ola Jakup and he was delighted to see us. The rest of the family were in Torshavn;

they should have returned the night before but apparently it had been too windy for the helicopter! We kept our rotors running, so it was a very quick hello and goodbye and we were gone. I hope I will return again. What a wonderful character.

We flew on south, passing the last of the islands, and I thought about life in the Faeroes, how they still have a way of life and values that most of the Western world has forgotten. Crime is non-existent and when I asked if the younger generation were leaving the islands for the bright lights of the cities, Ola Jakup had said, 'No, young and old, we love this place, we reckon there is nowhere better.'

Our next touchdown would be on British soil, Stornaway Airport on the Isle of Lewis, the most northerly island in the Hebrides, commonly referred to by locals as the Western Isles. From there it was a mere 63 miles to Plockton airfield where my mother and Gillian and Mark (my sister and brother-in-law) would be waiting. Q's parents were also due to be there, and many other friends. How strange it all was. How difficult it was to adjust to the fact it was nearly the end. I can understand the lone yachtsman, who, it is said, was approaching Plymouth after sailing around the world, and everyone was waiting there to welcome him home. He couldn't face it, so he'd radioed ashore to say he was going on.

In my case I would certainly be stopping, but the wrench was there after the close little world of me and my helicopter. I was full of wistful thoughts, but I was looking forward to being once more with family and friends. We had 268 miles to go to Stornaway. We had flown over more than 6,000 miles of water since leaving our own beautiful British Isles. Now, three months later, we were making our last long water crossing.

The hours went quickly by, and there in the distance was the tiny island of Sula Sgeir, a rock with a lighthouse and a helipad, no more. There was room for one helicopter only on the tiny helipad. I thought it would be fun to land, my first touchdown on British soil, but Q, with his faster machine and greater expertise, ducked in front and beat me to it. I flew on without stopping. Later in Stornaway I overheard him crowing to someone on the phone, 'Ha, ha – I was the first to land on British soil.'

We continued on, now with the scent of home in our nostrils. On the horizon I could see the most northerly tip of the Isle of Lewis, where we eventually caught up with Colin and journeyed on together to Stornaway. We were given a warm welcome by the man in the Tower. A couple of local newspaper reporters wanted to take pictures. I phoned Gillian, telling her – to ecstatic cheers – that we were in Stornaway, and gave our ETA for Plockton airfield just half an hour's drive south of their home (and five minutes by helicopter). Gillian said that John (her son) and Sasha would be there with baby Loris and that my mother and the Smiths had arrived and Mike was going to fly out to meet us. We had a cup of tea and a ham roll and were once more on our way.

On the short flight to the mainland I could see Colin to my right, silhouetted against the sun with the Western Isles in the distance. I thought back to all those months ago, the moment I had taken a last look at the white cliffs of Dover, and of all that we had seen and been through since. In a few days we would be home. We had set out to be the 'first solos' around the world: me, a woman in a helicopter; Colin in his microlight – and we were within reach of our goal.

Maybe without Colin I might have given up due to the tough flying, but more likely because of the endless stresses caused by the camera crew. I was happy for Colin, it meant so much to him. He was a real hero and a very brave one. I think in many ways he was immune to the camera crew and he had nothing in common with them. Colin, for the most part, was able to shut himself away from what he saw as an irritation. He became wrapped up in the challenge and saw the camera crew as there to make a film, a necessity to secure sponsorship. He was going to get around with or without them, and whatever they thought of him.

For me it was not that easy. Q had taught me to fly and I had counted on his loyalty and moral support. I expected him to feel proud that he had taught me. Yet, from the very beginning, as he showed at Battersea, I got no support. He felt a compulsive need to chip away at anything I did. I guess it was largely a case of not being able to accept the role of 'unsung hero'.

I found it profoundly sad. We had known him so long. He had been our guest many times. We were even related by marriage. We had shared some wonderful times, but there should have been so many more. Thank heavens for Heinz and Colin. Otherwise, God knows if I would have made it.

The last few miles passed swiftly. Mike Smith, Q's father, joined us in a Hughes 500 and we flew together to Plockton airfield, a small strip hugging the north-west coast of Scotland. The little village of Plockton behind the airfield has palm trees down the main street thanks to the Gulf Stream.

Colin went in first. I followed with Q on my left side. I was riding high, we had made our last water crossing and we were back on the British mainland. Everyone was waving and smiling, and I rushed to hug my mother and sister.

Pat Doyle filmed only Q greeting his family and then proceeded to interview only Q. Colin, whose family were not there, watched this filming charade, seething. It was disgraceful to deliberately cut off such a wonderful moment from our story, but I was too happy either to care or notice.

Gillian and Mark laid on a banquet. Twenty-four of us sat down to dinner, and then with Ann Mackay (arguably Scotland's leading piper lady) on the bagpipes, we danced Scottish reels into the wee small hours of the morning. I woke at 5 a.m., partly from habit I guess, but my arm seemed to be getting worse (it was a trapped nerve, and took months before it finally got better). I couldn't get back to sleep.

Daylight came. From my bedroom I could see the top of the mountains of Applecross catching the first rays of morning sun. It was going to be a lovely day. A day of relaxation – days of relaxation. The pressure was off, we were ahead of our final schedule. Our much revised arrival date at Brooklands was still four days away. Celebrations were in hand, we couldn't arrive early. But Colin wanted to press on south. He said strong head winds and deteriorating weather were forecast over the next few days. 'I've got a weather window and I really want time to visit with Jim Cunliffe and everyone at Mainair at Barton (Manchester). Jim has been so good. They all have.' So I flew him over to Plockton in G-MURY and helped him fuel his microlight, then waved him off as he headed south. I felt sad. Sad to be splitting up for the journey south, which somehow accelerated the end; the end of days of heading off into the unknown together – reaching for the far horizon, already rose-tinted in memory.

Gillian, Mark, Mike and Mary Smith, Heinz, my mother and I, had lunch in the garden of the pub at Plockton. The sun was shining and we ate the freshest of prawns and lobster with salad, beer for some and white wine for others, looking out over the small harbour. Q, James and the camera crew were with Sasha and John.

The weather held good, but, as Colin predicted, we had head winds for our journey south, but never more than ten knots and the visibility was good for most of the journey. My mother was travelling as far as Manchester's Barton airfield with Mike and Mary in the Hughes 500, so we were a flight of three helicopters.

We flew south, flying over familiar territory: the Isle of Skye, Ben Nevis and Loch Lomond. We had one brief stop at Oban airfield to the north of Glasgow to say hello to Paul Keegan who operates there, and who we knew well from many a stopover, and then it was onwards to Edinburgh from where we followed the coast south to Manchester's Barton Airfield, where we landed in what was to be the last of the sunshine.

The airfield was bathed in the late summer sunshine with lots of small planes and gaily coloured microlights on the grass parking areas. Colin was there, having celebrated in style with all the lads from Mainair – beers down at the pub and an Indian curry supper. My brother Peter was also there with the biggest of smiles. He collected my mother and the two of them would drive on south to welcome us the following day at Brooklands, where Simon and the rest of our families would be waiting.

We did a quick interview with the *Manchester Evening News* and were once more airborne, this time with an escort of two microlights, both from Mainair, who accompanied us for the first 20 miles.

The next 24 hours passed quickly, with an overnight stop at Wellesbourne Airfield where we all stayed at the nearby Arrow Mill Hotel, owned by Dennis Woodhams, a good friend of Mike and Mary's. Dennis laid on a grand celebratory dinner where a tired but triumphant team were finally united in the knowledge and happiness of what we had achieved. We all toasted each other. Colin was sitting at the other end of the long table and we raised our glasses to each other in silent salute. There were smiles and happiness all round. Just 77 miles to go to Brooklands and we would finally have made it round the world. All the pettiness, the irritations and aggro faded into insignificance compared to the enormity of the obstacles overcome, dangers surmounted and the world we had been so privileged to see. The great and the good far outweighed all else, and the realisation began to sink in that I was about to achieve what no other woman had ever done before – fly a helicopter solo around the world – and Colin would be the first person to fly a microlight solo around the world, major firsts which would be ours forever.

DAY 99 – 6 SEPTEMBER

Ninety-nine days had passed and this was our final morning. I woke to the sound of rain drumming against my window. As I dressed I was interrupted by several phone calls from newspaper reporters wanting interviews and was surprised and happy to see a report about Colin and myself on the BBC *Breakfast News*.

We set off for Brooklands in cloud, rain and turbulence. We planned to do two circuits of the airfield and finish off with a stylish fly-past down the runway. But, although the rain stopped and the cloud lifted as we approached Brooklands, the wind increased, meaning that low fly-pasts and circuits were going to be difficult for Colin.

Brooklands was in sight. We could see the crowd gathered below. Colin was being thrown about all over the sky. He said over the radio to me that if he could possibly manage to land after the first circuit he would. 'This is really dangerous,' he said.

'I'll follow your lead,' I replied. 'Good luck.'

Heart-stopping to the last, lurching and bouncing, he descended quickly and, to my immense relief, touched down safely on the first attempt. I followed him in. A couple of minutes afterwards, Q arrived in G-JEFA, followed by the Cessna. It was so turbulent that Heinz had to abort his first landing and do a go-around.

No sooner had I shut down than Nicola, my eldest granddaughter, came running towards me carrying a large bouquet of flowers. I could see Justin's smiling face behind her. Colin had his young son, Peter, and daughter, Sarah, in his arms, with Michelle close by. There were hugs and tears of happiness. Simon, Suze, Christy and Nick were there – our families and friends were all over us. Kathy Magee of Operation Smile had flown in from the USA; the press were everywhere and once more the band was playing.

Happiness and sadness, one emotion chased the other. Faces were blurred – so many dear faces. I realised how much I had missed them all and how very good it was to be home.

There was one wistful moment when I looked across to where our brave little aircraft were standing. Colin's microlight was already being dismantled; ignominiously folded up and boxed into a small trailer – our homes, our worlds for so many months now abandoned.

The cars were loaded up and goodbyes said to all the team, I headed for London, and Colin for Nottingham. We were on our way back to the real world, everyone in a hurry to avoid the rush hour.

APPENDIX

ROUTE, DISTANCES AND

Day	Date	From	To	Country	Total Miles	Daily Total Miles	Daily Total Hours
1	31 May	Brooklands	Rochester	UK	47		
	31 May	Rochester	Le Touquet	France	76		
	31 May	Le Touquet	Toussus	France	124	247	3.10
2	1 Jun	Toussus	Bergerac	France	330	330	2.40
4	3 Jun	Bergerac	Cannes	France	298		
	3 Jun	Cannes	Florence	Italy	237	535	5.50
5	4 Jun	Florence	Perugia	Italy	82		
	4 Jun	Perugia	Corfu	Greece	452	534	5.00
6	5 Jun	Corfu	Mikonos	Greece	329	329	4.25
8	7 Jun	Mikonos	Pafos	Cyprus	439	439	4.05
9	8 Jun	Pafos	Amman	Jordan	485	485	5.10
11	10 Jun	Amman	Hail	Saudi	462	462	5.35
12	11 Jun	Hail	Kuwait	Kuwait	400	400	4.20
14	13 Jun	Kuwait	Dubai	UAE	529	529	5.10
15	14 Jun	Dubai	Muscat	Oman	216		
	14 Jun	Muscat	Karachi	Pakistan	578	794	7.10
16	15 Jun	Karachi	Ahmedabad	India	368	368	3.05
17	16 Jun	Ahmedabad	Nagpur	India	432	432	3.25
18	17 Jun	Nagpur	Calcutta	India	610	531	5.55
20	19 Jun	Calcutta	Chittagong	Bangladesh	217	189	2.35
22	21 Jun	Chittagong	Chiang Mai	Thailand	520	520	6.20
23	22 Jun	Chiang Mai	Hanoi	Vietnam	390	390	4.20
25	24 Jun	Hanoi	Danang	Vietnam	475	475	4.35
26	25 Jun	Danang	Hong Kong	China	570	570	5.05
29	28 Jun	Hong Kong	Kao-hsiung	Taiwan	497	497	4.05
30	29 Jun	Kao-hsiung	Naha	Japan	577	577	5.35
31	30 Jun	Naha	Nanki	Japan	691	691	6.25
32	1 Jul	Nanki	Tokyo	Japan	347	347	5.00
50	19 Jul	Tokyo	Wakanai	Japan	744	744	7.35
51	20 Jul	Wakanai	Yuzhno	Russia	275	275	1.50
52	21 Jul	Yuzhno	Okha	Russia	490	490	4.05
55	24 Jul	Okha	Magadan	Russia	544	544	5.55
56	25 Jul	Magadan	Markovo	Russia	707	707	7.50
57	26 Jul	Markovo	Anadyr	Russia	215		
	26 Jul	Anadyr	Nome	USA	500	715	7.20
	26 Jul	Nome	McGrath	USA	319		2.15
	26 Jul	McGrath	Anchorage	USA	219	538	3.20
58	27 Jul	Anchorage	Yakutat	USA	373		
	27 Jul	Yakutat	Sitka	USA	230	603	9.00
60	29 Jul	Sitka	Prince Rupert	Canada	270		

DAY	DATE	FROM	TO	COUNTRY	MILES	DAILY TOTAL MILES	DAILY TOTAL HOURS
60	29 Jul	P.R.	Vancouver	Canada	468	738	10.40
61	30 Jul	Vancouver	Tillamook	USA	262		
	30 Jul	Tillamook	Eugene	USA	94	356	5.10
62	31 Jul	Eugene	Sonoma	USA	388	388	4.20
63	1 Aug	Sonoma	Oakland	USA	69		
	1 Aug	Oakland	Santa Maria	USA	218		
	1 Aug	Santa Maria	Los Angeles	USA	148	435	4.25
67	5 Aug	Los Angeles	Santa Maria	USA	148		
	5 Aug	Santa Maria	Blythe	USA	339		
	5 Aug	Blythe	Eloy	USA	190	677	7.05
68	6 Aug	Eloy	El Paso	USA	312		
	6 Aug	El Paso	Dell City	USA	70		
	6 Aug	Dell City	El Paso	USA	70	352	5.50
71	9 Aug	El Paso	Dimmit	USA	455		
	9 Aug	Dimmit	Laredo	USA	71		
	9 Aug	Laredo	Matamoras	Mexico	171	697	5.35
72	10 Aug	Matamoras	Brownsville	USA	11		
	10 Aug	Brownsville	Galveston	USA	304	315	4.55
73	11 Aug	Galveston	New Orleans	USA	283		
	11 Aug	New Orleans	Tallahassee	USA	355	638	6.25
74	12 Aug	Tallahassee	Miami	USA	451		
	12 Aug	Miami	Havana	Cuba	341	792	7.35
76	14 Aug	Havana	Nassau	Bahamas	200	200	3.50
77	15 Aug	Nassau	Palm Beach	USA	198		
	15 Aug	Palm Beach	Charleston	USA	459	657	6.45
78	16 Aug	Charleston	Brunswick	USA	140		
	16 Aug	Brunswick	First Flight	USA	197		
	16 Aug	First Flight	Norfolk	USA	67	404	4.50
79	17 Aug	Norfolk	Washington	USA	141	141	1.30
81	19 Aug	Washington	Westchester	USA	248	248	2.35
82	20 Aug	Westchester	Boston	USA	268	268	2.50
83	21 Aug	Boston	Montreal	Canada	248	248	3.55
85	23 Aug	Montreal	Sept Iles	Canada	463	463	4.50
88	26 Aug	Sept Iles	Kuujuaq	Canada	549	549	7.25
90	28 Aug	Kuujuaq	Saglek	Canada	210	210	2.35
91	29 Aug	Saglek	Narsarsuaq	Greenland	623	623	9.20
92	30 Aug	Narsarsuaq	Kulusuk	Greenland	441	441	6.20
93	31 Aug	Kulusuk	Reykjavik	Iceland	454	454	4.50
94	1 Sep	Reykjavik	Hörnafjordur	Iceland	201		
	1 Sep	Hörnafjordur	Vagar	Faeroes	291	492	6.35
95	2 Sep	Vagar	Stornoway	UK	268		
	2 Sep	Stornoway	Plockton	UK	63	331	5.00
98	5 Sep	Plockton	Oban	UK	63		
	5 Sep	Oban	Barton	UK	238		
	5 Sep	Barton	Wellesbourne	UK	94	395	4.50
99	6 Sep	Wellesbourne	Fairoaks	UK	74		
99	6 Sep	Fairoaks	Brooklands	UK	3	77	0.50

Total distance   26,886 statute miles   Total hours in air   287.80